Cont

Foreword **4**

Preface **5**

1: **Oxford, the Potteries to Liverpool to Sheffield** **7**

2: **Sheffield in South Yorkshire** **20**

3: **Education, Feminism and Europe** **54**

4: **Leadership, International Solidarity and Social Care** **83**

5: **Politics in the Public Sector** **118**

6: **Politics in the City** **159**

7: **Women and Conflict: The Miners' Strike and Further Afield** **202**

8: **Rate Capping and Local Government Finance 'Furthering Socialism in a Cold Climate'** **229**

9: **The Politics of Partnership** **257**

10: **The Way Forward** **294**

Appendix 1: Sheffield City Centre map 314

Appendix 2: Map of North Sheffield Area 316

Acronyms 318

References 322

Index 326

About the Author 338

Foreword

by David Blunkett

This is a fascinating testament, written from the heart and through the experiences of someone who rose to be a significant player in Sheffield: as a long-serving member of the leadership team and of the wider-city voluntary, education and political fields.

With her perspective as a former Labour MP, Helen Jackson looks back at the Sheffield city landscape at a significant time in its history, which was marked out as radical and progressive on the one hand, and effective in delivering for traditional supporters on the other.

Telling a good story is at the heart of bringing history alive and this book offers lessons for the future and an alternative narrative to the more familiar metropolitan-based authors.

Preface

This book was triggered by a talk I gave in 2014 to undergraduates and post-graduates at my former university about how useful studying for a history degree had been in my adult life and work. Preparing for the talk got me thinking about how integral history and politics are to each other, although at the time of the talk my conclusion was 'not a lot!' I had picked out five experiences to analyse from different decades of my 60 years of activity, in communities, campaigns, and as an individual, an educator, and in elected roles.

Afterwards, Selina Todd, the history professor who invited me, suggested I write about what I had said. I was wary – reluctant to write an autobiographical memoir, which I considered self-indulgent. I knew I could talk; but writing? However, I took up Selina's suggestion as a challenge to do something I had not done before. She recommended I have a chat with Professor Pat Thane, who listened and gave me wise advice not to go down the academic route but perhaps start to write a draft and see where it took me. She offered her help, for which I am extremely grateful. Of the original five 'Experiences' I picked one, 'My time in Local Government'. What took me onto Sheffield City Council, and eventually persuaded me to stand for election to Parliament 20 years later? Those years were, I thought, important for my personal and political development and, I believed, they were also historically significant.

Back at home in Sheffield I shared the idea with a few good friends, and I was heartened by their enthusiastic encouragement and support. Once started I couldn't let them down! Our joint recollections of the changes in the city and region were invigorating and the resulting project has become collective rather than personal. I am deeply indebted to the many individuals, including my patient and amazing family, who over the past five years have generously shared their memories, pictures, oral and written archives and time. They are not all well known, some sadly have died, but all were active in the events I describe. Without exception, their recollections of the years running up to the late 1980s in Sheffield and across South Yorkshire have recognised the intensity of the political culture of the period. The experience has impacted on their later lives, politics and careers.

My reflections have merged with theirs and added to the story of a woman in politics. The whole project has revived and deepened my political and historical understanding of the period, in particular of the under-recorded role of women. It enhanced my belief that any analysis of how local, national and international experience interacts needs to include the dimension of gender to fully understand history, politics and economics.

The actual production of the book has been fun and enjoyable because of the work of Jennifer Sayles of Sheaf Graphics and the friendly support given to me by Tony Simpson of Spokesman Press.

Helen Jackson
Sheffield, January 2021

CHAPTER 1

Oxford, the Potteries to Liverpool to Sheffield

We came to South Yorkshire from Liverpool in the summer of 1974.

Oxford to the Potteries '57-'67

I had learnt about Sheffield at Oxford University from two close friends. The first, Anne, arrived at St Hilda's College in 1957 at the same time as me. She was from Yorkshire as I was and studied chemistry. She had a slow speaking style, loved the moors around the city, held opinions rooted in practical realities, and had a wickedly sharp sense of humour. I liked all this and her direct way of talking. Tutors and students at Oxford women's colleges then were aware that the ratio of women to men gaining entry was around one to ten.[1] It stood to reason that we were cleverer on average than the young men of our intake. So, we were proud of our gender and had some confidence in our potential which helped redress other barriers to women's progression which were then still firmly in place, though the '60s beckoned and we read Katharine Whitehorn in the *Observer* avidly every Sunday. We were nearly ready for the acceleration of demands for more sexual and other freedoms in the next decade.

---

1. House of Commons Briefing Paper no. 616, 5th September 2015 by Paul Bolton states 12.5%.

The second was Keith, a history student like me from The Queens College who I went on to marry in 1960. In addition to Anne's Sheffield accent and characteristics Keith had a fierce loyalty to everything about his city, its industries and its working class people. He was proud of Hugh, his father, who had been an apprentice-trained silver finisher at Cooper Brothers until recently he had been made redundant. He was also proud and acutely aware of Mary, his mother's constant hard work as she struggled to make ends meet from her night shift work at Middlewood Hospital. He knew that his dad's redundancy had affected not just the family income but his pride and dignity as well. Keith arrived at Oxford aware that his educational background starting from the local elementary school and on to King Edward's grammar via the 11+ meant he also was in a minority of his intake at Queens. Again, it stood to reason that he might well be intellectually superior, and since he arrived straight from doing two years National Service in the Education Corps, he believed that he, like others of his age and background, were far more aware of social class reality than the 66% of his intake arriving straight from public school. Becoming a married couple, two months after my graduation, brought together our developing gender and social class identities into an affinity with politics on the left.

After graduating in 1961 Keith's work with the WEA took us to the Potteries, to the Welsh valleys and then back to Stoke-on-Trent. We both became sexually and politically active; he through his work, I through four pregnancies, two childbirths, and campaigning for better maternity procedures through the Association for the Improvement of Maternity Services (AIMS).[2]

2. Association for the Improvement of Maternity Services, a forerunner of the National Childbirth Trust.

This led me to join the Labour Party, which, in the Women's Section of Newcastle-under-Lyme constituency, was very active, but, during the 1964 general election, mainly involved making tea and sandwiches for the male canvassing teams. Our candidate was Stephen Swingler, who with his wife Anne were on the left wing. He was successful and Harold Wilson became Prime Minister.

Potteries to Liverpool '67–'74

We moved to Liverpool in 1967, he to a job in the Extramural Department of the University. My first memories before we had made friends there were of frequent visits with two young children on the top deck of a bus to Pier Head. We saw liners and freight ships from far off places; chased seagulls on the floating landing quays; and chatted to an older generation of Scousers on the benches about their memories of working on the docks and listened to their passed down tales of the slave ships docking there. We ate chips in the café and sometimes for fun bought return tickets on the Mersey ferry before going home for tea. The iconic image of the symbolic Liver buildings as we returned became etched in my memory; an emblem of the city of Liverpool's former establishment whose riches and status had come from trading and trafficking human slaves between Africa and the West Indies. Tate and Lyle sugar refinery, once dependent on their cheap labour for the production of sugar, still dominated the view north towards Bootle, and Manchester Ship Canal stretched away to the east, built to take the cotton crop, equally dependent on slave labour, to the mills of Lancashire.

As a historian I knew that the industrial history of a location shapes its culture and politics. Contrasts between the six towns of the Potteries and Liverpool docklands were everywhere.

Once acclimatised, and me again pregnant, we settled in Huyton five miles from the centre of Liverpool, but steeped ourselves in Liverpool's free-wheeling, rather chaotic, but vivid left-wing politics and wacky humour. Keith ran adult education courses for tenants' associations in Toxteth and Scotland Road. We had never seen such poverty as that of the depressing inner city streets of multi-occupancy Georgian houses between Toxteth and the University.[3] Liverpool City Council and the Labour Party seemed irrelevant to so many of the groups he met in his work. It felt distant and pompous. Tenants put up their own representatives at local elections, nearly ousting Labour establishment figures from the days of Jack and Bessie Braddock. This was before Derek Hatton and the Militant Tendency took hold. Local politics was becoming sour and embittered. The boundary between Liverpool and Lancashire also ran between Huyton and Prescot. The old village of Huyton and its church was part of Lancashire while the sprawling council estates spreading north to Kirkby and Knowsley housed Liverpudlians moved out from poorer inner-city Liverpool.

As well as helping to run playgroups for Keith's tenants' courses in the inner city, I joined Huyton Labour Party. I introduced myself at the Labour Party office and Arthur Smith, Harold Wilson's well-established agent, asked if I would help rejuvenate the ward we lived in. In due course I became secretary of St. Agnes Ward Party. I got to know and appreciate the politics of our Ward Chairman, Leo. He had worked on the docks all his life and was active in the Transport and General Workers' Union (T&GWU). I listened as he described the insecurity of dockland labour not knowing until the ship came in what work would be available, as Leo's wife spoke

3. Thompson, M (2020). *Reconstructing Public Housing*. Liverpool University Press.

of the uncertainty of what cash she would have to feed the family. Having never had a day off work for 40 years, his chest became bad within a year of retirement. Leo was overwhelmed with a mixture of pride and embarrassment when Harold Wilson came to visit him at home when he was terminally ill.

The Americans were losing the war in Vietnam, while the Wilson government avoided being drawn into it. London saw in Grosvenor Square violent demonstrations outside the American embassy in March 1968. Peter Jackson, MP for High Peak, Derbyshire and present at the anti-war demonstration described the police action in an adjournment debate:

> It had been agreed earlier that the leaders of the protest would hand in letters of protest. The leading group was headed by Miss Vanessa Redgrave. She appeared at the head of the march and made a request to hand in her letter of protest. I understand that her request was refused by a chief inspector. The vast majority of demonstrators were obviously not aware of this, but I am sure that those who were in the vicinity would regard that occurrence as something of a provocation.[4]

In Paris the May demonstrations were even larger. Enoch Powell's 'Rivers of Blood' speech triggered and solidified Labour movement alliances with the black and ethnic minority communities across the country. The Labour government went along with anti-racist demonstrations, taking on the National Front (NF) in a strongly insistent way. Equality measures in the name of socialism brought these themes to the fore politically.

---

4. *Hansard*, Vol. 762. 4th April 1968.

Wilson was popular with many within the Party. Campaigning was loud and vigorous. Without internet or social media, it meant marching; using loud hailers in support of pickets or striking workers locally; making leaflets, banners and badges for demonstrations; boycotting Outspan oranges to register protest against apartheid in South Africa. In general for political activists in the Labour movement, the enemy was unbridled capitalism and industrial establishments such as Barclays and Shell that invested heavily in the apartheid regime. The Anti-Apartheid movement stepped up its action against corporations by declaring support for a ban on arms sales to South Africa. 10,000 marched through London to protest outside the embassy in Trafalgar Square. I had convened a group in the constituency to make a HUYTON LABOUR PARTY banner, because we believed it was important to demonstrate in London with it as it bore witness to the backing of the Prime Minister for international justice.

More divisive, however, were the proposals in the 1969 White Paper, entitled *In Place of Strife*, which set out plans to force unions to call a ballot before a strike was held, and to establish an Industrial Board to enforce settlements in industrial disputes. The call 'Everybody out' followed by a show of hands before a 'lightning strike' was to be no more. Its name, a reworking of Nye Bevan's *In Place of Fear*, seemed somehow treacherous, and this frontal attack on the trade union movement was badly handled. Barbara Castle, who as Secretary of State for Employment drafted and

The Labour Party logo sewn on to the banner we marched through London.

proposed it, along with Harold Wilson was challenged by Jim Callaghan as the Cabinet was split. Collective solidarity had been shattered.

Election day 18th June 1970 had been a surprise for a start. We had rescheduled our camping holiday on the west coast of Wales so as to take the campaigning effort right through that hot summer spell to election day itself, ready to leave the morning after. What really shocked that night as we arrived home in the early hours was the racist message scrawled on our garden poster, and the memory of devastated bewilderment on Wilson's face as he met us after the count, as well as the realisation that Ted Heath had won. To cap it all, as we travelled west with trailer and children, the clouds gathered and the heatwave came to an end.

Liverpool to Sheffield '73-'74

On leaving Liverpool I had two immediate memories: the most recent was election day February 1974, knocking up the vote for Wilson, spurred on by the news early in the day, that, in contrast to 1970, the T&G were out strongly for Harold, with black cabbies across the city instructed to take all and sundry to vote. We were sure we were going to win. The other was hearing 'Quilapayun',[5] the Chilean folk group in exile, singing Victor Jara's socialist songs, interspersed with stories of his torture and murder following the military coup, which killed their President, Salvador Allende on 11th Sept 1973, as well as countless trade

5. 'Quilapayun' – a Chilean folk group formed in 1965, and inspired by social issues contemporary with the popular unity government led by Salvador Allende who were out of the country at the time of the military coup which killed him on 11th September 1973.

union activists and students. It was an emotional evening in a packed hall near Lime Street, along with an audience of Liverpool dockworkers determined to follow the example of Rosyth shipyard workers who, in solidarity with the workers of Chile, had blacked the shipping of spare parts for Hawker-Hunter Chilean military aircraft from Britain. We pledged to do what we could in support.

Once in Sheffield with three young children, I was again a newcomer. I applied for a primary school teaching job at Wharncliffe Side near the steel making town of Stocksbridge, to start in September, and joined the local Labour Party.

When the second '74 general election became imminent I went down to the Firth Park Labour Hall in the neighbouring Brightside constituency to introduce myself. This was full of friendly people from the massive council estates to the north of

Firth Park Labour Hall, now renamed the Harry Harpham Community Centre after the Brightside constituency MP who died in Februay 2016, less than a year after taking office.

Sheffield of pre and post-war housing for families from the slum clearance areas along the lower Don Valley. I offered to help and received a very warm welcome from Roger and Joan Barton and Jock and Betty Sturrock.

Brightside Labour Party had been in the national media for de-selecting their MP Eddie Griffiths shortly after the earlier February election.[6] Joan and Roger Barton live in the same house as they did then near Firth Park, and recently recalled this confrontation of 45 years ago and what issues had led to their disquiet. Roger explained that although Griffiths had connections with the steel industry he came from Wales, spoke with a Welsh accent, and did not seem to understand what it was like actually working in the industry. Joan was more forthright:

Roger Barton

> He wasn't interested in ordinary working people like us. We thought any of us could do just as good; the stories in the press about him playing golf with Tory MPs had put people off. He just talked down at us.

Jock, an engineer from Glasgow, and Betty Sturrock who also lived nearby echoed the Bartons' sentiments, but Jock admitted in retrospect: *'There was nothing really specific to complain about.'*

6. Eddie Griffiths MP, 1968-1974; Griffiths changed sides to support the Tories in 1979.

Roger described how he, Jock Sturrock and Clive Betts went to speak with officers of Lincoln constituency party where the struggle to de-select their sitting MP Dick Taverne[7] over his support for the European Economic Community had hit national headlines. They also took informal advice from Ian Mikardo, a left-wing member of Labour's national executive. After a number of weeks they were asked to make their case along with Mr Griffiths to a sub-committee of the NEC before the de-selection could be authorised. As it happened Ian Mikardo was in the Chair and it was agreed that the rules had been properly followed. They then went on to pick Joan Maynard as the candidate. Jock Sturrock became Joan Maynard's agent and thought her Trade Union credentials, albeit it in the Agricultural Workers' Union, rather than one of the steel unions, were in themselves a very sound qualification. Neither couple mentioned that being a woman had been a significant issue in her selection.[8]

The national Labour Party, alarmed by the constituency's bold approach, hoped this was just a local phenomenon. It singled the constituency out as being dangerously left wing in the eyes of many on the national executive committee. However, the NEC had to accept Brightside's decision. By carefully using proper rules and procedure, Brightside constituency offered an

---

7. Dick Taverne (b. 1928) was the Financial Secretary to the Treasury from '69-'70 in Harold Wilson's government and helped to form the Institute for Fiscal Studies (IFS) after Labour's defeat, in 1970. He later joined the Social Democratic Party (SDP) in the early 80s and is now Baron Taverne, a life peer in the House of Lords. Taverne was de-selected by Lincoln Labour Party in 1972, and in response he left the Labour Party and resigned his seat, thus forcing a by-election which he won in March 1973 and again in the February 1974 general election, standing as an Independent Democratic Labour candidate, but lost in the autumn '74, to the young Margaret Jackson, later Dame Margaret Beckett, MP for Derby North.
8. Agricultural Workers' Union from the rural constituency of Thirsk and Malton.

example that encouraged the movement for the mandatory re-selection of sitting Parliamentary candidates to gather strength. This combination of solidarity of purpose, discipline and careful organisation had made the South Yorkshire Labour and Trade Union movement a formidable force.

Back in the Labour Hall I had also told the Bartons and Sturrocks about my Liverpool experience and asked whether there was any interest on the left in Sheffield around Chile. Their response was clear and categorical: *'You need to go and speak to the Trades and Labour Council about that and see what they say'*. I followed this advice and went along to the T&G district office on Hartshead. Chile was placed as an item on the next agenda. I attended with another colleague, Steve Bond. When it was our item we were called in. The room was full and Cllr Bill Owen was in the chair with his shock of white hair. Bill looked me up and down and said:

> Right. You are welcome! Tell us about this item, 'Chile'. You'll then leave the room and we will discuss what you've said. We'll call you back in when we've done.

How formal! How un-Liverpool! No lively emotional discussion! However, when we were called in again the answer was definite, warm and positive:

> Well young lady! We liked what you said. Let us know what you want us to do in the way of support. Next business…

That was it. Support secured. A sizeable coach from Sheffield Trades Council took us to the second anniversary of the Chilean coup in 1975 on September 11th; trade unionists and political activists offered their hospitality to refugees forced into exile and negotiated jobs for them in the steel works and universities. Members of the City Council used their positions to ensure that English language courses and housing were on offer. Once settled in the city, not only were the Chileans made welcome, but more importantly their personal experiences and the politics behind them were a respected element in the Labour movement. They were 'one of us'. Friendship and solidarity followed.

The authority and confidence with which a political decision was followed up with well organised action taught me an important lesson. I felt proud to be part of something big and significant as I canvassed with the Brightside Labour team in the autumn general election campaign when Eddie Griffiths had not gone quietly but was standing as 'Independent Labour'.

The organisation within Brightside Labour Hall was meticulous. Clive Betts, as agent, was an economist fresh from Cambridge, young, bright and thorough. There were canvassing teams – mixed gender unlike ten years earlier in the Potteries. We methodically visited every house. At those displaying a Griffiths poster, we explained patiently that the Labour candidate was now Joan Maynard, not Eddie Griffiths, for political reasons, and would they mind exchanging their poster for our 'genuine Labour' one, ready to display with stickers at the corners. Once that happened we were happy to move on before returning to give a detailed house by house report to Clive Betts at the Labour Hall.

Clive Betts

The local *Star* newspaper ran a campaign against Joan Maynard, pictured at her home with a portrait of Lenin as a background. As a newcomer, I found the campaign impressively different from Liverpool politics. The pride of constituency activists in their local working class communities and in trade union solidarity came through with infectious enthusiasm. Joan Maynard beat Griffiths by 7,926 votes. It was a victory for energy and confidence.

The people we met in that first year had a strong bond of loyalty to the working class, which was matched by equally strong suspicion of establishments, and preparedness to challenge them. Six of them were much later Parliamentary colleagues in London or Brussels. This book celebrates the steep learning curve that started with an election victory in Brightside, developed my confidence as a political campaigner, whilst also delivering projects through the collective work and vision of many other individuals giving them wider significance.

CHAPTER 2

Sheffield in South Yorkshire

The Creation of a Socialist Community

At the start of the 1970s South Yorkshire did not exist. It was part of the West Riding of Yorkshire, whose population dwarfed the other two Ridings put together. Local authority boundaries had been virtually unchanged since 1894.[1] West Riding County Council's administrative headquarters were in neither Leeds nor Sheffield, Yorkshire's two largest cities, but in Wakefield, a smaller city, that lay at the heart of the coalfield, and close to the old Roman road north which roughly followed the present A1 through Leicester, Stamford and Doncaster, up to Pontefract and Ferrybridge, close to Wakefield and on up through Tadcaster, to the mediaeval ecclesiastical centres of York and Durham.

Redcliffe-Maud Report

The Wilson government set up a commission in 1966 chaired by Lord Redcliffe-Maud to:

> … consider the structure of Local Government in England outside Greater London, in relation to its

1. The Local Government Act 1894 introduced elected Councils at District level – urban (UDC) and rural (RDC) – and at Parish level. This was partly to address the significant population movements brought about by the industrial revolution.

> existing functions; and to make recommendation for authorities and boundaries, and for functions and their division, having regard to their size and character of areas … and the need to sustain a viable system of local democracy.[2]

Wilson accepted its main recommendations in principle, describing it as:

> a radical redrawing of local authority boundaries, not merely to reduce the numbers, but more important to end the division between town and country and recognise the requirements of planning and communication in the modern age.[3]

On taking office after Labour's defeat in 1970 the Heath government, although opposed to the abolition of so many county authorities under Tory control, accepted the principle of five new regional 'Metropolitan Authorities', covering the functions of planning and transport, and aspects of regional arts and culture. The new South Yorkshire Metropolitan Authority, (South Yorkshire County Council, SYCC) based in Barnsley, enhanced Sheffield's dominance in the region, and created new administrative job opportunities. South Yorkshire became an official entity and name for the first time.[4] Sheffield no longer felt subsidiary to the West Riding. Wakefield, at the heart of the Yorkshire coalfield, had closer road and rail links with Leeds and

---

2. Redcliffe-Maud Royal Commission on Local Government; Terms of Reference.
3. *Hansard*, 11th June 1969.
4. 'South Riding', in the novel of the same name by Winifred Holtby written in 1936, is a fictional area.

the woollen industry towns of Bradford, Halifax and Huddersfield than with Sheffield.

Despite the new County Hall of SYCC being located in Barnsley, Sheffield was generally accepted and viewed as its major political and economic unit. Sheffield local politicians and trade unionists felt like senior partners, but became more aware of distinct social and cultural differences among mining communities as they started to work with colleagues in the new Metropolitan authority. Barnsley people spoke a distinctly different dialect, boasted brass bands and/or male voice choirs in many communities, grew rhubarb and were bound together by their common history and work in the coalfield.

I am grateful to John Cornwell,[5] one of the few initial County Councillors who remained a member until its demise in 1986, for his insight and detailed descriptions of the early pre-operational discussions around the Shadow Authority. He explained how:

> Sheffield's initial attitude to SYCC appeared to be one of support provided they 'controlled' it – and the headquarters were in Sheffield. They lost out on the HQ being in Barnsley, but insisted that the Head Offices of the South Yorkshire Passenger Transport Authority (SYPTA) were located in Sheffield.

The first elections for the new Authority took place on 12th April 1973 and produced an overwhelming Labour majority. A 16-member Policy Working Party under the chairmanship of

5. John Cornwell, a former teacher at Ecclesfield Comprehensive School, one of the County Councillors who sat from its founding to its end along with Jock Sturrock and Alex Waugh, Chair of the Transport Committee.

Stan Crowther,[6] Leader of Rotherham Council, was established. New members from Sheffield included Sir Ron Ironmonger, its Council Leader,[7] and young enthusiasts including David Blunkett, Bill Michie, Jock Sturrock, and Peter Price. Clive Betts was later appointed an economic adviser to the SYCC. There was a significant absence of women. The group was to cover policy priorities for 'Planning, Transportation and Industrial Development'. They put together an outspokenly radical manifesto, whose final report included the hope that it would produce:

> … a sound Socialist basis for the programmes of the new County Council.
>
> Labour will be a local line of defence against the Tories, VAT and the Common Market, ready to go, centred on Jobs, Pollution, Transport, Planning and Prices.

John Cornwell emphasised that:

> Sheffield were always going to be the dominant force; they had the talent and the new ideas.

Buses and Cheap Fares

The same crowd of keen, young activists on the Sheffield & District Trades and Labour Party had already in 1972 discussed public transport policy in some detail. They had developed a

---

6. Stan Crowther, later MP for Rotherham.

7. Sir Ron Ironmonger 1914-1984. Memorial plaque erected in August 2020 reads, 'Freeman and Alderman of the city of Sheffield. He served the people of South Yorkshire as leader of the county and city council.'

scheme that included free fares for pensioners and a flat rate fare structure across the area that would be frozen at its present rate. This almost certainly was partly due to trade unionists returning from visits to the Soviet Union to tell of the efficient and cheap transport networks they had seen used in the urban areas there. As described later there were strong working connections between leading members of the local Communist and Labour Parties. This group of the newly elected Sheffield intake were adamant that these transport proposals would be given priority in the SYCC's first year, once its staff and Chief Officers were in place. The fares element of the transportation section of the manifesto promised that:

> The aim of the County will be to provide free public transport for the elderly, handicapped and disabled, as an immediate objective. This will be regarded as a first step towards the ultimate provision of free transport for all.

The proposals were to be funded by *'a realistic fares structure and subsidies'*, which since the Wilson government's Transport Act of 1968 were *'now accepted as a proper means of financing public transport, especially in those areas of transport provision with a social content'*.

Putting in place a policy that would affect the whole travel-to-work area made a lot of sense in terms of opening up the labour market. The policy was in operation throughout South Yorkshire less than a year later in 1975 when bus fares were frozen indefinitely. In 1974 Sheffield's Council Leader, Sir Ron Ironmonger, was elected Leader of the South Yorkshire Labour Group. John Cornwell reminisced that a number of the Chief Officers in the early days of SYCC who had moved over from the

West Riding thought *'we were MAD'*. He also described how Bill Rodgers[8] the Shadow Transport Minister:

> ... would ring Sir Ron from London when he knew a Labour Group meeting was taking place to beg him to 'look again' at the transport policy. But when it came to the vote Ron Ironmonger would be the first to jump up in support!

Almost immediately the policy proved very popular. Campaigning was honest and open about the cost to the rates because of the unity and conviction with which the Labour movement could boast of its efficacy. It also boosted Labour control of the three District authorities, Barnsley, Rotherham and Doncaster and Sheffield City Council in their annual elections throughout the period.

In the 1970s it was more unusual for women to drive a car than it is now – especially working class women. Hellewell[9] writes that car ownership in South Yorkshire was amongst the lowest in the country. 'BRAKE'[10] – a transport charity which focuses on road safety – informs us that:

> The number of women drivers has grown significantly since the 1970s when male drivers outnumbered female drivers by three to one. Between 1970 and 2000 the number of women

---

8. Bill Rodgers, Member of Parliament for Stockton-on-Tees (1962-1983), later Baron Rodgers of Quarry Bank, served as a cabinet minister in the 1970s, but defected from the Labour Party to form the Social Democratic Party (SDP) in 1981, one of the 'Gang of Four' alongside Shirley Williams, Roy Jenkins and David Owen who left the front bench in 1979 to launch the SDP.

9 See page 28.

10. www.brake.org.uk

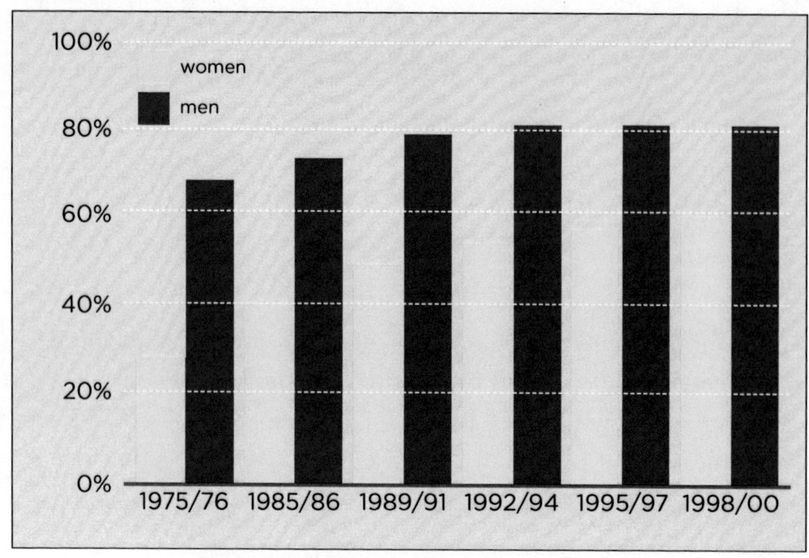

Share of full driving licence holders among all adults in England between 1975 and 2000, by gender

holding a driving licence doubled from 30% to 60%.[11]

It was a matter of some prestige in many Council estates to have a car parked outside, and the care of the car was commonly the responsibility of the man of the house, as reflected in TV adverts. Even if a woman had a driving licence she would often use the car for shopping or the children, but for longer journeys sit in the passenger seat.

With very cheap fares, less well-off families, the old, and women with young families were the obvious beneficiaries. Over the five years following its introduction, because of high inflation, the increasing value of the frozen 'flat' 10p adult fare, 2p for children,

11. Department for Transport, Current trends in and factors behind road use, 2015.

shifted the financial balance for many commuters, men and women, in favour of using public transport rather than their cars to get to work. It was a clear example of radical policy, introduced in the name of socialism, which especially benefitted women, though this was never used in the early days as its justification. It made good sense for everyone. It kept bus usage and income from fares high, and traffic congestion low. Sheffield became the least congested city of its size in the country. The environment benefitted. The ever-increasing number of passengers helped to justify the policy, to fund and pay for pensioner's free fares, and limit the rate burden. Today members of the public in the region hark back with nostalgia to the freedom the policy gave them and their families.

It also allowed the local authority to operate the transport budget with enough confidence in the increased numbers of bus users to place a regular order for new vehicles with the Leyland bus production company in Lancashire, and to build a close working relationship with that firm on the design of new, more environmentally friendly vehicles like the 'bendy-bus'. Councillor Peter Price, a member of the original group of future Councillors in Sheffield who proposed the fares freeze in 1972, described the Labour movement's pride in this achievement.

> School children could travel anywhere for 2p. Pensioners travelled free, adults for 10p. It was new and untried in this country. Later, bus lanes were created, shopping precincts pedestrianised, but it was the pricing that made the difference and as such was singled out for attention by supporters and opponents of the policy alike.

Public transport based on very cheap fares is indeed a working model of how public finance and purchasing power can be used for economic and social good. On the one hand it protects employment and boosts investment in manufacturing; on another it establishes a culture of friendly and supportive communities where young and old can afford to enjoy leisure amenities across the region. It reduces inequality because of being of universal benefit which helps poorer families and individuals more than the wealthy.

> The Metropolitan Counties lasted only 12 years, but during that time had a greater influence than any other on the provision and financing of quality public transport. Indeed, it is arguable that its very success led to its own downfall. Public transport is about the movement of people. In Britain public transport policy has been a political football lacking the continuity found elsewhere in the developed world.[12]

The fares policy came to epitomise the tag 'Socialist Republic of South Yorkshire' as Colin Brown spelt out in a *Guardian* article 6th January 1981 pre-viewing the upcoming third Metropolitan County election:

> The slogan was probably coined derisively by a local Tory councillor, though nobody seems sure today, but enterprising Labour councillors in Brightside constituency certainly cashed in on it. They produced badges proclaiming the Socialist Republic, that turned out to be best sellers at party conferences and rallies, benefitting local party funds.

---

12. Hellewell, Scott D. (1996). *South Yorkshire Transport, 1974-1985*. Venture Publications.

> There are no border guards, passport checks or even red flags arriving in South Yorkshire, and the Queen's head still appears on the currency. The one obvious difference between South Yorkshire and other Labour controlled areas is, of course, on the buses. South Yorkshire has the cheapest bus fares in the country. You can travel one stop for 3p or miles for 10p. The result has been an increased use of the buses.
>
> The county has followed its transport policy for half a decade, despite pressure from successive Environment secretaries to change or abandon it. The success of the policy has been held up by other Labour councils as an example of what can be done with the will and the money.
>
> South Yorkshire's policy is now under its most severe attack with a 30% cut by the present Environment secretary, Michael Heseltine, in the county's transport grant. The total cost of the policy will rise by £20 million to £60 million next year. But the County Council's ruling Labour group is adamant it will not change.

The cheap fares policy played a significant role in my own political development as I describe later.

South Yorkshire deserved to be proud of its acronym Socialist Republic, and the reason for it. A year later, in 1982, its loyalty to the policy was tested by the House of Lords ruling, known as the 'Bromley Judgement', that declared the GLC's 'Fare's Fair' policy for London Transport to be illegal. This was based on the 1969 Transport (London) Act rather than the 1968 Transport Act that covered SYCC and the Passenger Transport Authorities, but which also controlled fares. Joint work between officers from Sheffield and SYCC using statistics that showed continuous improvement of quality bus services and passenger numbers were useful in helping the GLC (Greater London Council) and Ken Livingstone to win their challenge in the courts. Underlying it was the South Yorkshire experience.

Boundary Changes and Political Cultures

The other boundary changes emanating from the Redcliffe Maud report changed the political culture. To the north of Sheffield, Wortley Rural District Council, the largest RDC in the country by population, was subsumed into Sheffield City. It covered a group of communities including the industrial town of Chapeltown, and a host of villages, once reliant upon metal trades and cottage industry as well as farming. It had a long history:

> The first local government unit within the district was the Wortley Union formed in the 1830s under the chairmanship of the Earl of Wharncliffe. It served the area between Sheffield and Penistone and set out to help and administer to the poor. Its business was conducted in the Wortley Arms, close to Wortley Hall, the home of the Earls of Wharncliffe.[13]

In 1895 it was split up and the Rural District Council was formed based at Grenoside, first at the Workhouse, and later in substantial offices after they were opened on Halifax Road in 1939. At its closure in 1974 it covered, with its 48,124 acres, a greater area than the whole city of Sheffield. Three new Sheffield electoral wards were created, Stocksbridge, Chapeltown and South Wortley. The remaining four wards of Penistone East and West, Dodworth and Hoyland, which joined Barnsley.

Penistone parliamentary constituency had remained roughly the same as when it was created in the 1894 reorganisation to accommodate the growing population around some of these major pits in the Barnsley area: Dodworth, Elsecar, Hoyland, Pilley and Silkstone. Penistone is an old market town with a large mediaeval church, on the drovers and later turnpike routes that skirted the eastern flanks of the Pennines, northwards to Huddersfield, Halifax and Skipton.

---

13. F*inal Report – Wortley RDC 1895-1974*, with Introduction by Chairman Cllr Ernest Fox.

Wortley Rural District Council's offices on Halifax Road, Grenoside, opened in 1939.

An archive of Ecclesfield Labour Party minute books from 1923 shows a new local political party gathering know-how, and funding their work and campaigning from whist drives, tea parties and dances, while the trade unions gathered their own experience during the years of depression, struggle, poverty and the General Strike. The local party also had the foresight to nominate their own member, Lady Mabel Smith, to be an MP. The divisional (constituency) meeting in Penistone, sadly, were not ready to put a woman forward. Had Lady Mabel, rather than Mr Rennie Smith, been selected by the Penistone Divisional Party she might have followed Lady Astor into Parliament as one of the UK's earliest women MPs. It was clearly a 'swing seat' in the clutch of elections after World War One, when the by-election in 1921 had returned its first Labour MP, with a majority of 576. After Labour gained the seat in 1923 with Rennie Smith, it was lost again in 1931 when the Labour Party split under Ramsay Macdonald.

Eva Ratcliffe and Ernest Fox, Council members at the time of WRDC's closure. Ernest Fox was Chairman.

Eva Ratcliffe lived in a Council bungalow in Ecclesfield, and was close friends of George and Rosie Bramald, a Labour Party couple I got to know locally in Grenoside, as an 'incomer'. Then in her 90s we would sit in her small kitchen where Eva would tell me about her father who had been one of the founders of Ecclesfield Labour Party. She had ensured that the old leather attaché case which held the archive of minute books and accounts from the 20s was preserved intact.

By World War Two Labour were in firm control in local elections and the 1945 landslide saw the constituency become a safe Labour parliamentary seat, until the December 2019 election demonstrated the vulnerability of many traditional mining areas, being 'taken for granted' by the Labour Party.

Thirty years later, however, bringing the three former Penistone wards into Sheffield brought a new political culture into the

Sheffield District Labour Movement. Stocksbridge was and still is a steel making town,[14] very proud of its specialist steel products. Chapeltown, closer to Rotherham and the Yorkshire coalfield communities, was dominated by what remained of Newton Chambers Engineering and former blast furnaces; railways and coal and coke works, and the Izal factory. The smaller villages, formerly part of Wortley RDC, had strong traditions related to metal working in the 18th and 19th centuries (see above), and their traditions and culture owed more to the wider area than to Sheffield. A similar impact was felt in the South East of the city where Sheffield drew in new areas from the Derbyshire coalfield.

Settling in: Penistone Constituency

Our new home in 1974 was in Grenoside a former quarrying and metal working village near Ecclesfield and in the Penistone constituency. As a newcomer and female political activist, I had to acclimatise to both cultural traditions, that of Brightside constituency – challenging and radical, and Penistone more traditional and dominated by the coalfield communities. Both traditions were very different from Huyton and Liverpool.

Penistone constituency meetings were held on Saturday afternoons. Women were expected to leave the meeting at a specific time – however interesting the debate – to prepare tea, sandwiches, cake and biscuits for a comfort break, before the MP, John Mendelson, gave his Parliamentary report. This, though irritating to me, was not seen as subservience by the other women, since the 'Women's Council' was a powerful voting

14. Samuel Fox, its founder, who developed the strong yet flexible steel to give Fox's umbrellas a national reputation.

force, dominated by miners' wives from the Barnsley end of the constituency. Most of the constituency's funding came from the multitude of affiliated National Union of Mineworkers (NUM) branches, still in existence despite earlier pit closures leaving the mine workings extinct. The NUM were in political control, and the history and culture of coal mining predominated. The majority of local councillors in the constituency, whether from Barnsley or Sheffield, were well established local figures, nearly all white, middle-aged and male.

A remarkable exception to this tradition, in gender terms, though also closely connected with the coal mining industry, had been Lady Mabel Smith, already mentioned, whose family, the Fitzwilliams of Wentworth Woodhouse owned many of the collieries in South Yorkshire. She went on to leave a valuable legacy to the area, as an educationist, devoted especially to girls and women's education.

A recent unpublished and detailed research paper by local historians Paul and Wendy Shaw has described her life in some detail.

> Lady Mabel Florence Harriet Wentworth-Fitzwilliam was born on July 14, 1870, at the Fitzwilliam's London home. She was sister to Earl Fitzwilliam, one of the richest men in England and a member of the privileged class, yet she became one of the great social democrats of South Yorkshire.
>
> She served on the West Riding County Council Education Committee for 30 years and was memorably described by a colleague as 'the feminine star in our firmament'. An officer of

Lady Mabel Smith (above centre and inset), described as one of the great social democrats of South Yorkshire.

> Wortley Rural District Council described her as 'one of the busiest people he knew – doing public work all hours of the day and often night'.[15]

Catherine Bailey in her book *Black Diamonds*[16] recounts how Joyce Smith tells how her aunt, Lady Mabel, became a socialist.

> When she was a child, her mother gave an annual party for the village children from the schools near Hoober Hall. They were invited for sports day and Mabel with her brother and sisters ran in these races. There was one village girl who was the same

15. Paul and Wendy Shaw members of Grenoside & District Local History Group.
16. Bailey, C. (2007). *Black Diamonds: The Rise and Fall of an English Dynasty,* Penguin.

> age as Mabel – she was twelve or thirteen – and they were great friends. One or other of them always won the races.
>
> One year her friend didn't turn up and Mabel said: 'Where's Janie?' They told her she had left school and gone into service and wouldn't be coming anymore.
>
> Joyce said that Mabel was horrified to think that while she was being taught at home by her governess, her friend had had to go into service. Mabel said at that point she made up her mind that she was going to get education for them all.

Former local residents, remember her serving soup for striking miners in Chapeltown market during the 1926 coal strike, almost certainly workers from the pits in her family's ownership. She served on the national Labour Party's Executive (NEC) in the thirties, and in 1951 aged over 80 was still an energetic independent thinker when she attended the World Peace Congress in Sheffield, and was criticised for this by Labour's NEC at the time. Her local Labour Party in Ecclesfield discussed whether to complain about it, but decided against because of her age. Clearly she was a remarkable character and, though unstated, a feminist, but with a very different political background from Sheffield Labour activists, or Joan Maynard the first woman MP in South Yorkshire.

Sheffield, City of Steel: An Industrial Culture

The special position of the Sheffield Trades and Labour Council in the local political culture cannot be overemphasised. A little known book, *Sheffield Trades and Labour Council – 1858 to 1958*, describes the roots of its radicalism. The book was sponsored by

'The Sheffield Bookshop', at 20 Matilda Street, in 1959 to mark the centenary of the Trades and Labour Council in 1959. Its four authors were: Bill Owen, founder of The Sheffield Bookshop, which advertised itself as 'Specialists for 20 years in books and pamphlets of interest to all Trade Unionists'; John Mendelson, Lecturer at Sheffield University,[17] ; Sidney Pollard BSc(econ) PhD, labour historian and lecturer at Sheffield University; and Vernon Thornes, secretary of the Trades and Labour Council for nearly 30 years, until his death in 1983.

Its back cover reads:

UNIONS – THE ONLY SAFEGUARD

From a letter addressed to the Trade Unions of Sheffield

23rd November 1841

Trades Unions … have generated a love of freedom, have knit together the victims of capital, when masters have forgotten honour and justice, and the world compassion and sympathy. When governments and religion were ranked with oppressors, Unions were the only barriers between the desolation of capital and machinery, starvation and the poor house.

G.J. HOLYOAKE

17. John Mendelson was later elected MP for Penistone constituency at a by-election in 1959 and held office until his death in 1978.

It shows that the Chartist movement was well supported in Sheffield but differed from other cities, such as Manchester, in winning support from the middle as well as the working classes. The quote below is from an early chapter.

> In the absence of large manufacturing establishments before about 1860, the social structure of Sheffield exhibited certain special features found elsewhere only perhaps in Birmingham and the surrounding Black Country districts. In the local staple trades, most men owned their own rooms, their own tools, had access to local sources of 'power' whether water, coal or manual, and decided themselves how many hours they would work. The artisan thus enjoyed a considerable degree of independence, and there was a continuous gradation from the skilled man to the 'little mester' or factor, up to the wealthiest manufacturer who themselves largely employed semi-independent outworkers, with no clearly marked social barrier along the ladder.

Pride in the skills of the many different trades was always evident: scissor grinders, cutlers, file smiths, steel casters, white-smiths all had their own trades. It defined Sheffield industry. Having a trade also meant having served an apprenticeship thereby becoming a 'working man' who deserved respect. No amount of exhaustion, dust, and danger from working with white hot metal took away from the empowerment that resulted. Rather the effort and danger added to his status. The authors' main concern was to stress the very early existence of Sheffield Trades Council and Labour Representation Committee, which had its first meeting in

1904. It recounts in meticulous detail how the affiliated branches doubled from 11 at the start of World War One to 25 by 1920, and continued to grow in influence through the 1920s. By 1926 links with the Labour Party were solid as Sheffield was the first major urban area to elect a Labour Council.

The four authors of the *Sheffield Trades and Labour Council 1858-1958* make little mention of women. The book fails to record that in 1851 Sheffield Women's Rights Association, led by Abiah Higginbottom of Pond Street, was one of the first groups in the country to collect signatures in support of the Chartist backed Parliamentary petition which included a call for universal suffrage. There is a brief mention of Mrs Gertrude Wilkinson, the first woman member of Sheffield Trades Council executive in 1918, who became President and encouraged the formation of women's sections in the TU branches in the area. It hardly touches other earlier aspects of Sheffield's political history, such as the influence of dissenters, whose George Street congregational chapel was closely linked with Carrs Lane chapel in Birmingham, from which the Reverend Robert Dale preached and promoted the 'civic gospel' which supported the Chartist movement and opposed slavery. Mary-Anne Rawson (1801-87) of George Street congregational chapel was a leading light in Sheffield ladies' anti-slavery society formed in 1825. Their anti-slavery petition in 1838 had no fewer than 25,000 signatures (three quarters of the female population). Once widowed she and her sister ran a school at Wincobank.

These details have been well researched by Clyde Binfield[18] and other academics – Matt Roberts of Sheffield Hallam University

18. Clyde Binfield, Reader in History, University of Sheffield.
Binfield, C. (1993). *History of the City of Sheffield. 1843-1993.* Bloomsbury.

Wincobank Chapel and schoolroom. The school was run by the Rawson sisters. Mary-Anne Rawson was a leading light in the ladies anti-slavery society.

and David Price of the University of Sheffield in his book *Sheffield Troublemakers.*[19] They are a useful reminder of other strands in Sheffield's history that contributed to its radicalism. Edward Carpenter (1844-1929) a poet and early promoter of gay equality and socialism, gets a brief mention in the 'Trades and Labour' history, as a

> … quiet idealistic Socialist who was to make many Socialist converts in the future, but remained equally without influence in 1887. When he opened his Socialist club in a Sheffield café in

19. Price, D. (2008). *Sheffield Troublemakers.* Phillimore Press.

> February 1887, not one of the prominent trade unionists of the SFTC (Sheffield Federation of Trades Councils) attended. Most of them were openly hostile.

Key Individuals – Men and Women

Bill Owen and George Caborn, just two years apart in age, were two dominant players in the Labour movement in Sheffield during the 60s and 70s. Bill in the Labour Party and George, a Communist, took each in different directions, Bill into local government, George to remain in the trade union movement and the AEU. They were the closest of friends. Both had deep-seated Socialist convictions, with an unusually soft, family-conscious, and liberal core. Neither drank much alcohol. Their reputations for integrity built respect from workforce and bosses alike.

Bill Owen, a dominant player in the Sheffield Labour movement.

Bill Owen is described by Michael Holloway in a book put together after his death as:

> ... a typical, if outstanding example of a generation of socialists who grew up in the 1920s and 30s and who educated themselves with the help of the WEA and public libraries.[20]

20. Holloway M. (1993). *Portraits of a City Father.* Sheffield Hallam University.

Richard Caborn pays tribute to Bill as '*a working class person who was probably one of the best read, best self-educated people in the city*'. In future chapters his commitment to education for all is described in more detail. A fitting tribute to Bill is the massive atrium within Sheffield Hallam University's main 'Owen' building, named after him. As Chair of Governors he had overseen the Polytechnic's transformation into a successful second university in the city. A powerful figure in the Sheffield Labour Movement he is remembered with respect and affection for his astute political acumen, tireless work and intensive knowledge of the rules of debate. Less recognised is his commitment to women's contribution to politics, and like Lady Mabel Smith to girls' education. Here, Holloway quotes how Bill describes the roots of his own socialism.

> My mother was the biggest influence on me. She was very good looking, a big woman and very outspoken. Her father was an Irishman working on the London docks and he was Keir Hardie's[21] election agent when he won the seat. Her father carried her on the shoulder at the dock strike in 1896, led by Tom Burns and Tom Mann – for what they called the docker's tanner.
>
> She became very active in the Labour and women's movement, became poll captain for the area we lived in. I used to do all the delivering of the Sheffield Co-operator Paper. I used to go to the election meetings as a school kid and enjoyed

21. Keir Hardie (1856-1914) born in Lanarkshire, Scotland. He stood for West Ham in 1892 as the Independent Labour Party candidate and won. An advocate of women's rights, free schooling, pensions and Indian self-rule.

> hearing the hecklers, not heckling myself, just listening.

Of his own education Bill writes:

> It was only after I left school that I started to develop mentally, through the Hillsborough Co-operative Fellowship, Arnold Freeman's Sheffield Educational Settlement, the Workers Educational Association and the National Council of Labour Colleges.[22]

As mentioned above Bill Owen founded the left-wing bookshop on Matilda Street, which Richard Caborn remembers visiting as a little boy, with his Dad, George Caborn. George Caborn and his wife Mary were a close couple with two sons, David and Richard. George, a lifelong Communist, well known and respected by thousands of steel and engineering workers, and by their employers for being principled, fair and true to his word, gave class politics an international dimension. He invited respected figures like Paul Robeson to sing at the City Hall. He was well read with very strong principles based on humanism, tolerance and fairness. Mary was a staunch Methodist, with equally strong moral values, and a 'Co-operator' like Bill's mother. She had worked as a cook at the local school and then as a dinner lady. Active in her union she was also heavily involved in Sheffield Co-operative Women's Guild.[23]

Richard describes his early years at home vividly. He tells how George went on a group visit to China organised by the

22. Freeman was appointed tutor for extra-mural studies in 1913.

23. Founded in 1883 by Alice Acland.

George and Richard Caborn.

Communist Party and his Union. He met Mao Tse-Tung, and was impressed and somewhat astonished to be offered a job there by the man himself, if he wanted one, because of his experience and expertise in the steel industry. On returning home Richard listened to his Dad telling his Mum all about this fascinating visit and has never forgotten Mary's reaction when it came to the job possibility:

> I've been with you all these years George and will do anything for the 'Cause', but I will NOT go to live in China.

The notion stopped there! Or perhaps not … The good reputation of the University of Sheffield for engineering and steel research and study continues. There are now 4,000 students and a Chinese speaking Vice Chancellor. One student is quoted as saying: *'I like Sheffield in particular because of its culture of diversity',* another appreciates its reputation for technology. Thirty-five years later, Sheffield's Council initiated a visit and a twinning link with Anshan, the site of one of China's largest steelworks, with cross-party support that included the Chamber of Commerce.[24] Richard Caborn is very proud of the city's Advanced Metals and Manufacturing Centre, whose foundation he championed as an MP which offers new apprenticeships and training. His childhood was imbued with his parents' joint commitment to their socialism, the 'Cause'. Apart from the visits to Bill's bookshop, he recalls the Saturday morning meetings of 'The Metal' where George met leading shop stewards from all the major steel plants. He was their leader and co-ordinated them with good humour and firmness as they met monthly as the Sheffield 'Confed', at the AEU (Amalgamated Engineering Union) offices. The 'Confed' was as significant a body as the Trades and Labour Council within the Sheffield Labour Movement.

George was a key player in the Trades Council acquisition of Wortley Hall in 1950 on a leasehold arrangement for an original annual rent of £50, as a 'residential and educational centre' for the Labour movement.[25]

It was a grand and beautiful country house, of 18th century design built in the latter half of that century and owned by the Wortley family, the Earls of Wharncliffe. It was taken over by the army during the war, after which it fell into disrepair. The post-war Sheffield Labour movement felt it was fitting for such a property to be owned and used by the working class and put in a successful bid to buy the leasehold. It needed massive renovation

---

24. See page 286.
25. Cornwell, J. (2011). *Voices of Wortley Hall: The Story of Labour's Home 1951-2011*. Wortley Hall Ltd.

Wortley Hall

to make it fit for its new purpose. Individual trades unions took on the sponsorship and renovation of separate grand rooms in the 18th century reception area. Experienced tradesmen repaired and re-decorated them with care in what time they had off from work. For the generation of friends we met in the Brightside election, Wortley Hall was where as children they had spent Saturdays and Sundays, playing in the house and grounds, while their parents had worked on the building. Its renovation was a source of pride in men, women and children working together each weekend not for money but for the collective good of the working class with a vision of an equal society as their goal, led by individuals of stature like the Caborns. It remains the venue for an annual New Year walk attended by over 100 people, children and dogs.[26]

Both Bill and George's goals of equality were wide. George established the Sheffield Campaign Against Racism (SCAR)

26. It had and still holds a luxurious sense of freedom, with its large laid out gardens, and endless corridors, for children to explore. It also now has a special link with the Sylvia Pankhurst Memorial Trust.

in the 70s with 'Windrush' socialist immigrants from the Caribbean. Women in the trade union movement at the time like Sylvia Greenwood in the T&G and Vi Gill in the AEU have described their huge personal admiration for how Bill and George helped them as women play their full part in the trade union movement by setting up women's groups within every plant and workplace, and ensuring they were given speaking roles at big meetings.

Vi Gill, now over 90, recently described how:

> George made me go on the platform to speak at a City Hall meeting. I thought I made a 'balls' of it, but George encouraged me.

She reflected on a later meeting she had been persuaded by George to speak at in Trafalgar Square: *'He said put some thought into it; write down roughly what you want to say and then practise! That's when you feel really good'*.

A third significant woman was Blanche Flannery (1921-2010). Like George a staunch member of the Communist Party, she concentrated her political efforts within the Trades council, leaving her husband Martin, MP for Sheffield Hillsborough, to promote left politics within the NUT and the Labour Party. Kate Flannery,[27] her daughter, described how Blanche took her politics from her father George Howson, a worker in the

Blanche Flannery

27. Later in the 1980s Kate Flannery became the Women's Officer for Sheffield City Council.

steel works who read a lot and quoted James Connelly – the Irish republican, and Edward Carpenter. He would take Blanche and her sister Marie to open air political meetings in Barkers Pool. She joined the CP at an early age and became an executive member of its national women's advisory group where she campaigned with vigour in the 60s for the Abortion Act. She felt patronised by London feminists she met who she described as *'middle-class, who told us Yorkshire women we were not allowed to call people "love" any more'.* She also described how her experience of life had given her an intense dislike of many trade union colleagues she would describe as misogynists, and indeed how, much later in life, after being elected the Chair of Sheffield Trades Council, she 'would have called herself a feminist'. Blanche was respected in the Labour Movement, in the 70s and 80s, often as Martin's wife and not enough in her own right. Martin Flannery[28] was from County Mayo. His mother Catherine, known as Katy, was from Sheffield, a former 'buffer girl' at a cutlery works on Solly Street. Martin left the CP to join Labour in 1956. He was a teacher, active in the National Union of Teachers (NUT), before becoming MP for Hillsborough in 1974. His politics, stimulated by the Spanish Civil War, led him often to quote Joe Albaya:

> Had the world united against the Catholic fascists in Spain World War Two would have been avoided.[29]

28. Martin Flannery 1918-2006

29. Joe Albaya, the Sheffield-born son of Spanish immigrants who travelled to Spain to fight with the International Brigades against General Franco's fascist Nationalists in the civil war.

Spring Bank Camps

I think the Spring Bank camps were first suggested by Jock and Betty, as a way of keeping strong the camaraderie we had experienced during the 1974 Joan Maynard election.

Jock Sturrock, describing his early move to Sheffield from Glasgow, for work in engineering became an active member of the AEU, and met his future wife, Betty, at a local dance near Brightside. Like John Cornwell he was an SYCC County Councillor from its start to its end. Betty was born locally from Labour voting parents and along with George Caborn's wife Mary was a key organiser within Sheffield Co-op Womens Guild.

Along with the Bartons, Joan and Roger, they organised a collective camp at Spring Bank Holiday on the Yorkshire coast near Hornsey Mere, which we and the family joined. Joan Maynard visited us. It established a tradition of annual Spring Bank Holiday family camping holidays, later by Ullswater in the

Jock Sturrock's election leaflet from 1952 for the City Council.

Lake District. At first many of the families came from the estates around Firth Park; working class, less well off and proud of it. Sheffield was then, and still is, one of the most divided cities in the UK by wealth and social class (see chart p.51). Others included David and Ruth Blunkett, Clive Betts, the Caborn family and their neighbours, and Bill Michie, all of whom would call themselves working class. There were others. Peter and Janet Price, John and Judith Cornwell, Alex and Pat Waugh. Keith and I were the incomers. Between us we brought at least 25 children.

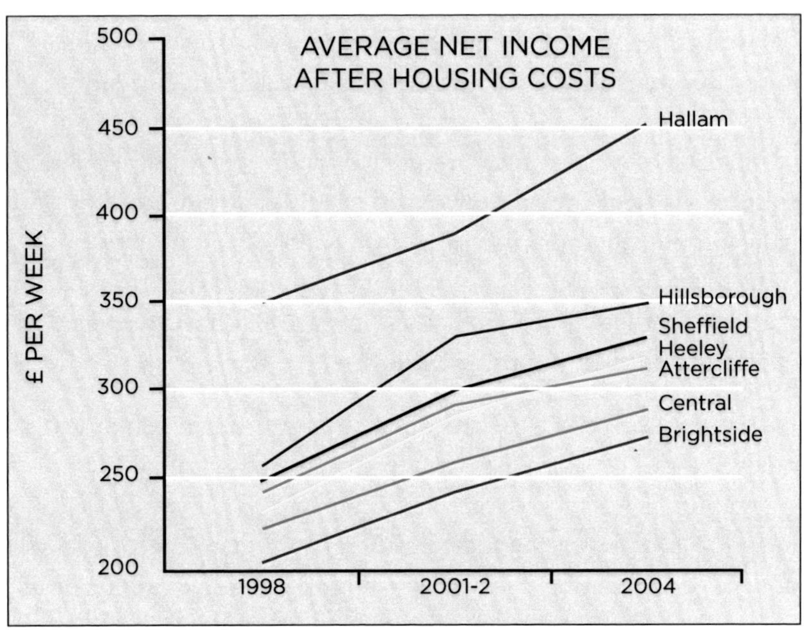

Taken from A Tale of Two Cities: The Sheffield Project, *by Danny Dorling et al. University of Sheffield, 2009.*[30]

30. Danny Dorling, academic co-author of *A Tale of Two Cities: A Sheffield Project.* Professor of Human Geography at The University of Sheffield until 2013 and later Halford Mackinder Professor of Geography at St Peter's College, Oxford.

A close network developed as the numbers grew to over 100 over the next ten years. By 1980 the crowd included the Chilean refugees and their children, community and youth work activists, including a group of youngsters on probation, more city Councillors, and many others. Some were caravanners, others like George and Mary Caborn as they grew older opted for B&B and watched the activities. Tents were pitched in a large circle to allow for continuous football or rounders. We climbed Helvellyn, went on pony treks, sailed on the lake and sang political songs around the bonfire on Bank Holiday Monday.

Political colleagues in Sheffield who were not involved would, in the 80s, refer to the 'Brightside mafia', usually in a friendly way. There was a hard-to-describe intimacy between the camp participants which created an undeniably strong cohesive political culture. Many of the group were on South Yorkshire County Council, but the camp itself was always a Sheffield initiative. It never encompassed the NUM nor political activists from Barnsley, Rotherham or Doncaster. It may even have deepened division with the other three authorities.

Politics was the link; a socialism based on wanting a better deal for the working class. The participants crossed boundaries of generation, gender, class, race and disability. Each family felt included and part of the same political movement, with work to do: election leafleting; Council meetings; teaching of adults or in schools; making badges; organising demonstrations, community action and trade union work. In recent discussions with the participants it was hard to find anyone who does not in retrospect feel there was something exceptional about the gatherings. They were in themselves a political expression of international, inclusive solidarity. George Caborn's rendition of Paul Robeson's song

Joe Hill went along with Victor Jara's songs, and the Chilean's chant *El Pueblo! Unido! Jamas sera Vencido!* and the South African national anthem *Nkosi Sikelela Africa.* Gender equality was part of the group's identity but again instinctive rather than explicit. Women and men climbed Helvellyn, cooked breakfast, played with the children and drank beer in the evening. Girls as well as boys played football, and everyone joined in the rounders.

It laid one of the foundations for the political direction in Sheffield over the next ten years into the 80s. The spirit, which can best be described as 'solidarity' came into its own in the early months of the new administration, and is the hard-to-describe ingredient in a successful political team and movement. It is well known that a divided Cabinet or Party damages the chance of good government and winning elections, and can point to this happening – as much today as ever. Why and exactly how a unity of purpose that is deeply ingrained into social culture adds effectiveness to political movements and programmes is less well researched.

In future chapters I examine in more detail why and how this personal unity played a part in bringing about social and economic change through local government, concluding that a common commitment to redressing inequality in all its forms, but starting with income and social class, was an essential factor.

CHAPTER 3

Education, Feminism and Europe

Despite the slender majority of Harold Wilson's government after the February 1974 election the mood in the country was supportive and his cabinet keen to pick up threads left unfinished when Heath took over in 1970. Re-establishing unity within the Labour movement after the discord over *In Place of Strife* was its first priority, then developing the Redcliffe-Maud reforms to local government described earlier. Three other major issues faced the government:

- firmly establishing the comprehensive principle introduced by the previous Labour government in all schools, and acting on the recommendations of the Russell report to develop adult education;
- building upon Ted Heath's commitments on Europe;
- maintaining the progress on equality issues to satisfy the growing influence of the race and gender equality lobbies.

Adult Education and the Russell Report

Education in South Yorkshire had moved from the control of the West Riding County Council headquarters in Wakefield, to the four Metropolitan Districts, expanding employment opportunities for public sector professionals in the education offices of Sheffield, Rotherham, Barnsley and Doncaster. Under the visionary leadership of Sir Alec Clegg, its Chief Education Officer, with Councillors including Lady Mabel Smith, the West Riding Education Committee had moved swiftly to implement the decision taken in 1965 by Tony Crosland, Secretary of State for Education, to request all local authorities to plan for the conversion of secondary schools to a comprehensive model.

Lady Mabel, had pointed out in 1934:

> Mass-thinking is a terrible thing, which is not really thinking at all. What we want education to do is to teach you how to think for yourselves. Then we shall get that finest of all things, collective thinking. This means everyone thinking out problems for themselves and then pooling them together so that we get a great whole. Then we shall have an educated democracy, which simply means people who are able to think for themselves.[1]

She believed that comprehensive schools would help to achieve this aim, and that education and politics were inextricably linked. By the 1970s the 11+ had been abandoned in the West Riding.

The Labour movement in the UK had always encouraged and been reliant upon the education of working class adults. Ruskin College in Oxford was:

> Founded in 1899 it aimed to provide university-standard education for working class people to empower them to act more effectively on behalf of working class communities and organisations.[2]

1. Her Hebden Bridge Grammar School Speech Day 1934, Paul and Wendy Shaw.
2. Ruskin College. www.ruskin.ac.uk

Today women make up the majority of mature students, but early adult education institutions assumed that their students would be men. The Workers' Educational Association (WEA), founded by Albert Mansbridge in 1903, was initially named as an *'Association to promote the higher education of Working Men'.* It was closely connected with R.H. Tawney, an eminent Oxford economic historian and advisor to the Labour Party on education policy, who was tutor to the first WEA tutorial classes at Longton, Stoke-on-Trent in 1908, shortly after Tawney married Jeanette Beveridge, sister of William Beveridge.

Adult education had inspired my husband Keith from his early days after leaving school, when he was called up for National Service and served in the Royal Army Education Corps. His experience of teaching working class adults in the regular army who, as he put it, '*were failed by the education system*', pointed him in the direction of his future career. Keith recalled how

> Our first home together after we left Oxford in 1961 was in the Potteries, where I was based as tutor trainee with Oxford Delegacy for Extramural Studies, which worked closely with the North Staffordshire District of the WEA, in the Tawney tradition. The training programme operated on an apprentice system where I learned through teaching under supervision of senior tutors a wide range of courses, including evening courses, day release courses for miners, potters and engineers, and residential short courses at Wedgwood Memorial College run jointly by the University and the WEA.

We found that the Potteries community in the 60s was very proud of its historic connection with R.H. Tawney. Its district office was in Cartwright House, so-named because the first of Tawney's classes was formed in response to a request by local people who flocked to an occasional extension lecture by Tawney on the Puritan Revolution, sponsored by Longton Borough Council, whose clerk, E.S. Cartwright, was convinced that *'there was a proven need to establish tutorial classes in the Potteries'.* Of his time in the Potteries Tawney wrote:

> The friendly smitings of weavers, potters, miners and engineers, have taught me much about the problem of political and economic sciences which cannot easily be learned from books.[3]

Three members of the WEA District Committee, much respected by its district secretary Eric Tams, were elderly women from the Potteries area, Nellie Mould, Eve Rowley and Winifred Myers. They were active in the Labour movement, and ran the local branch of the Co-operative Women's Guild.[4] They made us aware that manual work in the pot banks had from the beginning used women's as well as men's labour. We found that it was common for women as well as men to go to the pub in the evening and it was frequently they who decided whether another beer could be

---

3. R.H. Tawney quoted in *To Build A Blair* by A.J.Davies, (1996). (Revised ed.). London: Abacus. p. 176.

4. Co-operative Women's Guild founded in 1883. In 1889 Margaret Llewellyn-Davies took over as president and had new aims for the organisation. By now it was recognised that women were making the spending decisions in most working households; and they were choosing to spend the bulk of their money at Co-operative stores where they could get their 'divi' once or twice a year. Llewellyn-Davies wanted to harness this spending power (known as 'the power of the basket') and use it to push for change within the movement and for broader political change. (Kate Woodward – Co-operative Women's Trust.)

afforded. They, and we, believed that women might have been amongst Tawney's first students, though women's presence within the WEA was seldom mentioned in its early days.

After Keith's training year we moved to South Wales, another powerful WEA area, where he taught in the mining 'valleys', and our first child was born, but we were tempted back to the Potteries after 18 months, where Keith was proud to be appointed Tutor in Charge of the newly opened Tawney House adult education centre in Longton. He was able to follow up some of the development ideas inspired by his original time there. He described how his *'eyes had been opened to what a remarkable educational development day release had become. Negotiated between employers and trade unions, they gave manual workers the same opportunities for learning and personal development, in prime time, not at the end of a day's work, as is commonly available to professionals.'*

The question Keith addressed was: *what about people who are not in a trade union and not even in the labour market?* We recognised that adult education counter-balanced unsatisfactory earlier schooling and, for women especially, was useful when they wanted to explore their potential and improve their skills before re-entering the labour market after having children. From Tawney House he established day-time tutorial courses specifically for women for which my friends and I ran a crèche.

The WEA in the Potteries also worked closely with Keele University in organising courses at Wedgewood Memorial College, a residential college owned by the WEA at Barlaston, just outside Stoke. Keith's role there included teaching on trade union courses and national trade union residential courses and summer schools. He recognised this as another example of how opportunities could be given to working class adults, as they normally were for professionals who had already received substantial educational resources. He continued to develop these ideas in his work at Liverpool University Institute for Extra-mural Studies, organising a programme of 'Second Chance to Learn' courses in conjunction with Home Office Community Development Projects which included a residential element.

Ruskin of the North – Northern College

Tony Crosland was Harold Wilson's Secretary of State for Education 1965-67. Both he and Wilson acknowledged the importance of these developments in further education and founded the 'Open University' in 1970 to make access to further education more easily available for everyone, through outreach learning. Ten years later in 1980, Willy Russell's play *Educating Rita*, set in an Open University tutorial room, was a box office success and later turned into a film. At the same time another initiative of the Wilson government, the Community Development Project, was set up in 1969, by the Home Office. One of theses projects was Coventry Workshop with which Keith worked closely. Thise initiative:

> ... consisted of 12 local action research projects across the UK, linked to their local authorities, supported by local university research teams – seeking to turn around economically deprived areas through new ways of mobilising local people to solve their own problems in collaboration with more responsive public services.[5]

---

5. Carpenter, M. *Community Development Journal.* Volume 52; Issue 2: pp. 247-268.

Crosland and Wilson also established a Commission to review Adult Education headed by Lord Russell whose Report was published in 1973. Its recommendations included *'one further long-term residential college in the North of England'*, which became commonly known as a 'Ruskin of the North'. Its foundation was to draw Keith and our family back to his home town of Sheffield. While exploring the development of South Yorkshire politics in this period, Northern College has constantly cropped up as playing a key role in developing awareness of the importance of race and gender as well as class within socialism. Its reputation for delivering meaningful political education grew rapidly after it formally opened in 1978 and it strengthened a pride in the region's political awareness. Its roots, foundation and early years are worth recalling for their contribution to socialism in South Yorkshire. Keith's contribution to a book about its history described its background:

> R.H.Tawney … noted that all major educational movements have themselves been representative of social movements across classes. Northern College is distinctive in being the only major new educational institution for adults to be founded in the last few decades through the initiative of a social movement that is the Labour movement in South Yorkshire.

Keith Jackson

> The College's approach to adult education was developed out of this alliance by education

> workers influenced by the new and old social movements of the 1960s and1970s – the post-war Labour movement, the women's movement, the events of 1968 and the student movements, and the black power and consciousness movements. These origins were vital to the successful establishment of the College and profoundly influenced its teaching and learning programme. A value base and practice, transparently and overtly committed to collectivist and mutual organisations, has been apparent in the College's work throughout its short history. This is most clearly demonstrated through an examination of the short course programme over the past 25 years.

It was 18 months before the staff posts were advertised, during which time I settled into Sheffield politics, the Chile Human Rights Campaign and teaching infants, while Keith commuted, continuing his 'Second Chance to Learn' work in Liverpool.

Professor Richard Taylor[6] echoed how the 'second chance' movement played a part in the creation of the College:

> Karl Marx argued that 'Men make their own history, but they do not make it just as they please; they do not make it under circumstances created by themselves, but under circumstances directly encountered, given and transmitted from the past'.
>
> The creation of Northern College, in one sense, is a prime example of this constructive interaction.

---

6. Director of Continuing Education at the University of Leeds.

> Without the commitment of a small number of key people to the central idea – and without their persistence, collective working and inspiration – the College would not have come into existence. Equally the right configuration of objective circumstances, social, economic and especially political, needed to be obtained to make the development successful.

Bill Owen was a member of Sheffield Education Committee along with Peter Horton, an academic who chaired the Committee. It was an all male group but, along with Michael Barratt Brown, then senior lecturer at Sheffield University responsible for industrial studies in its adult education department, and Bill Carter, a senior officer in the Education Department, they were well placed to champion the new movements in adult education. They had been to London to lobby the Russell Commission about a 'Ruskin of the North', and were delighted when they heard of their success. They badly wanted it to be in Sheffield or, second best, somewhere in South Yorkshire though in the initial bid they tactically pressed for it to be in Yorkshire. They started looking for suitable locations.

Another stately home in the countryside, known as Wentworth Castle, Stainborough, between Sheffield and Barnsley, much bigger than Wortley Hall, had become a teacher training college for women after the war. Barnsley had scheduled the property for closure for cost reasons. Wentworth Castle[7] lay in impressive grounds and was famous for its long gallery facing south –

7. Thomas Wentworth, 1st Earl of Strafford, 1593-1641, was a leading advisor of King Charles 1st – Privy Councillor and Lord Deputy of Ireland. He was attainted and executed.

Wentworth Castle built by Thomas Wentworth, Earl of Strafford whose statue stands in the grounds, became home to the Northern College in 1976.

one of the finest, and longest in the country. After protracted negotiations to fend off bids from Lancashire, financial deals with the four authorities involved were completed, supported by the new South Yorkshire County Council. Northern College was established there in 1976, staff were appointed and it opened its doors in 1978 with Michael Barratt Brown as its principal. Keith became its Senior Tutor, responsible for its community and short course programme. He recently described how he saw it as a privilege to be working with Michael Barratt Brown, an immensely well-respected academic, and leading figure in extramural work, including industrial day release programmes in South Yorkshire, but also as an opportunity to bring together that tradition with the possibilities opened up by 'community adult education' programmes, that for him had been inspired by his work in Liverpool and previously in the Potteries.

At a conference of the Society of Industrial Tutors in 1974 Keith had outlined how a new 'northern Ruskin' could use short courses, closely dovetailed with community organisation and activity, to advance the original Ruskin aim. He organised his first short course in conjunction with Sue Atkins, a young woman appointed by Bill Owen in 1968 as a youth worker in Burngreave, one of Sheffield's most diverse working class communities, poor in financial terms, but rich in dynamism. Her background was in youth theatre in Uxbridge and Leicester. She described how the residential element had been an inspirational factor for the young people on the course, and strengthened her belief in community development:

> Young people have to know about discrimination and build their own confidence through having pride in their community. One of my principles, she said, is never to write anything about a young person, his or her character, or prospects without it being jointly owned by that person themselves.

Sue Atkins was later to play a big part in developing a Community Work Apprenticeship scheme in the city, to spread these principles.

Keith recognised that progressive local authorities, along with the sponsorship and support of trade unions, would be able to combine the residential element of the College, adult education, and communities in new ways.

Michael Barratt Brown recognised the contribution made by the short course programme in his contribution to *Portrait of a City Father*. 'We made two big changes from Ruskin. *We tried to have equal numbers of women, and we put as much emphasis on short courses and short course students as on the longer courses*', stating with conviction that Bill Owen *'was always concerned to aim at 50:50 balance, and the only way to do that was to accept that while men could come and leave their families behind, often women couldn't'.*

The College obtained a Joseph Rowntree Foundation grant for a crèche and persuaded local schools to accept children on a temporary basis while their mothers, or sometimes fathers, studied on short courses. Because some students were single parents, it offered accommodation too for their children. By 1981, 100 children had used the crèche. The immense importance of women's and girls' education was explicit from the start. It was also a testament to the growing influence of the feminist movement seven years after the College's foundation. With the additional support of *Educating Rita* and the Open University it proved excellent publicity for women's place in adult education.

The location of the College on the outskirts of Barnsley placed it at the heart of the South Yorkshire coalfield and the pit communities. Its establishment was another way that Sheffield learned more about the coalfield areas of South Yorkshire and vice versa. The residential element, in particular, of this highly political educational initiative, brought together people from a wide range of ages, industries, and communities in common learning experiences, enhanced by socialising in the bar, located in the former cellars and wine vaults of this historic building, former home to the local aristocracy. Northern College was in itself a major political achievement which in part derived from, and importantly contributed to the region's political culture.

Jol Miskin, an educationist with 40 years WEA experience, put it well when I interviewed him for this book:

> Northern College opened up the space for working class adults, with limited resources, to explore issues confronting them and to consider solutions. All within a friendly, beautiful, peaceful, free and well resourced setting. What is more, decent childcare ensured access for women. It really seemed a sort of equivalence to what the upper middle class take as a given at the universities which 'service' them: Oxford, Cambridge, Durham etc. It felt wonderful, exciting and, most importantly, liberating. And lest we forget, for many it was the closest they'd get to a genuine holiday.

The following chapters illustrate a number of examples of how the College played an important role within the years covered by this study.

Feminism and Women's Liberation

Active women, like myself, were slow to get involved with feminism. Experience in the Potteries of men-only canvassing, and in South Yorkshire, women-only tea making, had put me off separate Women's Sections in the Labour Party. Kate Housden, a former student from Northern College's second year intake told me recently, *'I would never have seen you as a feminist when*

I first met you at Northern College'. She was right, although I attended and enjoyed left-wing and feminist songs and drama, both in Liverpool and Sheffield. She also told me how, as the administrator of 'Red Ladder' Theatre Company, the college had not considered her to have enough trade union experience to enrol on the trade union course, which she had applied for, and was offered instead a place on the community and society course. The antipathy amongst working class activists on the left to Women's Liberation, described earlier, was significant; class mattered more than gender.

Despite women's sections of trade unions in factories being supported, collective organising by women outside the official Labour movement was either not recognised or treated with suspicion.

To find the roots of feminist thinking and campaigning, related to paid work in Sheffield, we have to look to community based movements and womens co-operatives outside the industrial leftist structures of trade unions and political parties which this study has so far described. The first major Women's Liberation Movement conference in the UK was held at Ruskin College in Oxford in February 1970. Of its first four demands:

- equal pay;
- equal education and job opportunities;
- free contraception and abortion on demand;
- free 24 hour nurseries;

the first two directly linked the movement to the labour market, the second two indirectly as they would open up greater access to paid work for women. So it is not surprising that some of the founders of the Sheffield Women in Manual Trades group were focused on ways to remove gender stereotyping within the labour market. They have described how in the early 70s, their motivation came mainly from their own ambitions to work in traditionally male dominated occupations. They joined an existing group of feminists in Sheffield who had already established a women's film co-operative in 1975, using media and film to campaign for abortion rights, described in more detail in Chapter 6, and the women's print co-operative, founded in the late 70s, based at Common Ground which was used for publications in the miners' strike.[8] Maureen Storey worked with Womens Aid to help establish one of the first Women's refuges in the city. They campaigned collectively, outside trade union or council connections, but closely linked with the gay liberation and anti-racist movements, to expand women's training opportunities and challenge discrimination and domestic violence. Their regular meetings in pubs attracted around 50/60 people from a variety of backgrounds, including young students from the university.

The stories of three of them, Rose Ardron, Sheena Clarke and Roz Wollen, are varied and relevant to the book's study of the Labour market.

Rose Ardron was from London. Her mother, from Boston USA, was aware of feminism, and had read Simone de Beauvoir's *The Second Sex*, which, although written in 1950, only began to be read widely in English in the mid to late 60s when it was first translated from French. At first Rose was especially interested in women and health and admired the book *Our Bodies, Ourselves*, written and published by Boston Women's Health Book Collective in 1970. Her partner, Matt Tatlow, was an architect in a building collective, at a

8. See page 210.

time when legislation establishing Housing Improvement Areas meant there were grants available for work on old houses such as rewiring, taking out lead pipes, insulation, introduced in the late 1960s by the Wilson government. Rose joined him as a building worker in his projects. They lived in Burngreave, (described earlier, see p. 64), quite near the city centre. She met **Sheena Clarke** when putting in a bathroom in the terraced house where Sheena lived. Together they knew of a small vegetarian café, 'Brick Rabbit', where they got to know **Roz Wollen**. They remember vividly how they discussed feminism and Women's Lib, and read books published by the feminist publisher Virago there. The women were middle class, from outside South Yorkshire and not initially members of any political group, nor active in the trade union movement, yet they knew they were pioneers of important new thinking not just about the role of women in the labour market and non-traditional trades but in wider society. They joined the growing Sheffield Women's Group and started a newsletter.

Rose Ardron working on Sheena Clarke's home.

In 1975, following Labour's Sex Discrimination Act, Barbara Castle established the Equal Opportunities Commission (EOC), and the Equal Pay Act came into full implementation, though equal pay in practice did not. A national group, Women and Manual Trades, was formed in London. Juliana Bethlem describes its formation:

> We had our first meeting at Essex Road Women's Centre. It was organised by myself and Jane who was working in the same mixed building co-op as me. She had just been sacked because they were unresponsive to her needs to accommodate her children and I also left. I was a self-taught builder part-trained as an architect. Jane was a plasterer. Mary Clemmy also came – she'd been involved with building the Women's Centre – and a few other women. We first called ourselves 'Women in Traditionally Male Jobs'.

The following year they had an exhibition stand at the National Women's Liberation conference in Newcastle which Roz Wollen attended, and in 1977 the Sheffield group received a grant from the Equal Opportunities Commission of £500 to produce a pamphlet, whilst the EOC also granted £2,500 to an affiliated Sheffield co-op to make a film about a girl who tries to be a car mechanic. Sheena and Roz attended Manpower Services Commission (MSC) TOPS courses at Handsworth, and Rose at Barnsley skills centres.[9] Sheena Clarke went to learn engineering and received a small learning allowance. She and Rose described how:

> Many young women and men were trained through those facilities. Applications for courses were made through the job centres. The small learning allowance was especially helpful for single parent. They could learn a really useful skill at the same time as qualifying for a bit extra money.

9. MSC skills centres set up by the Wilson government in 1973.

Sheena Clarke became a Sheffield City Councillor in 1983 and was given the job of steering through and launching the Council's in-house Positive Action Project, which exposed the extent of gender bias within the workforce. She pushed for the creation of a new Women's Unit to work very closely with the Race Equality Unit, where she helped to co-ordinate from within the local authority many of the campaigns initiated by the Women and Manual Trades group to improve the MSC skills centres' equality practices.

Rose decided to get a building qualification through Barnsley skills centre. She used the Sex Discrimination Act to challenge the practice in that institution of turning women away from such courses. She remembers a light-hearted comment by one of her interviewers: *'Well what would happen to you? You'd probably get raped in the loo.'* Instead she was taken on by Sheffield Works Department as an 'Improver' on a shorter term basis than a full apprenticeship. In 1981/82 she saw the advertisement (see Chapter 6) for jobs in the new Employment Department of the city council and decided to apply. '*I was amazed and excited to be successful'*, she commented. *'I suppose the interviewing committee, Cllr Bill Michie and Jude Stoddart, were interested in my background and variety of training experiences'.* She started work in the equal opportunities team, later becoming a key player in winning European Social Fund (ESF), grants for proposals including the Women's Joinery Training Workshop at Shirecliffe FE College.

The third groundbreaker, Roz Wollen, had links with the national group, Women and Manual Trades, and took the lead in the newly established Sheffield branch which had received acknowledgement at the Newcastle conference. Those involved in the Sheffield group, which was quite small, realised they were challenging locally accepted stereotypes. Coming neither from Sheffield nor the Barnsley area further north, they knew nothing of the fight Lady Mabel Smith had put up in the West Riding committee against married women having to leave their teaching jobs before the war because their place was 'in the home', which she lost, or her views that girls should learn woodwork and boys cookery.

Roz went on to establish a successful car repair garage called Gwenda's with two other women,[10] which is described in Chapter 6. While her colleagues went on to teaching posts, she became the AA's only female patrol person in the north of England. The AA was running a highly successful 'I know a man who can' publicity campaign and Roz's job was well-timed. Photos of her in the local papers wearing the regulation brown jumper and beret were a powerful means of breaking the gender stereotype.

'I know a (wo)man who can!' After establishing her own successful car repair garage, Roz Wollen went on to become the AA's only female patrol person in the North of England.

10. Ros Wall and Annette Williams, see page 181.

Roz followed this up with a teaching career at Sheffield College and went on to be pivotal in setting up the Sheffield Women's Development Trust, established in 1995, whose biggest project was a training centre for women in non-traditional trades (WINTT) in the Burngreave area of the city which still runs women's courses in building trades. In 2009 she received an Honorary Doctorate at Sheffield Hallam University which has a unit Women in Engineering, Science and Technology (WEST). She continues to campaign and to raise money for student bursaries, and celebrate students who complete their courses.[11]

The three women's stories illustrate how feminists brought fresh ideas into the traditional Labour movement at a time when the labour market was on the verge of catastrophe with steel plant closures, and then the coal crisis.

This book covers a time when men and women were rapidly becoming aware of the scale of change in society, the labour market and the economy, partly, some would say mainly, because of advances in reproductive technology. Contraception had long been widespread in the UK, though not wholly effective nor talked about in public. There were class differences in women's access to contraception, due to cost, before the pill, which became available in the early 60s but was only offered free by the NHS in 1974. It was common, at the play groups in Toxteth, Liverpool in 1968, for women to arrive with their children and a pocket full of contraceptive pills which they had on prescription from visiting their GP, and covertly share them among friends or sell them.

11. www.westskills.org.uk.

Other working class women like Vi Gill, active in the AUEW and Sheffield's trade unions, simply became pregnant and struggled to make ends meet as single parents. Blanche Flannery, Vi, and Sylvia Greenwood and many others joined trade union campaigns against low pay and to strengthen maternity leave, abortion rights and training opportunities for women.

> In an economic downturn women are expelled from production much faster than men. It has been argued that women only work for 'pin money', yet we know that a married woman's wage is essential to the family budget. Statistics show that the number of families with income below the poverty line would be trebled if it were not for the wife's wage.[12]

The practical impact of the pill on women's lives, whatever their social class, changed the labour market. The psychological impact of easily accessible contraception for all women was and is much harder to assess. It lies at the root of the stereotyping of work in the labour market which had been there long before the pill. The phrase 'pin money' to describe women's wages was commonly used in the 70s and 80s, and earlier suggesting that women's earnings merely paid for extras, while men's pay funded important essentials. It affected the expectations of men and women about pay, work and status in the labour market. Caring was women's work and could therefore expect to be low-paid, often cash-based, part-time, maybe under 16 hours a week, temporary employment. It also encouraged employers to overlook the career progression of their female workforce because

12. Blanche Flannery, in a speech at rally in the Sheffield City Hall, May 14th, 1980.

of their expectations that a period of maternity leave might be imminent. These assumptions continued despite the important changes to gender and race equality legislation introduced by the Wilson governments of 1964-70. Abortion was made legal in 1967, in the same year as homosexuality was partially legalised; a second tranche of race relations legislation was passed in response to Enoch Powell's provocative speech in the West Midlands and Martin Luther King's murder in the US, both occurred in 1968; divorce law reform in 1969. Barbara Castle's significant influence in cabinet was evident as she moved swiftly to see through the Equal Pay Act in 1970 before the election had to be called. I am indebted to Pat Thane's clear and insightful description of the progress made in the sixties and seventies towards equality in society.[13]

> Shifts towards greater equalities and cultural change were promoted and expressed by an exceptional range of collectively organised groups – workers, feminists, gay activists, nationalists – organising and campaigning against perceived disadvantage more actively than at any time since the beginning of the century, but not in formal political structures, whose membership dwindled. It was a time of lively intellectual and cultural ferment when many new possibilities seemed to be opening, with uncertain outcomes. A generation that had grown up since 1945 mostly better educated, better off, more confident and less deferential than older generations challenged established values in various

13. Thane P (2018). *Divided Kingdom: A History of Britain, 1900 to the Present.* Cambridge University Press.

ways, seeking to transform the culture, not just for themselves but for everyone.

There was good reason for these developments to have a positive impact on individual girls' and women's job prospects and their gender awareness, place in society and the economy.

Internationally, movements for change were taking hold: colonial government was giving way to independence in Africa; black immigrants from the West Indies or Yemen were working in steel and engineering plants. There was a vigorous black section from the Caribbean in the T&GWU working on the buses, who developed their own cricket team complete with a cricket ground and pavilion in Ecclesfield. Unlike the feminist movement, trades unions in Sheffield, partly through the work of George Caborn and Bill Owen, together with a strong West Indian Association and some active work in the community, took the lead in establishing Sheffield Campaign Against Racism (SCAR) in response to some of the worrying tendencies led by Enoch Powell in the West Midlands.

A decade later an industrial dispute at Grunwick over trade union recognition by Asian women led by Jayaben Desai, manual workers in a print factory at Dollis Hill in North London, brought women's and race equality campaigners together with the Yorkshire NUM and other trade unions. A large group from Sheffield travelled down in a bus to demonstrate and cheered the Yorkshire miners.

Two years after Grunwick, the UK elected its first female Prime Minister and in 1981, at the other end of the political spectrum, women started the Greenham Common Peace Camp against nuclear weapons.

A workforce of predominantly Asian women were joined on the Grunwick picket line by the NUM and other trade unions members. It was a dispute which brought women's and race equality campaigners together like never before.

These moves forward on the wider dimensions of equality in the 60s and 70s were happening in South Yorkshire and across the country. They were substantive, positive, and largely embraced by the Labour and Trade Union movement. However, as I conclude later, serious concerns remain, that all these reforms are yet to be fully implemented and normalised, including equal pay, fair treatment for black people and communities, freedom from domestic violence, and are therefore fragile and open to change by reactionary regimes at any time or place across the world, especially in the informal or 'gig' economy in the UK at present, which the Conservative government makes no attempt to regulate.

Europe

During the seventies a closer link with Europe emerged with a degree of cross-party support to ensure that the terrible wars of the first half of the century would not recur. The European Coal and Steel Community, formed by the Treaty of Paris in April 1951, between France, West Germany, Italy, Netherlands, Belgium and Luxembourg, and a precursor to the EEC, (European Economic Community) was opposed at its outset by the Labour movement. Herbert Morrison explained that, *'the Durham miners won't wear it'*, because it might weaken the independence of the NUM and trade union collective bargaining. The UK did not join or sign the Treaty of Rome which established the EEC in 1957. The position changed when the Tory Prime Minister Harold Macmillan appointed Edward Heath to 'submit an application and lead negotiations to enter the Common Market'. Ted Heath's own top priority was to set in motion a closer relationship with the European Community. This was vetoed by Charles de Gaulle. Under Wilson's government, talks resumed in 1967, whilst the majority of the Labour movement remained opposed. In Sheffield and the South Yorkshire coalfield, although the region participated and benefitted from the Coal and Steel Community's policy in its early days, opposition remained, as the Labour manifesto for the SYCC 1973 election made clear.[14]

Harold Wilson took a different approach whilst disagreeing with Ted Heath, arguing with some passion for a longer-term view: that European unity was here to stay, and should be welcomed in the name of peace and stability. There was an intense debate

14. See page 24.

in Huyton Constituency Labour Party before the 1970 election, when he listened to those of us opposed to joining the Common Market on socialist grounds, before responding, again with passion, that protecting workers' rights for the long term would be more certain if we worked from inside the six nations rather than outside, insisting that in order to fashion a socialist Europe in the future we should be part of its establishment, not shouting from across the Channel.

Heath never persuaded many in the Conservative Party to share his enthusiasm even though the CBI and most of his party supported joining. However, shortly before the 1970 general election was called and after he had become the Conservative Party leader, negotiating membership was included in the Conservative Party manifesto. Once elected Prime Minister he undertook many of the negotiations himself and became good friends with Georges Pompidou, the new French President. Before the subsequent parliamentary vote on whether or not the UK should become a member of the EC, he said: *'Tonight, when the House endorses this Motion, many millions of people right across the world will rejoice that we have taken our rightful place in a truly United Europe'.*

Decimalisation was introduced in 1971 amidst considerable protest. Proposals began for the possibility of direct elections to a European Parliament. On 1st January 1973, the UK joined the European Community (EC), as the EEC had become in 1967 along with the Republic of Ireland and Denmark. The Labour Party remained divided. Wilson as Leader managed a precarious situation with considerable skill. Labour's manifesto in 1974 promised to:

> … renegotiate Britain's terms of membership, to be followed by a consultative referendum on

For a YES vote	No official position	For a NO vote
Conservative Party Liberal Party Social Democratic and Unionist Party Vangard Unionist Progressive Party (NI)	Labour Party	Scottish National Party Plaid Cymru Ulster Unionist Party Dem. Unionists Alliance Party National Front Communist Party of GB
The majority in the referendum of 67% in favour of remaining on a turnout of 64% was decisive.		

> continued membership under the new terms if they were acceptable.[15]

Cabinet members were allowed to campaign publicly against each other. Seven of the 23 members of the Cabinet opposed membership.[16] Wilson did not remove the Whip from MPs or members of the Cabinet who opposed continuing membership and he depended on a coalition with the large majority of the Tories to support the legislation required to set up the referendum in 1975. The Labour Party did not campaign on either side.

In Sheffield, all the cars which took the victorious Brightside Labour Party to their first Spring Bank Camp in 1975, except one, sported **Vote 'No'** stickers. Nevertheless, South Yorkshire as a whole voted **'YES'** but with the smallest margin of any region in the country. I conducted a recent informal survey of people mentioned in this book, who were old enough to vote in 1975,

15. This phrase was repeated almost word for word in Labour's 2019 manifesto.

16. Tony Benn; Barbara Castle; Michael Foot; Willie Ross; Peter Shore; John Silkin and Eric Varley.

most of whom were connected to the Labour movement. They voted 'NO' by 2:1.

Gradually decimalisation became normal and arithmetic simpler. Legislation to introduce European elections by direct universal suffrage was signed in 1976 and after ratification, came into force in 1978, with the first elections the following year. The argument in favour of closer links with the EC became more persuasive to coal and steel communities like South Yorkshire, as job losses and unemployment started to take hold. Richard Caborn, amongst others on the left who sported NO stickers in 1975, considered standing for election to the European Parliament three years later.

Two candidates were selected from the South Yorkshire region in the first UK-wide election to the European Parliament held in 1979. Richard Caborn, who at the time chaired Sheffield Trades and Labour Council, was chosen to represent Sheffield, and Norman West from NUM for South Yorkshire. Elections were held on the same date as the General Election that brought Thatcher to power after the so-called winter of discontent. They were both elected. Richard was impressed by the inspiring idealism he found in the Socialist Group of the new European Parliament. He worked closely with Barbara Castle, now no longer an MP, and other members of the Group, led by Jacques Delors. They worked to adapt the criteria through which EC grant aid, such as the European Social Fund would be distributed to fit their socialist principles. The politics of social class was expanding into wider demands for equal opportunity and positive action within the labour market.

The late Rt. Hon. Robin Cook MP wrote in his letter of resignation to Tony Blair on 17th May 2003, over Iraq:

> As our foreign secretary I was impressed by the energy and skill with which you ended Britain's isolation from Europe and achieved for our country equal status and influence with Germany or France. I am dismayed that once again Britain is divided from our European neighbours. As president of the PSE [Party of European Socialists] of which the Labour Party is a member, it troubles me that I know of no sister party within the European Union that shares our position.

This suggests that Harold Wilson's pragmatic long-term approach was vindicated. His retirement in March 1976 of his own volition as he approached his 60th birthday felt premature and surprising. His leadership style concentrated on canny and careful discussion with colleagues and adjustment when necessary, aiming to deliver real and radical action, which integrated measures to lessen class inequalities with concerns about wider social inequalities in a very effective programme in government.

The three sectors examined in detail, adult education and the founding of Northern College, feminist movements, and the first European referendom cover a variety of issues which all laid a foundation for subsequent reform that took place through local government in the following decade.

CHAPTER 4

Leadership, International Solidarity and Social Care

Leadership

Until 1979 when national elections brought Margaret Thatcher into Downing Street and other British politicians into the European Parliament, political programmes seemed to override the role of individual party leaders, partly because of the relatively short time leaders held their position, or the fragility of their Parliamentary majorities.

The Heath-led government took over from Harold Wilson unexpectedly in 1970, interrupting a developed political programme of reform. Heath himself was a relatively new Conservative Party leader having been elected in 1965 following Alec Douglas-Home who held the position for only two years after Harold Macmillan's long term in that office. Heath's agenda was markedly different from Wilson's, including curbing trade union powers, denationalisation, continuing the programme of Beeching cuts to the railway system, and means testing welfare, but his policies hit many obstacles and his tenure was short. As we have seen, local government reform, equality and education reforms set in motion by Labour were not wholly abandoned or reversed. In 1974 when Wilson's government took back control, his cabinet team could continue to implement other planned projects, like equal pay, the Russell Commission reforms, and the stream of Home Office funded urban regeneration policies through the Urban Programme and 12 newly created Community Development Projects despite a very narrow Parliamentary majority. Wilson also established the planned Manpower Services Commission, with its youth opportunities training programme and skills centres.

When after two defeats Heath was forced to resign in 1975, and Margaret Thatcher won the leadership of the Conservative Party, she vigorously set about moving the party's policies and programme to the right. Sale of council houses, cuts to welfare, privatisation of local government, and curbs on trade unions were all in preparation, but as a shadow leader she could not deliver on these policies. After Wilson's sudden resignation brought in a Callaghan-led Labour government, with similar commitments, but without Harold's knack of holding the Party together, and knowing when to go the country, the shaky majority, dependent on the Lib/Lab pact was unstable, internal differences intensified and Labour's defeat was not unexpected.

At home in Sheffield, we believed that to deliver effective democratic political change, collective culture, embodying clarity, drive and unity of theme and purpose should override the role of any individual leader. Walking in the local woods with David Blunkett on a Sunday with our dogs – his dog was good friends with our dog, and we knew him, Ruth and their young family well – our political discussions were about how to develop progressive projects through local government including the short-course political education at Northern College. They were positive and enthusiastic often leading to new ideas, but far more often about policy than leadership, since at regional and local level leadership changed hands without much political upheaval.

In 1974 Sir Ron Ironmonger moved to lead SYCC and was replaced as leader of Sheffield City Council by George Wilson, a member of Brightside constituency with strong working class credentials. His style was more populist, but the political programme remained similar.

An International Dimension

Sharing our home with Chilean families gave an international flavour to our political discussion. The refugees were from different Chilean political groupings, and a wide range of jobs, education and professions. Many were still students, and loved to discuss politics. They had all been active within Allende's Popular Unity movement in Chile and were buoyed by Salvador Allende's electoral success in forming a government, and equally devastated and angered by its violent overthrow with the active support of the US, and the ensuing brutality they suffered under the military regime of Pinochet. We, also political activists, were horrified yet fascinated by their experiences.

Pedro Fuentes came to Sheffield in 1975 followed later by his family. He has vividly described what this meant for them:

> The Cuban Revolution demonstrated that socialism could be achieved in our lifespan. It showed us that the road to socialism was there, it was a matter for us to get together and fight for it. It was a dramatic change, and opened up a wider perspective for my school mates, friends, and family. The final result of the general election in 1970 was fantastic! We gathered together in the centre of Valparaiso – hundreds of people, a

full night of joy, congratulating ourselves, and I remember thinking the windows and the doors are starting to open up – to open completely, it is here! We can march and let's enjoy it together, let's embrace it. The feelings on the following days were of a type of self confidence. My head was buzzing with the idea of walking in our neighbourhood, and in the city centre saying 'Well this is us now, this is us!' It was great!

On the day of the coup 11th September 1973, I was in Santiago, 1,670 miles away from Arica, where I was working. In the morning I put the radio on, and there was Allende making his famous speech, denouncing the treason of top army officers, asking people not to resist the coup. It was his 'goodbye speech'. Soon after, the flow of Military Orders started to be broadcast. I saw the very low flight of the British Hawker Hunter aircraft towards the South. They had just bombed the Presidential Palace and the killing field had started.

I was detained at my parents' home and then transported to Arica where I went through torture, interrogation, solitary confinement, and finally –'luckily' – landed on the part of Arica's jail which had been turned into a so called concentration camp. It was one of the approximately 1,170 concentrations camps and clandestine centres for detention and torture in Chile. After nearly two years in prison, I received a letter from the British

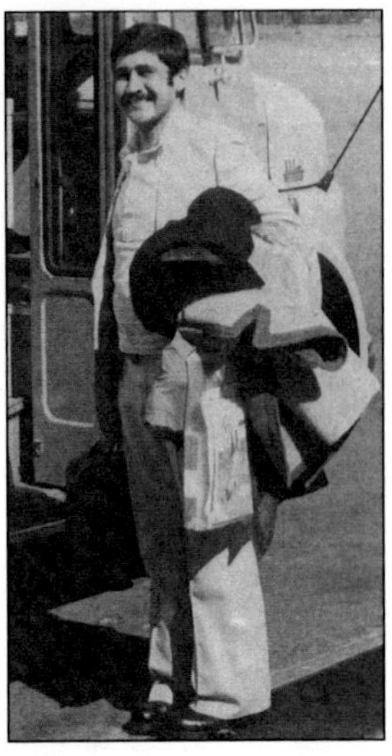

Pedro Fuentes pictured on his way to the airport and a new life in the UK.

Embassy in Santiago saying that I had been granted a visa to live in the UK if I wished to.

I arrived in the UK in October 1975. After a short stay in the Sinclair reception centre for Chilean and Latin American refugees, in Shepherd's Bush, London. I and another 'compañero' that I had met on the airplane in Santiago got on a coach with destiny Sheffield! When the coach arrived at the old Bus Station we were welcomed by two fellow Chileans and two British people. It was a cold and dark night in November. After introductions Nick Howard invited me to come with him to his house, and Tom Owen did the same to my friend Luis. When Nick and I arrived at his address, I was welcomed by his wife, and his children: two daughters and a son. I was given the bedroom of one of the daughters. That night began an experience for me of what was going to be a long journey of new friendships and most of all sincere and transparent solidarity from the Labour Movement.

These Chileans were not just young male revolutionaries. Their wives and children were able to follow their husbands, freshly released from prison, into exile. First hand accounts like Pedro's about the Popular Unity government led by Salvador Allende, that generated hope and optimism after his election victory in 1970, struck a chord with us in the Sheffield Labour movement, fresh from the recent general election victory in October '74, which had played a positive role in securing their release and safety. Glasgow dockers' action in blacking the delivery of spare parts for Chilean fighter planes[1] had inspired Judith Hart, the new Secretary of State for International Development in the Wilson administration, to redirect funds intended to support Santiago University to the Chile solidarity movement which set up a Europe wide system whereby political prisoners were given the option of exile in lieu of continued imprisonment.

Soon after the election I was contacted by the Chile Solidarity campaign to see if we were able to host one of the refugees recently arrived in UK. We agreed. Bernabe Alvarez, Ester, his wife and Barney their 4-year-old son, were the third family to come to Sheffield. We rearranged the bedrooms, so that our children slept in the attic and they settled in. Their story differed from Pedro's. Bernabe worked at the *Popular Unity* newspaper as a photographer. He had witnessed the morning after the coup in Santiago, and realised his place of work was deserted. He had no resources or money, and a wife and young child to care for. For some months he tried to get by using his camera to take portrait pictures for the identity cards which had become essential for every Chilean to possess. After some months he

1. A heartfelt documentary film *NAE PASARAN* was made in October 2018 by Felipe Bustos Sierra. It is about the decency and moral courage of a group of Scottish Rolls Royce workers and trade unionists. In 1974 they had downed tools, refusing to repair jet engines for the Chilean air force in protest against the bloody military coup that had toppled the government of Salvador Allende.

decided to travel to Peru to get away from the constant danger. He sought asylum and Ester, now pregnant and Barney managed to join him. Travel to Europe was agreed and they landed in London. Once in Sheffield they settled in as part of our family, teaching us how to make the perfect 'empanada', a meat pie with an olive inside. After completing their short English course Bernabe was offered work at Shardlow's engineering company where the union influence was strong. Barney got to know our children and the local school offered him a place once he was 5 years old. We travelled to Liverpool together in September 1975 to remember the victims of the military coup (11th September 1973), and protest against the Pinochet regime. Natalie was born, and although it was lovely to have a baby at home again, a house became available shortly afterwards in the Attercliffe area, where they still live today. Other families followed to live with us in Grenoside over the following eight or nine years, and on the whole we found the community supportive, if somewhat surprised! Luis Silva, a self-employed copper miner, who fled across the Andes to Argentina where he was caught and imprisoned, was sponsored through Peter Heathfield, the NUM organiser in north-east Derbyshire. Juan from the same prison in Arica as Pedro, had corresponded with our local Labour Party before he arrived, followed by Ana, a dress maker who cooked delicious fried rice. Later, they went to live in Liverpool. Another temporary lodger, Mario, had been a member of Allende's armed forces, and had been badly tortured and damaged. He was silent and lonely. He sought comfort roaming through the Grenoside woodlands that reminded him of back home and wrote endless sheets of poetry. He now lives in Chile. Finally Roberto and Eysen, who also had children of school age, stayed for some time. Their son, also called Roberto, wrote us a moving letter about his memories of sharing life with our family, when he was 21.

The Chilean refugee community soon joined in Sheffield life and made the city their home.

My role in the Solidarity movement was to work within its Human Rights committee to match up names from those listed as political prisoners, with trade unions or organisations in Sheffield who would likewise offer to sponsor an individual, help them into suitable work and offer temporary hospitality in their home. We would contact an appropriate trade union or institution, including the AUEW for industrial workers, the University and Labour groups for students, the NUM for former miners, and so on. We would then write to the prisoner, directly to their prison governor with a copy to the CIIR (Catholic Institute for International Relations) which helped to arrange their release and travel overseas. It was very exciting to receive a letter from Chile, for example from Juan in Arica prison (Bernabe helped me with the Spanish). We met them in person at the bus station as Pedro describes.

Political aspirations and international solidarity became part of our home environment and social activities. Listening to their stories, told in broken English and many gestures, with our children in the background, sharing our household with their families, hearing from the women as we cooked our meals together about the terror of the coup, and listening to inspiring songs and music of Victor

Jara, murdered in the stadium where he had performed to packed crowds of Allende supporters, left a deep impression. We were proud that the election of the Labour government in 1974 had really made a difference! Pedro described how:

> Soon I started to feel completely at home, in terms of the political and economic dynamic of this city. Politically, the 'Socialist Republic of South Yorkshire' was an ideal place for us Chilean refugees. In the early 80s the Red Flag was flown on the Town Hall on May Day. Later the Chilean flag would fly every 11th of September at the top of the Sheffield Town Hall as homage to victims of the dictatorship. There was a strong Sheffield Chile Solidarity Committee group chaired by Roger Barton, with Helen Jackson, Peter Heathfield Secretary of Derbyshire Union of Miners, and many others.
>
> With its 7 hills Sheffield resembles Valparaíso, my home city, whilst the industrial sectors were more like Concepcion with its coal mining, heavy steel industry, and the weather... All this provided a kind of cushion to our landing onto our new hometown, with our one-way passports forbidding a return to Chile, partially alleviating the baggage of loss, suffering, frustration and the moral dimension of change.
>
> Our community members in exile used to be militants of different political parties back home, but now everybody shared the same ideology which facilitated both individual and the group's

involvement in support of social and political activities. Its prevailing theme was guided by clear political, ideological and moral focus: ***solidarity!*** This was particularly the case after the general election of 1979 which brought Margaret Thatcher into government as we saw her clear sympathy with the Pinochet regime's neo-liberal economics. Members of the community brought the Chilean national flag to demos and events of that political period. An indicator of the actual integration process into Sheffield's community was the slow disappearance of the Chilean flag in such events, although individual members of the community continued to participate. Chilean coal miners in exile actively supported the long Miners' Strike of 1984-85. With our community unanimity we involved ourselves in a plethora of national and local events, whether demonstrations, pickets, marches, fund raising, or international delegations.

A large majority of Chileans in this region, and elsewhere, were extremely eager to leave the state's support mechanisms by engaging in training, further and higher education and employment. The second generation of Chileans have also done this confirming a positive trend, so that university students, teachers, young professionals, workers, shanty town dwellers and trade unionists, supported by the local solidarity movement and many individuals, have all made this city their home.

Solidarity! Many Chilean members of the Sheffield community, including Pedro Fuentes, joined us in local social and political activities.

The Chilean refugee community joined in Sheffield life soon after they arrived. Many found work in steel works negotiated for them through shop stewards committees, whether driving a horizontal crane, furnace men, working in the melting shops, or as cleaners. They were encouraged to put their names on the council house waiting list by the local authority, which agreed to pay the accommodation costs of a 'Saturday school' run by themselves to ensure their increasing number of children learnt about their Chilean background and fluent Spanish as well as the English they were learning at school during the week. Isilda Lang spoke recently about her arrival in Sheffield in 1977 from being a nanny with a military family in Chile, loyal to President Allende, whose eldest son was condemned to death and the family maltreated.

As she described the trauma of her experience and her exile as a refugee in Sheffield she told me how she first had the idea of making a patchwork from pieces of material and their memories of life in their homeland:

> I was able to get a job with 'Sheffield Homestart'[2] because of my former work and training in Chile. We lived and worked in the Burngreave area of Sheffield, and I made friends with the wife one of the local vicars,[3] who wondered what she and the community could help with. We together decided to collect wool and material so that we, along with the local community, could make pictures – patchwork scenes, known in Chile as *arpilleras* – using knitted shapes and scraps of material of our memories, and our journey to Sheffield. What started with a simple idea grew with members of the local community joining in. Recently I was proud that our work was exhibited not just in Burngreave but also in the city's Millennium Gallery, and elsewhere when Joan Jara[4] came to visit.

Isilda's story is an important example of how welcoming political refugees has expanded Sheffield's culture and gave meaning to its present title as the first 'City of Sanctuary' in the UK.

2. The charity offering support to vulnerable families over difficult times.
3. Urban Theolology Unit, founded in Sheffield in 1970.
4. The widow of Victor Jara the musician and song writer, killed in the stadium that had been turned into a prison after the Chilean coup in 1973.

A Chillean 'Arpillera' called 'Jornada de Nuestras Vidas' ('Journey of Our Lives') a large patchwork made by the Grupo Andes.

A Personal Experience

In 1978 after the sudden death of John Mendelson, MP for Penistone, who had supported our work for Chile, a by-election was called. David Blunkett, who had stood in the unwinnable Sheffield Hallam constituency in 1974 as a very young candidate, made a serious bid for a Parliamentary career when he was nominated for selection. He lost by a single vote to Allen McKay, a member of NACODS, who was backed by NUM.[5] Later he often said it was the best thing that ever happened to him, as he learnt so much more about politics, government and leadership from remaining in local government.

5. Allen McKay, Member of Parliament from 1978 until he retired in 1992. Refer back to Chapter 2 and strong influence of miners and NACODS in Penistone.

The same year as John Mendelson died, Penistone constituency were debating South Yorkshire's bus fares policy, after a South Yorkshire delegation had met Minister of Transport, William Rodgers in London to persuade him drop his opposition to the cheap fares policy, arguing that the successful second SYCC election result the previous year had illustrated its popularity. They returned, rebuffed and angry. I had spoken at the meeting about how it keeps family costs low. As a result I was asked by the constituency to be our delegate to the annual Labour Party conference in Blackpool.

It was my first conference. Also, I realised later with surprise, it was the first time I had ever been away from home for a whole week without Keith or the children on a non-family related

The Winter Gardens, Blackpool, venue for my first Labour Party conference.

activity since I was married, and I was nearly 40 years old. I travelled by train on a pooled fare system agreed between the national Labour Party and British Rail which meant every delegate across the country paid the same fare (a good transport policy in itself!) I had been told to arrive in Blackpool early on Saturday to attend the 'transport compositing meeting' to decide which resolutions were to go into the transport composite motion to be put to conference. The meeting was fairly large, almost all male, and chaired by a Trade Union official from a non-transport union. As we went around the room, we each introduced ourselves. I stood up to speak briefly for Penistone. Our simple sentence was duly incorporated into the motion. I sat down pleased and satisfied with the outcome.

What happened next was a shock. The meeting continued to debate who should propose and second the resolution. There followed long, sometimes impassioned speeches from union delegates from ASLEF, T&G and NUR as to whether the motion was most relevant to railway unions or should as usual be moved by the biggest, the Transport and General. Tempers rose, time ticked on. I almost left to explore Blackpool, when the Chairman stood up to intervene:

> 'Right!' You can't agree so I propose that the composite transport resolution is put to conference by the T&G,[6] and, because of all this

6. This was known to be the last Labour Party conference before Jack Jones retired as General Secretary only to become a long standing President of the National Pensioners' Convention. He had fought in the Spanish Civil War against the fascists; he was chief economic spokesman for the Trades Union Congress and one of the authors of the Social Contract. Jones was also instrumental in the creation of the Advisory, Conciliation and Arbitration Service (ACAS) in 1975, and was a member of the National Economic Development Council from 1969 to 1978. He died aged 94 in 2008.

> argument, one of the constituency comrades will second it. We often hear the accusation in the Party that we in the trade union section dominate too much. Where's the young woman from Penistone who talked about the buses?

I put up my hand.

> You'll second it then. Is that agreed?

It was dinner time, and no-one quibbled.

Not until conference opened the next day did the full implication dawn on me. I sat in my allocated seat and listened to the debates. I became terrified! I noted the brusque way in which speakers who carried on after the red light were stopped in mid-sentence. I did not want that to happen to me. Gradually I realised it was not just me in front of this massive audience. I would be the delegate from Penistone with a resolution about cheap fares. That helped! I had a job to do. Back at the B&B I recalled our constituency debate that led to this very scary situation: the County Councillors had been extremely angry and upset by a speech made by the Secretary of State for Transport, Bill Rodgers, expressing disapproval of local authorities who subsidised bus fares at a cost to rate-payers. In South Yorkshire we knew how popular this was. As I told the constituency, it only cost our three children 12p to travel to Hillsborough and back. The bus passengers were friendly and conductors kept an eye on unruly youngsters. The children learnt how to be independent. Old people on a pension could visit their families by bus for nothing. That kept communities together and the elderly mobile. Importantly – at the last County Council elections, South Yorkshire had been one of only two Metropolitan Counties to hold their Labour majorities, which indicated its popularity.

This is what I planned to say. I practised out loud countless times with meticulous attention to my watch. But there was a snag. How was I to tell conference just how angry and let down we all felt with the Minister sitting right behind me on the platform without sounding disloyal to the Party? Should I point at him, or mention him by name? I got through the speech giving the platform behind me a quick glance as I made our criticism clear. To my great surprise there was applause – which cost some seconds as it nearly put me off completely! I finished just as the red light came on, and left the platform shaking but feeling high as a kite. The main resolution was passed and cheap fares had won applause!

I enjoyed the rest of the week, and sadly never came across the Chair of the compositing meeting to thank him. Long afterwards I realised that I had spoken with conviction because I was using MY experience, as a woman with a family to win the argument. That had given me confidence. I have never forgotten how this one challenge made such a difference to me, a woman, away from her children for the first time doing something she had never done before. It was probably the end of my school teaching career. I stood for election to the city council the following May, knowing that feeling of ownership and collective achievement in helping to develop a policy made it possible to speak with confidence and conviction in public.

David Blunkett

The experience increased my admiration of the efforts of David Blunkett to overcome the barriers of disability to perform so effectively in political and public life. He recounts in vivid detail

David Blunkett

in his autobiography[7] the struggles of his family's working class roots. David was brought up on another of the council estates around the Firth Park area; a small child with a serious disability, only four when he went to a boarding school for the blind in Sheffield, and aged twelve when his father was killed in an accident at work leaving his Mum struggling to make ends meet. As he describes, it was his Grandad Williams, who was political and used to read news items from the *Daily Herald* to him as a boy.

> From listening to him I picked up much of my political awareness and developed an early interest in the wider world.

After his father's death he attended a boarding secondary school in Shrewsbury where he remembers being rather rebellious and keen to try anything despite his blindness. As he approached school leaving age it became clear to him that only a limited range of careers (such as piano tuning) were considered suitable for youngsters with visual impairment. He hated being stereotyped because of his disability, got a job with the Gas Board and used evening classes and hard work to prove them wrong, gaining 'O'levels and economics 'A' level.

Back in Sheffield he again faced obstacles. In his words:

> The Department of Education and Science weren't very encouraging about visually handicapped

7. Blunkett D. (1988). *On a Clear Day.* Michael O'Mara Books Ltd.

> people becoming teachers except in special schools or in music.[8]

After passing more 'A' levels he entered Sheffield University. With Bernard Crick[9] as his tutor, and work with Bill Hampton in the University Extramural Department, he graduated with a good honours degree in politics. His time with Bernard Crick at Sheffield University left him certain that he wanted to make a career in politics in order to change things. He married Ruth Mitchell who had grown up in the same Brightside neighbourhood as David. Ruth was a tireless reader for him and kept him up to date with all the local and national news, supporting his high ambitions. He obtained a teaching post at Barnsley FE College travelling by train from Chapeltown station with Clive Betts, another former neighbour. His route to success through post-16 education was a personal fight and an achievement that put my small scale experience in Blackpool into perspective.

Writing later in 1981 he described his analysis of its impact:

> When you're handicapped you're desperately trying to assert your independence; to assert your ability to do things on your own and to do them well. In asserting that maybe you over emphasise the point. But I'm less abrasive now.[10]

The suppressed frustration behind these words are similar to how Roz Wollen described her feelings after qualifying as a

8. *Local Government Chronicle*, 1981.
9. Sir Bernard Crick, 1929-2008, Lecturer at Sheffield University and from 1971 at Birkbeck.
10. *Local Government Chronicle*, 1981.

car maintenance fitter, and finding it impossible to get work. The same sentiments were felt in ethnic minority communities around the country especially as unemployment increased and black youngsters found themselves always at the tail end of job searches.

Social Care

After his unsuccessful selection bid for the Penistone by-election, David Blunkett put all his energies into an innovative social care initiative. This involved developing two 'Elderly Persons Support Units' (EPSUs). One was at Ecclesfield close to where we lived. The Council used land available for housing to add new bungalows to the significant amount of older persons accommodation built by the former Wortley Rural District Council. They were centred around a purpose-built hub, with office space for home help services for the wider area and a lunch club and day centre, with space for GP outreach surgeries. It stimulated further sheltered housing in the area, so that by the 1991 census, Ecclesfield Polling District had the highest number of over 80s in the city.

This was a project that was simple, practical, affordable as well as radical, and put in place after listening to working class people in communities. The Home-Help service and 'meals-on-wheels' were free or very cheap; the GP practice and facilities were close by, and sheltered bungalow rents affordable. It helped most those who had least. A model of social care that brings local government and NHS care for older people together is as rare and necessary now as ever, and David was well aware that he was breaking new ground, creating Labour Party policy and putting it into action. In its field of social services it was as bold as cheap bus fares in transport. In both, the underlying stated principle was one of equality across communities and social classes. It went unstated that the main beneficiaries were women. In an article based on an interview for *Community Care* in November 1981, by which time he was Chair of the Social Services Committee of the Association of Metropolitan Authorities (AMA), David explained what he had gained from this work:

> We now have to ask how we involve people in the services we have created; how, for example the community can be involved more in facilities like homes for the elderly and handicapped so that they really are community homes – perhaps by having adult education as a part of day centres; opening up the space we are now getting in schools because of falling rolls for other purposes; having real involvement for staff and resident; making social workers and home helps community based not just in offices, but working with and through communities and feeling they are part of them.
>
> It's difficult not to sound evangelical about this but we do really have to go back to basics.

David Blunkett did not articulate in his early writing that his social care model for older people was especially appreciated by women because it focused on poorer families, where women, unpaid, bore the brunt of care, and because women were more likely than men to live to old age, and to be poorer. Because equality policy was in its infancy, like the initiators of the fares freeze, he and others did not make such points explicit, but it is significant that David instinctively recognised gender and racial inequality in the labour market and society, and was invariably on the side of the victim, but he did not speak out about it, any more than he referred to his own visual impairment.

1980s New Challenges

In 1980, I was elected Councillor for a safe Labour Ward, Owlerton.[11] I left my job in the Remedial Department at Ecclesfield Comprehensive. Traditionally the Labour Group met the day after the election at 5.00pm, not an easy time for women with a family, to choose its Officers, and Executive. I had not realised that the former leader George Wilson was about to stand down. There was tension as the vote for leader went narrowly for David Blunkett rather than Bill Michie, who became the whip. Joan Barton, also from the Brightside constituency, took over as Chair – the first ever woman in that position. I went home pleased for her and excited to be a part of it all.

Joan Barton

Many factors, including the change of Leadership in May 1980 brought new ideas and momentum for change into local government in Sheffield. One was the collective solidarity within the local Labour movement around a left-wing political doctrine,

11. This was an 'all out' election for the whole council, which in Sheffield happened only after substantial boundary changes. My close colleagues became George Burrows and George Mathews all representing Owlerton.

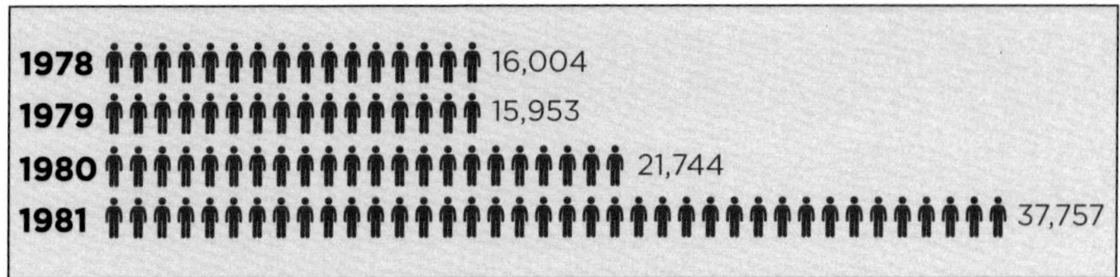

The total number of unemployed in Sheffield 1978-1981 (above) and job losses reported by industry 1979-1981 (Below).

	1979	1980	Jan-Aug 1981
Metal manufacture	822	3,248	3,868
Metal goods	564	1,581	2,467
Engineering	210	1,048	950
Other manufacturing	332	813	656
Construction	332	370	652
Other services	470	846	356
Total	**2,730**	**7,906**	**8,949**

designed to create a more equal society, which had built up in the 70s through political activism and social contact. Another was the dramatic job losses in local industry that shocked the whole city. The steel strike of 1979/80 saw a crowd of 1,500 pickets outside Hadfields, one of the largest steel plants. Even in the sleepy steel town of Stocksbridge workers marched through the streets. The need for urgency and political action was palpable.

A third trigger for change was that the clarity with which the Thatcher government outlined free-market principles demanded a swift and equally clear political response, creating added urgency and a new radicalism at both ends of the national political spectrum. Personified by Margaret Thatcher on the right, Tony Benn and Michael Foot on the left, demands for action intensified. A fourth was undoubtedly an influx of politically driven individuals from outside Sheffield, previously employed within mainly the public or voluntary sector and already politically active.

Keith Jackson and David Blunkett have described these years eloquently,[12] and other authoritative commentators and academics at the time and since have spelt out how Sheffield was not acting alone. It was a product of the rise of a 'Labour Left' in the 70s and early 80s, upbeat and new, driven by an ideology based on grass roots activism and deeply opposed to the expressed ideology of the Thatcher government at national level.

Leadership and clarity of policy came together. Statements from the Leader made Senior Officers throughout the Council aware that they were all expected to work to the manifesto, which was tabled before each Programme Committee for debate and discussion. Overnight study days were organised for the ruling Group Executive and Senior Council Officers at Thornbridge Hall in Derbyshire. At one such gathering in the winter of 1981, during a heavy snowstorm which kept us all imprisoned there overnight, we struggled out to the local pub in the evening, but disaster struck as David Blunkett lost his dog's lead in a snow drift. This was not quite the same as camping by Ullswater but had the same effect of developing solidarity and consensus.

Although some senior officers felt it was not within their traditional brief, others embraced the new culture readily, partly because the manifesto had added credibility with Council Officers because of the wide consultation process it represented. It was indeed impressive. It had been put together collectively within the

12. Blunkett D., Jackson K. (1987). *Democracy in Crisis: The Town Halls Respond.* Hogarth Press.

formal channels of the Sheffield and District Trades and Labour Party (described earlier). Working groups were established, bringing in academics, tenants, representatives from ethnic minority communities and the unemployed, and trade unionists from the private and public sectors, all with specialist experience, knowledge and ideas.

Howard Capelin arrived with his wife Nicki from London along with hundreds of other civil servants in 1979 as the Manpower Services Commission were establishing their new headquarters in the city. He described the manifesto working party arrangements as:

> … stunningly liberalising. Trying to think and argue things through gave a 'point to politics'. Getting to grips with what was going wrong with an atrophied Labour Party made you clearer about the stuff you really wanted to change as a would-be Councillor.

Howard had helped the Labour team in his local ward in London in the '79 election. He recently recalled:

> I was thinking it was the worst thing in the world to have lost that election to Thatcher, but once here I was surprised that on the Council there were lots of things going on and a mood of 'We can do this'.

Manifesto working groups discussed action rather than theoretical politics. Action points included:

- How to establish a Centre against Unemployment?
- How to defend the bus fares policy in the face of government attack?

- How adult education courses could be used to consult swiftly with as many people as possible, such as tenants in housing policy, or young people in black and minority ethnic communities so that they felt part of the movement for change.

The serious riots in Brixton in April 1981, followed by those in Toxteth, Liverpool in July of the same year raised tensions and focused minds on racism in urban areas. It gave prominence to the issue of Equal Opportunities for all regardless of gender, race or disability. The manifesto stressed the need for positive action to redress inequality in the city **and** within the Council workforce through seven pledges to:

1. Develop specific employment projects that better meet the needs of disadvantaged groups in Sheffield
2. Appoint a special officer to work with ethnic minority groups on issues of discrimination, including those affecting employment
3. Encourage training and re-training courses to better equip women to return to work and take up job opportunities
4. Commit itself to act as a model equal opportunities employer by acting positively toward women, ethnic groups and the disabled
5. Act on behalf of the disabled to ensure minimum employment quotas are observed in the local authority and increase their opportunities for employment
6. Encourage and promote the development of childcare facilities in the City
7. Develop its policy of job-sharing to assist those, particularly women, who do not wish for full-time employment but can

> play a useful part by working on a shared basis. It will publicise its scheme and work towards achieving the same rights and protection for part-timers as full-time employees.

Recollecting the uncertainty and distaste felt by colleagues in the local Labour movement towards feminism, these statements were a step forward in recognising the over-arching nature of the goal of equality for all, within a socialist programme of action.

The intensity, creativity and breadth of political debate left little room for splits. In Liverpool the 'Militant Tendency' were challenging local government as being too rigid and traditional, but in a noisy ideological and theoretical way, without the emphasis on action and wide consultation, which delivered sound, carefully costed and radical projects. It became a power struggle with a Council establishment for its own sake. In Sheffield the discipline within the Trades and Labour Council remained intact with close involvement by a wider community.

Municipal Enterprise

Events moved swiftly. We believed, as newly elected councillors, that we had a political mandate to take the lead as one of the bigger local authorities in reviving the city's economy, society and culture along socialist lines. David spoke for the collective Labour Group and Trade Union movement as he named the fresh approach 'Municipal Enterprise'. Building on the model of social care for older people, described above, the term went wider than local government and included other public authorities including the Health Authority. Like the bus fare policy it encompassed a wider area than Sheffield. The employment crisis meant that it also covered the labour market, industry and the economy. He needed close advisers who would develop the radical thinking and enthusiasm into well worked out proposals. The place to start was the local authority. The objective was to bring its whole culture and way of working into line with our thinking.

David Blunkett, Keith and I discussed these ideas at length on our Sunday walks. Keith helped put together three strategy papers 'Towards a Social Policy', 'Alternative Economic Policies' and 'Implementing a Local Economic Strategy for Sheffield'. The papers were discussed in a Members and Officers Strategy Steering group. On 25th July 1980, the Policy committee approved the preparation of an Economic and Employment Strategy, and a Social Strategy under the direction of two Member/Officer Steering groups that would report to the Urban Strategy Panel. Both groups would co-opt relevant individuals from outside the council: academics, community leaders and trade unionists. Preparatory documents made clear that: *'the aim of the strategies is to encourage, and provide a vehicle for, the development of a corporate approach to economic and social matters and not to plan in detail what will happen'.*[13]

The organisation of the work, co-ordination, providing the necessary impetus, much of the input about how to go about it, not the content, would be the responsibility of the two temporary principal development officers in the Corporate Management Unit. It stated:

a) to succeed there will need to be a co-operative effort by all relevant departments.

b) two senior officer posts would be created for which Urban Programme funding would be sought.

---

13. Discussion note by Head of Corporate Management Unit. 1st draft. Economic and Social Strategies, 18th August 1980.

c) the strategies were responses to 'a new style of political leadership'.

The initial suggestions were amended and developed. A third post in the central administration team was agreed, a Research Officer responsible directly to the Leader. Differentiation between the two strategy groups was discussed. Economic and Employment, to be chaired by Bill Michie, and would focus on 'short term action' to respond urgently to the rapidly rising unemployment. Social, chaired by councillor Rev. Alan Billings,[14] would have a longer term focus of 4/5 years. Advertisements for staff to organise both groups appeared in the *Guardian* in October 1980 making their political aims clear. Employment and Economic would:

> … seek to create employment by identifying the needs of Sheffield people and examining new ways in which they may be met by local skills and productive capacity including municipal enterprise, co-operatives, and planning agreements.

Social strategy would:

> … guide the local authority's work in the general direction of positive discrimination and by linking traditional departmental provision will co-ordinate the direction of resources to meet political objectives.

14. Rev. Alan Billings, presently South Yorkshire's Police & Crime Commissioner. As a City Councillor he became Chair of the budget sub-committee under George Wilson's leadership, becoming Deputy Leader when David Blunkett won the leadership. He was the vicar of Broomhall, and then Walkley, leaving the Council in 1986. A member of the 'Faith in the City' Commission, under the chairmanship of Sir Richard O'Brian.

Paul Skelton was appointed to the Economic and Employment brief. He was a community development worker with a background in Town Planning who worked for Coventry Workshop, one of the Community Development Groups (CDGs) funded by the Home Office. It was co-operative based; salaries, policy and costs were shared. He had experience of bringing together tenants and trade unionists to design housing schemes and community facilities, and had also developed an 'eye' for suggesting new uses for derelict buildings that the interviewing committee believed would be useful, in the rapidly increasing number of former industrial sites in the city.

His application pointed out the potential difficulties in making too sharp a distinction between economic and social strategy when the city was traumatised by job losses, which had massive social impact, and stressed the need for close liaison between the two groups, and for further research to *'explore in concept and*

CITY OF SHEFFIELD

PRINCIPAL OFFICER

(ECONOMIC AND EMPLOYMENT STRATEGY)

£9,000-£10,000

Sheffield City Council wishes to appoint a Principal Officer, fo
years in the first instance but with the intention of renewal, to
a new Economic and Employment Steering Group consisti
Councillors and Officers and co-opted members incl
representatives of industrial management and the L
Movement in Sheffield and local educational and training b
The Steering Group will seek to create employment by iden
the needs of Sheffield's people and examining new ways in
they can be met by local skills and productive capacity inc
municipal enterprise, co-operatives and planning agreements.

The City Council is looking for applicants whose experience e
them for both research and development. The officer will e
that the necessary background information is available t
Steering Group in which decisions can be made and will als
ordinate the necessary steps by which employment initiative
plans can be developed. No particular professional qualifica
required; more important is vision, insight and commitment
City Council's approach and policies.

**Further details from Corporate Management Unit, Town
Sheffield S1 2HH, Tel.: (0742) 734072. Closing dat
November.**

City of Sheffield

PRINCIPAL OFFICER

(SOCIAL POLICY STRATEGY)

£9000-£10000

The City Council has decided to formulate an explicit Social Policy Strategy to guide the local authority's work in the general direction of positive discrimination and linking traditional departmental provision. The Strategy will provide the framework within which individual Council policies are prepared and will co-ordinate the direction of resources to meet political objectives. A Social Strategy Steering Group made up of councillors, officers and co-opted members from within and outside the city, will guide the direction of the work.

The council is looking for a Principal Officer for two years in the first instance but with the possibility of renewal, to provide the continuing thrust and co-ordination for the detailed work. Councillors and officers are strongly committed to the success of this new venture and it offers creative and exciting possibilities for the right person. He/she must have the intellectual ability for work at this level and the capacity to relate to councillors with strong political views. No particular professional qualification is required but past experience of this type of work will carry weight.

Further details from Corporate Management Unit, Town Hall, Sheffield, S1 2HH. Telephone (0742) 734072. Closing date 7th November.

Job ads that appeared in The Guardian in October 1980.

practice' the links between industry and the community, and to develop *'a clear analysis of the class nature of the key issues facing the city, whether it be unemployment, housing or public transport'.* His statements were openly political in a way that today would be considered out of order for a senior official in the public sector. They looked to the future:

> We are increasingly going to see the inability of the local authority to solve many of the major problems of the working class. Therefore whilst Tory government policies will continue to seek to close down the room for manoeuvre and in so doing will further sharpen the problem and contradictions … If Labour councils like Sheffield don't develop further their relationships with the working class through the development of more explicit strategy then the problems will remain.[15]

Geoff Green lived locally in Walkley near the University. A friend suggested he might be interested in one of the posts. He was offered the Social Strategy task. He warmed to the political aspirations of the advertisement. He was at the time influenced by the book *Beyond the Fragments: Feminism and the Making of Socialism* by Sheila Rowbotham, Lynne Segal and Hilary Wainwright.[16] Lynne Segal reflected in an article for *Red Pepper* magazine in May 2013:

> Our feminism was never separate from attempts to make sense of the broader political landscape.

15. Paul Skelton was interviewed for his role as Principal Officer for Economic and Employment Startegy, on Wednesday 19th November 1980.

16. The book's back cover describes it as *'the most sustained argument for a reappraisal on the left of all its traditions that has yet come out of the women's movement in Britain'.* Published by Merlin Press in 1979.

The third post of Research Officer caught the eye of **Frances Homewood**, then a member of theatre company, 'Red Ladder', which was later based in Leeds, one of whose productions I had seen and admired back in Liverpool. She was a declared feminist. As she explained recently:

> I had been part of the team in London who established the first Women's Refuge at Essex Road. I really enjoyed working with Red Ladder but was looking to move to a job closer to policy development. I was very surprised to be shortlisted!

I asked her about the interview and who was there.

> They were all men. I heard Alan Billings describe the purple trousers I was wearing to David. I didn't really know what they expected so told them how we had gone about developing the Essex Road project and our work with the community. I was amazed and excited to get the job

All three shared the ideals and enthusiasm of the Labour Group, and occupied an office near the Leader's office in which they made themselves easily available to Councillors, other Officers and those outside the Council with whom they were working. It was a shock to the Town Hall establishment. Paul described how members of the Council, but especially from the Labour Group, would often drop in to discuss issues. Bill Owen was a frequent visitor, as was Alf Meade, and Peter Wood (a bus driver), all Councillors outside the 'Brightside mafia' and its Spring Bank camping network. These local politicians may have found the tightness of that group, with its strong political assumptions and collective loyalty, quite difficult. Discussing options and policy with the strategy officers was important.

For the Chief Executive and his senior officer team it was disturbing. It challenged his authority and accustomed ways of working. Exchanges of memos about how the work of the new officers should be authorised, given their brief of building links within and outside the council with non-traditional partners, tell an interesting story. They portray the tension that built up in the first year. For example, an initial concern was about council notepaper being used *'in connection with a Housing Workshop's series of meetings about which I had no prior knowledge, but really the reason I commented was out of concern about whether Town Hall resources were being used properly'.*[17] Town Hall communication was generally by Memorandum on paper prepared by a shorthand typist. Numerous records of meetings were exchanged.

The situation was exacerbated by an incident when Liberal Councillors explored the joint office of the strategy team in their absence and rummaged through papers. A *Star* headline followed: 'Labour denies Politburo claim', referring to a Liberal accusation that the named officers had jumped the Council House queue by accepting temporary tenancies in the 'hard-to-let' Broomhall area flats. It described them as:

> three research officers, selected for their political views and working from a special 'operations' room next to Council Leader David Blunkett's office, who have been working on the next Labour manifesto and on a Labour campaign on marginal wards.[18]

---

17. Memo, Chief Executive to Mr G Green, 12th May 1981.

18. *The Star*, 11.11.81.

The Tories joined in. Councillor Graham Cheetham was quoted as saying, *'We have been compiling a dossier for weeks on activities in the office which is known as "Red Square" to other officials in the Town Hall'.*[19]

By 16th December the Chief Executive lost patience accusing the three of:

> … still failing to grasp the difference between working for the Council, as you do, and working for the Labour Group, as you do not.[20]

David Blunkett intervened to cool the atmosphere before Christmas in a note to the Chief Executive about:

> … managerial lines of accountability with which some apparent difficulty appears to have been forthcoming.

He kept to formalities, suggesting use of existing Policy A or A1 meetings of Labour Members and Officers so that:

> Officers will be asked to be present and the whole agenda be presented as such, they will then be asked to leave and the meeting will break into an Executive or Labour Group. I had hoped to avoid the necessity of following this course if action, which is used to a much greater extent by the South Yorkshire County Council, as it seems unnecessarily bureaucratic.[21]

---

19. *The Star*, 12.12.81.

20. Memo from Chief Executive, 16th December 1981.

21. Memo from David Blunkett, 22nd December 1981.

In the New Year the Chief Executive responded with yet another suggestion in a paper, 'Accountability and Work Practices of Strategy and Research Officers in the Corporate Management Unit, 21st Jan 1982', that the strategy officers should be split, separating Social from Economic and Employment and both from the Research Officer. This was strongly resisted by all three who valued working together in their central location in the Town Hall, easily accessible to members. They felt it greatly enhanced the speed with which they could turn ideas into action and project proposals.

Paul Skelton recalled these ongoing tensions:

> I shall never forget how supportive David [Blunkett] was at the time. He never wavered. The same was true of Alan [Billings] and Bill [Michie] as well.

Frances Heywood and Geoff Green strongly agreed about the support they enjoyed from the political leadership. These initial key officer appointments indicated the determination with which the new administration, Leader and Labour Group intended to involve all mainstream officers in driving through its programme. It was a simple but important structural change which set the scene for change at the top level of the institution.

The following chapters describe the way in which a culture change was achieved within the local authority, so that radical ideas were turned into action over the next four to five years.

CHAPTER 5

Politics in the Public Sector

Strategy into Action

The three people appointed to lead the way to municipal enterprise, Geoff Green, Paul Skelton and Frances Homewood brought new ideas and edge from the world outside Sheffield. I am indebted to them for their comments and archive material which has helped inform some of the detail of process and progress. They were professional, yet undoubtedly politically motivated. They challenged existing policy and proposals for the future, and the manner of operation. Their experiences in community development and women's liberation brought new inspiration into the public sector, exposing the conventional culture of local government as top-down. This was challenging to a Labour movement, rooted in worker solidarity in a very masculine industrial world by demonstrating that there were other aspects of socialism to explore. The ensuing tensions with the Chief Executive and other senior officers in the authority were inevitable as they came together with Sheffield City Councillors to pursue a common agenda for action. A Fabian tract produced in October 1983 by Geoff Green and David Blunkett, *Building from the Bottom: Sheffield Experience*, developed this theme. I have picked out some key general points:

> We argue throughout that we can only win – the *battle for Labour* – by reconnecting economic issues with social issues …
>
> Our key aim is to reinstate the central relationship between alternative economic policies and a social strategy. In short we should produce for need …
>
> Local government has a vital part to play in persuading people to relate their local experience in workplaces or communities to broader advance to a better society …
>
> Conservatives distinguish between productive private sector and a non-productive public sector. It follows then that candy floss is productive, an extra stair rail for a handicapped person is not. Rubber ducks, plastic gnomes and fruit machines create wealth; council houses, school text books and wheelchairs dissipate it. Home helps are costly public spending; 'Home Angels' which only the rich can afford – a 'wonderful service' …

The message was clear and simple, albeit little reference to discrimination faced by women, black people nor the role of adult education.

They and subsequent staff appointed in the first eighteen months after Blunkett became leader of the City Council, in 1980, all describe the five years of Sheffield City Council before the end of the miners' strike in 1985 as exceptional. They appreciate David Blunkett's leadership role, but also recognise the strong, yet friendly, collective mood of solidarity within the Labour movement that was important in delivering a momentum for change, and clarity in its defining principles.

During their first year the two strategy groups took different directions. The Social Strategy Steering Committee met regularly, was well documented and produced reports. Rev. Alan Billings, Council Deputy Leader, adopted a quizzical style of chairing. He put an introductory paper before the first meeting of his steering group that asked questions of the new committee:

> What is a Social Strategy?
> What does 'positive discrimination' mean?
> Is it possible / desirable / workable?
> Can we ever know?[1]

The minutes of the Committee's meetings confirm that co-opted members including Alan Walker[2] at Sheffield University and Roy Bailey,[3] the folk singer and academic, played a significant part. They consisted of interesting, theoretical debates. Neither Rev. Billings nor Joan Barton, both senior Councillors who sat on the committee, could recall much of the meetings, or much discussion of Positive Discrimination. In the minds of these politicians, rather than the academics and others attending from outside the Council, the group's significance was marginal to their core political programme of action. However, Councillor Alan

1. Agenda item 2, Social Strategy Steering Committee, 4.11.80.
2. Emeritus Professor of Social Policy and Social Gerontology, Sheffield University.
3. Academic and folk singer, Roy Bailey (1935-2018) took up material provided by the many performers and writers he met on his travels, each drawing on the traditions of protest of their own country. With songs from Si Kahn, Robb Johnson, Ray Hearne, Geoff Pearson and Leon Rosselson among others, he wove the threads of his own distinctive themes and causes: denunciation of war, political repression, injustice and the impoverishment of working people and minorities. (*Guardian* obituary. 20.11.2118.)

Wigfield, the Chair of Family and Community Services later a lecturer at Sheffield University, and Cllr Pat Heath were the major players from the Labour Group. Alan Walker in particular was influential in using the work of the strategy group towards developing projects which linked evidence from poverty indices to the need for and provision of health and social services.

Early in 1983, the Social Strategy Steering Committee brought together *'City councillors who sit as a minority on Sheffield Health Authority with other representatives drawn from progressive health organisations in the city'*, to work on a Health Plan for Sheffield, based on detailed figures broken down by ward and poverty indices. Statistics drawn from the 1981 census provided ward by ward figures broken down by gender and age of the population. This showed, for example, that at age 55 numbers of women and men across the city were more or less equal, but by age 70 there were 4,000 more women than men. They could measure the impact on the areas of the city maintaining the Council's Elderly Persons Support Units, described in the previous chapter which integrated local authority managed housing, home help and community services, with GP and other NHS support for elderly people. This confirmed that the beneficiaries of this model of social care were, in numerical terms, mainly women.

Geoff Green recalled with pride the 'People's Campaign for Health' which was a product of the strategy group and quoted David Blunkett's attack on the Health Services Act of 1980 which removed the requirement for local government *'to fund all essential services'*, and instead empowered it:

> … to allocate money towards meeting any shortfall in a variety of other ways including jumble sales, raffles and appeals. What is needed is an alternative

economic policy geared to meeting social and health needs – providing social support and community facilities. This should not be seen as desirable but unaffordable benevolence that is only possible in an economic upturn.

PEOPLES CAMPAIGN FOR HEALTH

BULLETIN 1

The NHS – A Major Achievement

Before the war socialists and others campaigned vigorously for a national health service, free at the time of use and available to all at time of need. Older people will remember those grim days before 1948 when private treatment meant that the great majority could only afford to see a doctor as a last resort. The NHS liberated people from those fears by helping all people according to need rather than ability to pay.

Principles Undermined

The NHS, is, and always has been, denied the funding necessary to provide an adequate national service. This bulletin explains why the Health Service in Sheffield, as in the rest of the country, faces a major financial crisis. The principles of a universally available service are being challenged politically and ideologically. If the battle of ideas is lost, if the basic principles are diluted, then economic cuts soon follow. Take 3 examples.

(a) **Increased charges.** The principle of a service free at time of use has been undermined by the Government's belief that people (that is, 'scroungers') will exploit it unless they have to pay a charge. In the last 3 years prescription charges have risen well ahead of inflation.

PRESCRIPTION CHARGES

(b) **Privatisation.** Introduces into the Health Service the ideas of a market place economy and a two tier service. According to the Government, the twin challenges are "freedom of choice" and "efficiency"—those who can afford to pay for a better service should have the choice, and the market forces which provide the NHS with drugs in return for huge profits could more "efficiently" provide other services like laundry and cleaning.

(Frank Reynolds in *Punch*, 1925)

Doctor. 'WHAT DID YOU OPERATE ON JONES FOR?'
Surgeon. 'A HUNDRED POUNDS.'
Doctor. 'NO, I MEAN WHAT HAD HE GOT?'
Surgeon. 'A HUNDRED POUNDS.'

(c) **Charitable Funding.** The Health Services Act of 1980 removes Government responsibility to fund all essential services. Instead, the Department now "allocates" money "towards meeting" the expenditure. The shortfall has to be found locally, and health authorities are now empowered to raise money through jumble sales, raffles and appeals.

The Alternative

"What is needed," according to the Leader of Sheffield City Council, Councillor David Blunkett, "is an alternative economic policy geared to meeting social and health needs—providing social support and community facilities. This should not be seen as 'desirable but unaffordable' benevolence that is only possible in an economic upturn."

The People's Campaign for Health's first Bulletin, published in 1983.

The Economic and Employment Strategy steering committee met less regularly. After its second meeting, confidential papers were leaked to the media, which made Cllr Bill Michie wary of regular meetings.

Its work was action orientated. They applied for MSC money to help fund a Sheffield Centre Against Unemployment.

They intervened in an industrial dispute at a small engineering works, Snows, which the management wanted to close or relocate while the employees wanted to run it themselves as a workers' co-operative. The workers staged a sit-in and were all summarily dismissed. The strategy group supported the workers and helped finance the creation of a co-operative called 'Mons'.[4]

4. Mons (Snows backwards, almost).

A meeting of the 'Mons' workers' co-operative, including Chair John Smilie (centre) and Bill Michie (right).

A New Department

Six months into its existence and exactly one year after David Blunkett took over the Leadership, the Economic and Employment Strategy Group brought a proposal to the Policy committee to establish an Employment Department separate from the Corporate Management Unit and Planning, with a new Employment Committee. The argument was two-fold:

First, that the sudden upturn in job losses (see charts on p105) most obviously in the steel and engineering sectors justified urgency, and second, that the devastating impact on the incomes of countless families in working class communities was causing a traumatic social crisis. The Council therefore had a duty to explore **every** potential avenue of job creation and protection in new and imaginative ways.

Core funding for staff would be found from 'Section 137' – a clause in the Local Government Act 1972 which gave local authorities *'Power to incur expenditure for certain purposes not otherwise authorised'*. Neither Sheffield City Council nor SYCC had used it previously. The preamble included two conditions. One emphasised that spending in relation to any activity for which there were existing local authority powers should come from the relevant budget; the other specified that the expenditure should be *'commensurate with the direct benefit to their area or any part of it or all or some of its inhabitants'*. The definition of 'commensurate' was spelled out in a schedule that detailed the complex formula whereby this should be established, but which was generally referred to as 'the equivalent of a 2p rate'. The Department was given an initial annual allocation of £2.5m.

These Terms and Conditions were significant. Section 137 resources could fund new policy making posts. Putting them together in a new Department created a collective stimulus. Because most ideas and projects they came up with included existing local government powers, like Education for training projects, Social Services to support the unemployed, Arts and Recreation for new jobs in cultural industries, the new Department was involved with every area of Council activity. Its chief effect was felt by the Planning Department. David Skinner[5] became its Chair in 1982 and was ready to build a close working affinity with the Department's new Chief Officer. This became the main focus for the Strategy Officers; Paul Skelton split his working time 50:50 between his strategic role in the Corporate Management Unit and heading a Municipal Enterprise team in the Employment department.

David Blunkett and the Labour Group were still very new, so the Department had considerable political influence. Whereas the

5. David Frederickson, formerly David Skinner, was a City Councillor in Sheffield from 1978-1987. He left the Council to train as an actor.

expansion of the Corporate Management Unit was a challenge for the Chief Executive's team, the new Employment Department and Committee shook up the whole authority as it gave every Council Department a duty to focus on jobs.

An advertisement appeared in *The Guardian* on 17th June 1981.

CO-ORDINATOR
£14,853-£15,861

We wish to appoint a Chief Officer, responsible to a new Employment Committee, to set up a department to help strengthen and develop the local economy and tackle the effects of the re-structuring of the manufacturing base of the city. Priority is to be given to preventing further job losses, creating socially useful and accountable employment and supporting the unemployed and those threatened with redundancy.

This will be done by bringing together existing industrial and employment development functions, as well as promoting relations with the local workforce to use its skills, experience, and productive capacity to defend, generate and expand employment. Assistance will be given by providing land, property, finance, information, technical advice, and training (in conjunction with other departments); exploring partnerships, municipal enterprise…

A degree/professional qualification and proven success at a senior level is essential. She/he must have the intellectual capacity to relate to Councillors with strong political views and be committed to the Council's approach and policies.

Skelton, who drafted the advertisement, described the position as 'Co-ordinator' because of the way the team was expected to work within the local authority 'from the bottom up' and with relevant groups in the city.

John Benington applied to head the new Department. He was a visionary academic at Warwick University, and had also worked with Coventry Workshop.[6] He felt a strong accord with the political aspirations of the new administration.

So far the changes to the local government institution in the first year of Blunkett's leadership were structural but they offer some lessons for political action in general. Challenging the existing patterns of town hall bureaucracy was a necessary pre-cursor to liberating it to implement fresh strategies for the public good. Using the term 'Municipal Enterprise' demanded that officers champion the socialist approach. It required the bureaucracy to change the manner and style in which they operated as a large public employer. They were expected to listen and be responsive to the public. Close engagement with shop stewards and their trade unions, unemployed workers and community activists was essential. David Blunkett wrote a Foreword to the 1980 Urban Programme submission three months after he became leader in which he explored the changes he was working towards.

> If the Urban Programme submission is not to be dismissed by everyone as a minor appendage to the day to day work of the City Council it must

6. Coventry Workshop, see p58. The Community Development Project was a research project initiated in 1969. It was a neighbourhood-based experiment aimed at finding new ways of meeting the needs of people living in areas of high social deprivation by bringing together the work of the social services under the leadership of a special project team. https://discovery.nationalarchives.gov.uk/details/r/C9253.

> be seen as an opportunity to examine and interlink the policies and programmes of the Council as a whole. This document is therefore not merely a submission for a relatively small amount of financial aid, but in a wider context.
>
> The City Council places the highest priority on economic measures which accept the belief that in tackling deprivation, inequality and social injustice, it is fundamental change not palliatives which will tackle causes not symptoms, aiming at prevention rather than cure.

He concludes:

> If we are to have any impact on the needs and aspirations of the people of Sheffield, it will require their involvement. Without the backing, enthusiasm and commitment of ordinary people, strategies will remain on shelves; hope will turn to frustration; good intentions will appear as cynical disregard. To set out on a long journey without a map would be foolish, but to have no idea of why or where you are going would be an act of ultimate despair. The present programme is only a start in the process of gearing resources to coherent objectives and it is important that the process of review should be an ongoing feature rather than an annual hiccup in the authority's calendar. Everyone has a part to play.[7]

---

7. Use of Urban Programme funds are described in a later chapter (see page 273).

When inevitable tensions arose between these political objectives and paid officials' perceptions of their role, politicians argued that norms of working should not hamper wider goals. The 1982 manifesto, described earlier, was to be put before each main committee after the local elections in May 1982, for comment and agreement.

The work of establishing a new grounded and bottom-up structure continued to transform the whole local authority into a more coherent and politicised body. As described earlier, Sheffield Trades Council had, through George Caborn, established SCAR (Sheffield Campaign against Racism). The Local Government Act of 1966 gave authorities the right to attract grant aid for:

> Special provision in the exercise of any of their functions in consequence of the presence within their areas of persons belonging to ethnic minorities whose language or customs different from those of the rest of the community, such as expenditure in respect of the employment of staff

Using these funds the Council appointed Mike Atkins[8] to a post in 1982, which eventually became the Race Equality Unit in 1985, and was also located close to that of the leader, chief executive and strategy officers. His small team included two significant women from the black community, also very active in the women's movement, Dorothy Dixon-Barrow and Senni Varadkar

Dorothy Dixon-Barrow

8. Mike Atkins, a member of the West Indian community, who had studied at Coleg Harlech residential college of adult education.

It was the way in which new projects were delivered, as much as their content, that was radical. It is worth describing in some detail how three such activities within the Council established a model of how to turn political ideals into action which especially benefited the lowest paid workers in the Authority.

The first, based in the Personnel Department, addressed pay, the second addressed widening employment progression through Adult Education, the third related to the Public Works department and had an impact within the building industry and public sector housing and its tenants.

Positive Action: A Pay Audit of Sheffield City Council

Jude Stoddart, the newly appointed deputy to John Benington in the Employment Department, and Frances Homewood within the local authority's Central Policy Unit, had built a substantial section on equality into the 1982 Labour manifesto. They were feminists and Jude had considerable research experience from her previous work with the Equal Opportunities Commission (EOC). Although the Trades and Labour Council was still dominated by men, its leaders, Bill Owen, George Caborn and Dan Sequerra[9] were happy to be guided by women on the detail of equal opportunity aspirations. John Benington and the Strategy team in CPU had persuaded the two Strategy groups to come together to hear Cynthia Cockburn[10] speak on her publication *In and Against the State*. I vividly remembered her overnight stay with us before speaking at a conference Keith had organised and being

9. Dan Sequerra, then Chair of Sheffield Trades and Labour Group.

10. Cynthia Cockburn, 1934-2019, author of *In and Against the State*, published in 1979, a collection of articles about community development and women.

surprised as we talked long into the evening, that she seemed more interested in my busy life with three young children and what my aspirations were, than about her lecture the following day.

The 1982 manifesto included seven pledges through which to redress inequality in the city and within the Council.

Items 2, 4, 5 and 7, below, relate to in-house activities.

2. Appoint a special officer to work with ethnic minority groups on issues of discrimination.
4. Commit itself to act as a model equal opportunities employer.
5. Act on behalf of the disabled to ensure minimum employment quotas are observed.
7. Develop its policy of job-sharing.

They were measurable and therefore outcomes were specific. A Positive Action Steering Committee was established to oversee the work chaired by Cllr Sheena Clarke. Isabella Stone was recruited from the EOC where she had been a colleague of Jude Stoddart, and started work in the Personnel Department as a 'Positive Action Research Worker', in November 1983. A new chief Personnel Officer had recently been appointed.

Isabella Stone's initial task was to undertake a gendered analysis of pay within the Council, Department by Department. Her work was detailed and methodical. In 1983 she produced a statistical profile of gendered pay. Its Introduction reads:

> This statistical profile provides a broad picture of the earnings and distribution of (non-teaching) men and women working for Sheffield City Council. It is part of a one-year research project,

which began in November 1983, set up to collect together statistical information about men and women working for the City Council, to identify the barriers to women's job opportunities and career development which exist within the Council, and to make recommendations to the Council as to changes in policy and practice that need to be made in order to bring about equal opportunities for women. It was jointly funded by the Employment and Personnel Departments.

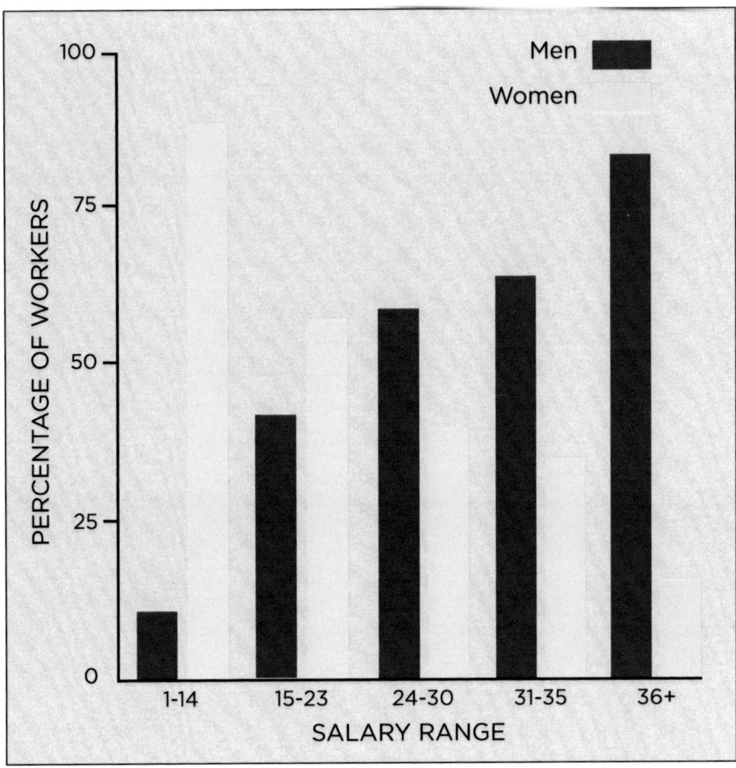

Distribution of men and women within the salary ranges. Taken from Positive Action Report, Statistical Profile 1984; Section A: Salaried Workers. (Sheffield City Council).

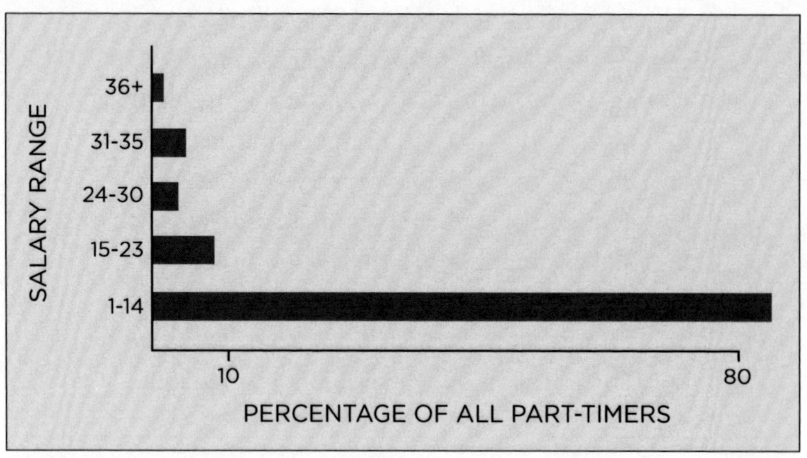

Distribution of part-timers across the salary ranges. Taken from Positive Action Report, Statistical Profile 1984; Section A: Salaried Workers. (Sheffield City Council).

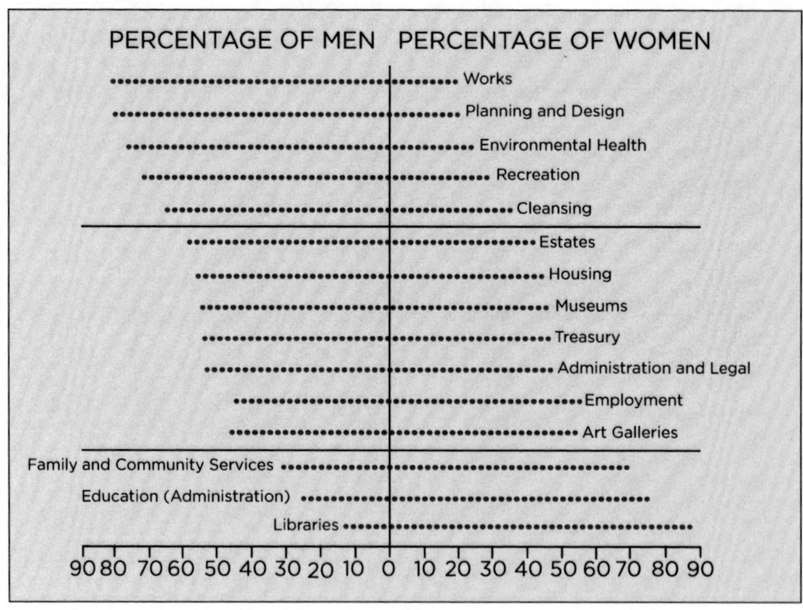

Distribution of men and women within departments. Taken from Positive Action Report, Statistical Profile 1984; Section A: Salaried Workers. (Sheffield City Council).

Isabella mentioned recently how important it was that she was based in the Personnel Department, under the Chief Executive and Leader, to give her the necessary credibility over large departments like Treasury and Education, especially for the first year as she collected the data. The final report of the 'Positive Action for Women Project', together with its Statistical analysis, was completed in 1984 as a joint project of the Employment and Personnel Departments.

It uncovered huge pay differentials. 88% of salaried employees on the lowest pay scale were women, whilst at the highest levels the figures were reversed. 96% of salaried part time workers were women, '*who are even more concentrated in the lower salary ranges than are women workers generally … the vast majority (84%) earn less than pro-rata of £5493pa.*'

The statistical profile was only the first part of the project. The second was:

> … to identify, by means of case studies in different Council departments, and by examination of various centrally developed policies and practices, the barriers to women's job opportunities and career development within the council.

The six case studies are described in detail.

To take, for example, the City Treasurer's department, which employed 463 men and 213 women but found that less than half (44%) of the women earned below £5493pa, whereas half of the men (49%) earned more than £9,000pa. They included:

> - Interviews with staff responsible for recruitment and selection, designed to a) understand the process involved; and b) to discover the attitudes in the section.

- Interviews with managers designed to a) understand the process involved and b) discover the attitudes of these individuals to women working in the department and in particular their suitability for promotion.

- Interviews with women working in the department to gage their perception of opportunities for women, and group interviews with all Data Preparation operators, about their working conditions; their experience of training; their promotion prospects; and their aspirations.

The report found there were basically five routes into the Treasury:

1) People employed to do a specific job such as data preparation operators, typists and machine operators and, increasingly, the counter cashiers. They are generally 'set apart' from the rest of the department and are not integrated into the overall progression paths. They are 100% women.

2) Professional accountants who enter already qualified, or as graduate trainees who will do their Institute of Finance qualification over 3 years on block day release. Of these 6 of the 60 entrants are women (an unusually high proportion we were told).

3) A group who enter as 'juniors', and gradually work their way up to gain qualification through several years of day release. Of these 86% were male and 6% female.

4) Those also entering as juniors, but, rather than progressing through the department by means of professional qualification, become the 'clerical stream'. These can progress as far as grade 5, but then meet a block as moving to grade 6 requires further assessment.

5) Those entering as computer specialists with a view to remaining and progressing in that field. Of these only 6 of the 46 programmers and analysts this year were women.

Isabella summarises as follows:

> The 'dead-end' jobs in City Treasury, with few or no opportunities for progression, are held exclusively by women.
>
> The 'core group' of workers recruited as 'juniors', diverge in 2 directions
>
> (i) higher qualifications and higher paid jobs – these are predominantly male
>
> (ii) into clerical jobs requiring no or lower qualifications, and are graded scale 5 or below. These are predominantly women.
>
> The professional accountants are predominantly men.
>
> The computer specialists are predominantly men.
>
> Recruitment interviews for applicants for grades 1 and 2 take place by an officer who described the qualities he was looking for as 'the willingness to get on', the 'right attitude and looks' and an ability to 'fit in with our way of working'. Another describes his view that 'when a woman decides to have a baby, she decides to lose her career', and that 'their [women's] money is often additional to their husband's so they don't need to go for higher jobs'.

Of course, times have changed and many of these approaches would not be compatible with the Equality Act introduced by Tony Blair.

The methodology however was significant, as they included findings based on individual interviews, and meetings with groups of lower paid employees. For example, Appendix II, a chart based on 33 interviews with part-time Town Hall cleaners about their jobs before and after marriage/motherhood, is particularly instructive as an example.

> All of the women with children had taken a break from work for a time when their children were small. One woman who had been working full-time as a short-hand typist before leaving to have her child said: *'Ten years ago you didn't take a break and then come back to your job. It just wasn't the done thing.'* Another said, *'I only came out for the money and that's it'.*
>
> For most of the women their work experience between their break and their present job had been characterised by moving in and out of a variety of more or less insecure low paid part-time jobs … Because of this experience, most interviewees consider the Town Hall cleaning job better paid and with better conditions than comparable jobs in the private sector, which is why they had stayed in their present job.
>
> *'This is like a real job. You get holiday and sick pay.'*

It was a chance for low paid women workers to talk about their jobs and what they meant to them. It was a practical means of building from the bottom. The face-to-face friendly approach gave the study's conclusions credibility.

The third part was 'to develop recommendations for change in policy and practice'. To quote again from Sheena Clarke's Introduction to the final report:

> With 17 Council departments, each with a different function, and 23,000 workers in a range of jobs, a research methodology had to be devised which would produce material broad enough to give rise to generalisations about women's experience as Council workers, but at the same time detailed enough to promote a better understanding of the practices which make that experience one of relative disadvantage.

They identified six categories of women workers, which would, they hoped, 'collectively provide a picture of what life is like for women working for the Council'. In this way discrimination on grounds of race was also highlighted. The categories were:

- Part-time manual workers;
- Low paid white collar workers;
- Middle grade clerical/admin workers;
- Women in non-traditional manual jobs;
- Black women;
- Women who had left the council's employment for maternity reasons.

Then they selected departments or departmental sections which would provide the most illustrative data: Town Hall cleaners; City

Treasury; Housing Department; Works Department; Education Department – maternity leavers.

The material relating to black women was also collated during the course of each case study, and by means of a series of meetings of black women working throughout the Council. Their experience is described in all of the case study summaries as well as in the case study specifically relating to black women.

The report commented on the 'double discrimination' faced by black women as well as women in non-traditional jobs.

> A black woman cleaner as well as being compelled to take low-paid, low-status work for the same reasons as other women do, may very well be allocated the least desirable tasks within that job, and have less chance of progression to a different job than will white women, because of racist attitudes.

Criticism of the mechanistic way the 'disadvantaged' were divided into 'women', 'ethnic minorities', and 'people with disabilities' used two telling examples:

> At a meeting where the recruitment of a Council officer to work with the black community (a section 11 funded post) was being discussed, white male officers consistently referred to prospective candidates as 'he' as if, as long as the requirement to recruit a black person was being fulfilled, there was no need take into account any other area of positive action.
>
> At another recruitment day to attract 'disadvantaged' young people into Council craft

> apprenticeships, all the black youngsters who applied were male and all the girls who applied were white, because no effort had been made to ensure the representation of black girls in either the 'ethnic minorities' or the 'girls in non-traditional jobs' group.

The Positive Action Final Report, completed in just over one year with remarkable speed, threw a spotlight on very uncomfortable facts, which sent waves through the Labour movement and Council. Sheffield Trades and District Council maintained their somewhat sceptical view of 'London' feminists, who might have little understanding of women's lives in working class council estates. But this was work from within its own local authority!

'Take Ten'; Paid Educational Leave

Running concurrently with the Positive Action Project was 'Take Ten', a paid educational leave initiative.

Its roots lay in a series of part-time social studies courses named 'Second Chance to Learn' in which Keith Jackson taught along with Martin Yarnitt through Liverpool University's Extra-Mural Department. Their conclusions identified:

> Three key priorities on which we should campaign:
>
> > give greater attention to the needs of women,
> >
> > confront our own racism as white teachers directing the curriculum,

> address the issue of paid educational leave.[11]

It linked with the new atmosphere in the Town Hall, rejecting old paternalism, and brought together Council workers with the communities where they lived through adult education. The future tutors recounted how:

> After a day long seminar in December 1982 called by the Central Policy Unit, in conjunction with Northern College, on 'Adult and Continuing Education Policy in the Local Authority and the Community', the Policy Committee approved a 'programme of continuing education on a paid-release basis' for all its employees. A curriculum development group was established reporting to the Policy Committee which included representatives from trade union, Personnel and Education Departments, Northern College and tutors from adult education.

Graham Birkin, Cathy Burke, and Steve Bond were three of the four tutors on the Sheffield courses. They are still enthusiastic about the programme, and recently described the scheme as *'one of the most productive teaching/learning experiences of their working lives'*, recalling how *'councillors, under the new leadership of David Blunkett were wanting to counter the negative effects of years of paternalism towards the workforce and the public, in a way that enabled them to become "ambassadors for the Council", understanding the services they were providing, and the issues, and arguing the case (for Labour) whenever they came into contact with the public.'*

---

11. Yarnitt, M., Mace J. (1987). *Paid Educational Leave and Low Paid Workers 'Time Off to Learn'.* Methuen & Co Ltd.

> Graham was team leader of the programme, but in line with the way he lived out his politics, he rejected the hierarchy implied by the job title and informally shared the difference in his salary among other members of the team.

Graham Birkin

> Gently but firmly, and with a great sense of humour, he encouraged participants to develop their own interests and potential. No single course was the same, and a large part of the content was decided upon in discussion with the students.[12]

Basically, the scheme agreed between Personnel and the trade unions, offered Council workers one day off per week for ten weeks, with pay to attend the course. The maximum number of students in a class was 36. Over the first year around 270 employees went through the scheme. Cathy, Steve and Graham described the challenging recruitment efforts they made, discussing the course with groups of clerical workers and cleaners. As with the Positive Action project the methodology was intensely people-centred and action based, using individual interviews and discussion groups. The initial leaflet stated:

> With TAKE TEN you can
>
> - Learn how the local authority works, how your job fits in, and what it means to local people

12. Burke, C. Graham Birkin obituary. *The Guardian*, 18th August 2020.

- Find out about ways to change things at work and in your neighbourhood
- Work together to gain confidence
- Look at how our lives and the choices we make, as women have changed.
- Find out about your rights as a part-time worker
- Have more information about your health
- Think about how to make the most of your abilities and where to go from here

Final recruitment for 'Take Ten' was therefore done through face-to-face groups and discussions, rather than on management recommendation. Preference was given to workers without any post 16 school or college educational experience, and within that sector, the lower paid had priority. Consequently the main beneficiaries were women and ethnic minority workers.

It is well described in Chapter 8 of *Time Off to Learn* (ibid) which opens with the students' own words.

> We were suspicious of the leaflets inviting us to take a day off a week for ten weeks. It was strange to be asked to study subjects which interested us and could be of our own choosing. What was it all about? What was the Gaffer's angle – giving us time off with no apparent advantage to him? We who swept the city's streets, cleaned the toilets, did the filing, mowed grass verges, and the numerous humdrum, irksome, important, but under-valued jobs that have to be done by that proverbial 'somebody'. No-one ever gives us 'owt'! We were wary, but we took a chance.

> We were going back to school – a place we had gleefully left at the ages of 15 or 16. On reflection it was a stranger experience than we had bargained for. We were expected to investigate all sorts of social problems, and where possible did this in a practical way.

They concluded that:

> It has proved that the community spirit is not dead. It has given us the ambition to want more.

The education delivered displayed a depth and thoughtful insight into lower paid work and workers within the public sector. The residential element led many to use the experience as a route out of the lower echelons of Council work as it allowed time and space for debate. Keith's recent comment on reflection was: *'I think this was the most ambitious of all the Northern College initiatives during my time there'.* Cathy Burke thoughtfully concluded her reflections:

> The key impact lay with community-based education, by enabling each student to better understand their own community and the political relevance of that understanding.

Direct Labour and the Works Department

Municipal Socialism – Six Years of Labour Rule in Sheffield: 1926-1932,[13] a small booklet written by Alderman E.G. Rowlinson[14] and with a Foreword by Rt Hon Arthur Greenwood MP,[15] was rediscovered and re-printed in 1982 by the Sheffield Women's Printing Co-op to celebrate 50 years of Labour rule in Sheffield. David Blunkett wrote an introductory tribute to the new edition:

> This Manifesto stands as a tribute to the will and courage of those who had to face unthinkable odds, both in personal and political life. It is an irony of fate that it is exactly fifty years on that with unemployment and cuts in living standards reminding people so vividly of the 1930s, the Anti-Labour forces raise their heads once again to throw back the forces of progress that have made Sheffield the best city in the United Kingdom in which to live.

The Foreword by Greenwood describes how:

> Sheffield was the first great Municipal Borough in the provinces to return a Labour majority. It was

13. Published by Sheffield City Council Labour Group in 1932.

14. E.G. Rowlinson, 1882-1941. He moved from Chesterfield to Sheffield to work at Sheffield railway station and led the Amalagamated Society of Railway Servants (ASRS) in the railway strike of 1911. (Mathers H. (2018). *Dictionary of Labour Biography*. Vol; VI: pp. 235-236).

15. Arthur Greenwood, 1880-1954. Churchill paid tribute to *'his patriotism, his unselfishness, and his personal charm that made him a man of whom it may be said that in the wide circle of his acquaintances there were few who were not his friends'.* (*Hansard*, Vol. 528; 15th of June, 1954).

> a Socialist Council, believing in the principle of collective effort.
>
> It extended the operation of direct labour and established and developed Municipal Printing Works.

The pamphlet emphasises the economic benefits of municipal enterprise and Sheffield's trading departments. In the trading departments, Labour increased the services and reduced the costs so that the benefits of municipalisation should be 'for the many and not for comparatively few' wealthy ratepayers.

An emphasis on direct labour runs through the pamphlet, describing how the administration had saved money through its policy of bringing building work and other services such as Printing, Architects and Surveyors, and Municipal Insurance under its direct control. They set aside an annual 2d rate (£20,000) to purchase land with a payback over 60 years, with which they bought sites such as Beauchief Abbey – an historic monument, a neighbouring golf course used by the public, and sections of woodlands – for public enjoyment. They helped build Sheffield's reputation as one of the 'greenest' industrial cities in the country.

Even earlier, Ecclesfield Labour Party minutes echoed this in a resolution passed unanimously at its meeting on 28th November 1922:

> This meeting of the Ecclesfield Labour Party respectfully suggest to the Council[16] the advisability of conducting future building

16. Wortley Rural District Council.

> operations by direct labour as we are of the opinion that by following that course and eliminating all private contractors better and cheaper houses could be built and employment could be found for a large proportion of local ratepayers.

The ideology behind Labour local authorities expressed in the pamphlet engendered a proud, often pompous aldermanic approach to local government, not only in Sheffield but across the country in Birmingham, Bristol, Bolton, even smaller Burslem – one of the six towns that now comprise Stoke-on-Trent with their imposing Town and City Halls.

This was the sort of creative approach to budgeting Sheffield Council were also trying to encourage, with its call for a new 'Municipal Enterprise'. Fifty-five years later, Margaret Thatcher's ideology of free competition in a market economy was equally clearly defined, and totally different. A clash over direct labour was inevitable. One of Thatcher's first moves on taking office was the 'Planning and Land Act 1980' which introduced compulsory competitive tendering for everything except the major housing maintenance contracts.

After barely one year on the council, David Blunkett suggested I take over as Chair of the Works Committee from John Senior who had suddenly died. This was a shock to me and I suspect an even greater shock for the Director of Works, who had never imagined working with a woman Chair of Committee. We travelled to Blackpool together a couple of weeks later to attend my first annual Association of Direct Labour Organisations (ADLO) conference, where he was a senior figure. He looked embarrassed as he cautiously introduced me to his colleagues from around the country as his new Chair-Woman. He was clearly doubtful whether I was up to the challenge of the new legislation, which was driven by the aim of putting direct labour in the firing line. I listened and learnt from him on the journey about competitive tendering which assumes that the lowest price wins. He explained how it was common practice for informal deals to take place between companies, including the works department bidding for work, so that a small number of large firms cornered the market. A pretence of not knowing who was the 'winner' was maintained. Tendering had always been assumed for new council house building but not for the mass of modernisation and other building work now included in the new legislation.

The two years I spent in this position remain one of the most intense learning curves of my life in three fundamental respects. Grasping the pressures of managing such a very large budget, with its tendering, contracting, purchasing and employment contracts was hard but gave me a grounding in local authority finance. Learning enough about the variety of trades, skills and technologies within the building industry to appreciate the importance of standards of quality, safety, training, was fascinating, and overseeing fair trade-union negotiations was certainly a challenge. All three were new to me.

As Chair of the Works committee one of my first tasks was to Chair a seminar, 'The New Direct Labour Laws', on 4th July 1981 organised by the two new strategy officers, Paul Skelton and Geoff Green along with the Director. Those invited included management and workers in Sheffield's Direct Labour Organisation, together with councillors, members of the Trades Council, Tenants Federation and others committed to supporting the principles of direct labour. The main outside speakers were

Tosh Flynn,[17] and senior officers from the Chief Executive and Treasurer's department. We all had to learn fast.

The need to balance and tailor a large budget in the face of new legislation was a big challenge. Sheffield Works Department in 1980 covered all building trades and the highways workforce and employed 3,000 workers – 90% male on a weekly wage, well organised in a shop stewards committee that was 100% male. Its annual turnover of £3 million was the fourth largest in the country, Glasgow being the largest. Sheffield's Director, and Chairman John Senior were leading figures in the national body ADLO. They and the shop stewards were as one in their vocal commitment to direct labour for public good.

A different type of learning curve included understanding a woman's position outside family and teaching. I was thrust suddenly into a world of manual and male work. I had never before been so acutely aware of my gender. It even got in the way of meaningful communication. I had to put older managers at their ease by asking about their families in a way they saw as normal conversation with a woman, before I could establish a useful discussion about the best way of achieving high productivity in a maintenance contract. I had also to persuade workers that I, a woman, really did want to know how to become an expert joiner, bricklayer or plasterer, and experience their pride in their trades. At my first meeting with the Director he was flummoxed by how to address me. 'Madame Chairman' – no good; 'Mrs Jackson' – too formal; 'Madame Chair' he didn't like.

---

17. Tosh Flynn, Institute of Local Government and Birmingham University. Author of *Economics, Capital and Class* (1981) and joint author of *Direct Labour Organisation: Implementing the New Legislation*.

'What did you call my predecessor?' I asked. *'Why John, of course!'* he replied. He felt uncomfortable with 'Helen' whilst for me he answered happily to 'John'.

The shop stewards were easier. Some I knew through the wider Labour movement and first names over a drink were natural. But at work or in a joint negotiating committee, such informality was not possible. In desperation on one occasion as I chaired the monthly Joint Negotiation Committee (JNC) one of the shop stewards blurted out *'Mother Chairman'*. They understood the threat posed to their jobs and wages by the Planning and Land Act but were concerned that the workforce also needed to understand this, and its implications for the Department. With my Deputy Chair, Councillor George Burrows, we were determined to put a socialist focus onto the task. At the core of this, we reckoned, was listening to and learning as much from experienced workers amongst the senior shop stewards in the department as I was receiving from the equally experienced senior management.

David Blunkett had announced that he wanted every Council employee to become an ambassador for Council Policy in this new environment, so we suggested to the Director a programme of workers' meetings, depot by depot, in order to explain the threat and respond to their questions. The Director was extremely uneasy about direct contact between elected Councillors and the workforce, insisting: *'It's not appropriate for you as Councillors to speak directly to **my** workforce'*. However, he was equally adamant that we would have to reduce bonus pay to win tenders, whilst the shop stewards were clear that better explanation to the workforce as to why this was necessary was essential to avoid industrial action over reduced bonuses.

We suggested that we would hold the meetings anyway at the invitation of the shop stewards unless, as we preferred, he would authorise them. The private sector in the building industry, meanwhile, were rubbing their hands as they looked forward to winning more public sector contracts. On financial grounds, there was no time to lose.

We assured the Director that the meetings would not in any way usurp his management role of negotiating the details with the trade unions, but that as the elected political representatives we were best placed to explain a political problem not of our making. The Director said we could not afford to lose an hour of the working day, so it was agreed to hold the meetings before work commenced at 7.00 am. A further obstacle was the lack of meeting spaces at the depots, so we agreed that they would be informal with no need for chairs and out in the yard if necessary. George and I visited over 30 depots between October and November of 1981, often in cold weather at dawn! Any doubts I had about speaking in public evaporated as, daily, I explained that the purpose of the new legislation was to undermine direct labour in local government, and that we were determined to continue to win the necessary tenders to maintain our present strength. Each meeting was chaired by the local union shop steward. At most meetings the audience was 100% male. After all, only men in the council workforce took home bonus pay!

Afterwards I gathered that one concern about the meetings among shop stewards and also management was that I would be shocked by the semi-nude pin up pictures of women in the depot offices. We were told that one woman manual trades employee had raised the matter in the new Department newsletter, *The Tannoy,* the shop stewards had initiated in July of the previous year. I was curious to meet her!

I have since come across Rose Ardron's letter, *A Birds Eye View of Porn*:

> *'Don't swear. There's a lady present.'*
>
> *'Oh, Sorry love. I forgot you were here.'* If I had a pound note for every time this happens I would be a rich woman by now …
>
> However what I CAN do without is the weird and wonderful display of female anatomy that graces the walls of cabin joiners shops, stores and depot offices. I find these pictures of women offensive and degrading. Women are not sex objects, technicolour fantasies to be used as wallpaper. When men see us this way its no wonder some feel free to beat us up and rape us. As things we have no feelings, we do not count. Stop for a minute – is this what you really think about us, brothers?
>
> Its very difficult to write this without sounding like Mary Whitehouse. You can't expect people to change their attitudes over night, but its time to make a start. The Works Dept. is not only a man's world, it's a woman's too. Women are strong and useful people, not just a nice bit of stuff for men to stare at. So next time you are passing that 1977 dog-eared calendar still hung up on the stores, remember – beneath every woman's curve, lies a muscle.

The response from the Personnel Section, in the next issue, February 1981, is even more revealing:

> I read with amusement Miss Ardron's letter in Issue 2, in which she attacked the many men who post up pictures of semi-nude ladies at their place of work.
>
> She really should have directed her comments to the women who actually flaunt their bodies as a means of living and not to those of us who like to look at their pictures. She cannot possibly deny the fact that if she was so fortunate to be beautiful and figurely attractive she would prefer to earn a living that way and not as one of the lads on the tools.
>
> Miss Ardron has yet to appreciate that to break up the standard daily procedure for us pen pushers, it is pleasant to occasionally gaze and make comment concerning pictures of attractive large breasted ladies pinned up on our wall.
>
> No matter how much she will try, Miss Ardron will not achieve equality until she condescends to pinning up posters and calendars of semi-nude males at her place of work.
>
> B. Hebblethwaite,
> Personnel Office

Rose described recently how upsetting she found this official response. She explained that its institutional nature, not the attitude of her working colleagues that was the problem: *'I was very grateful, for the support of one or two of the senior shop stewards, especially Tommy Latham, a joiner from Knutton Road depot, over the row'*, she emphasized.

The correspondence may have increased the interest and attendance at our meetings. I remember standing on a table on one occasion or sometimes we were in the yard outside in the cold. After the first few meetings, the tension with management lessened and the local foremen and managers also came to hear what we had to say and join the discussion. Twenty years later as an MP, individuals would come to my advice surgery saying *'I remember you when I worked for the Council. You came to our depot!'*.

Listening to workers at these meetings about the close affinity they felt with Council House tenants was interesting. After all they would say:

> We live or were brought up on a Council estate,
> we should get the Tenants' backing as well.

As Councillors we also wanted to involve the growing tenants' movement in working class communities. Jock and Betty Sturrock or Vi Gill took pride in their working class Council estates. They remembered the excitement in their families when their pre-war rented streets were condemned as unfit, and they became eligible for a Council home. Post war housing estates had mains drainage, flush toilets, gardens and running water from a tap in the kitchen – luxury compared with their previous housing. Council tenancies were more secure than in the private sector, and rents less volatile.

Tenants and Workers

With the help of the new Municipal Enterprise Officers in the Council's Central Policy Unit, a Committee called the Joint Works Group was established, consisting of representatives of the workforce and of tenants' associations. The group became a novel way of building from the bottom up and of listening to Council workers together with tenants from working class estates. Tenants' representatives were mainly women, 'Collective Consumers' who appreciated the role they were playing, at a time when the government was trying to bribe them all to become individual home owning consumers by subsidising the right to purchase their rented homes through Right to Buy legislation. One of our speakers was Jane Darke[18] who had written about how important it was for women to be involved with the design of their council homes at an early stage. As mentioned earlier, Sheffield is a very split city. By 2001 in Brightside constituency, 15 years after tenants had been given the 'right to buy', 48.4% still lived in council-owned houses, whereas in Hallam constiuency the figure was only 11%.[19]

The Committee was advisory, but its minutes went to monthly committees of both Works and Policy. Our working relationship with the Director was now smoother. A recently appointed director of the Personnel section of the Works Department was positive about the new committee. Managers as well as shop stewards attended. The Director of Works agreed that he or a member of his senior team on the management side would attend. An important component for both workers and tenants were short courses organised and delivered by Northern College which in many cases led to new educational opportunities and career paths.

18. Taylor, G. (1984). *Making Space. Women in the Man Made Environment.* Matrix – A Group of Feminist Architects.Pluto Press.

19 Dorling, D., et al. (2009). *A Tale of Two Cities: The Sheffield Project.* University of Sheffield.

The Director of Housing however was more uneasy about involving *his* Department or *their* tenants in the new Committee. He argued that Housing, as the Authority's landlord, had its own housing revenue account to determine what rent its tenants should pay and what costs would go into maintaining the housing stock. The Works Department were basically in a contractual relationship just like any private firm. The Director of Housing argued that he already planned housing policy from the bottom up, bringing tenants into aspects of the management of their estates through a new system of 'Area Based Management', where tenants met housing officers, but not Works department staff and workforce. Area Based Management had indeed helped to defuse something of the more traditional top down culture among Housing Officers, the belief that they knew what was best for their tenants. He thought the minutes of the Joint Works Group were not relevant to his Housing Committee and would confuse their relation with tenants. We from Works did not agree that collaboration between the Works Department workforce and tenants would confuse matters or be subversive. Matters such as responding to the competitive tendering requirements in a way that could protect Council jobs were, Housing officers claimed, political and maybe were the business of Councillors on the Housing Committee, but certainly not of tenants, nor the workforce of the Works Department. Such views challenged the fundamental notion of direct labour as described in the 1926-1932 pamphlet. Ideologically, they took local government further and faster down the road of outsourcing. They refused to attend or recognise the Committee, so the Joint Works Group carried on regardless.

These three examples: the pay audit, paid education leave, and direct labour, were all ways in which officers were operating in a different way than before. It was an important preliminary to changing the culture of a city, which follows in a subsequent chapter, but a number of obvious conclusions emerged from the Pay Audit and Take Ten, and the Joint Works group which still have relevance.

First, they succeeded because they affected Council employees, suggesting it is time to revisit directly employed local labour as a way of celebrating work, good quality safety standards, equal pay and employment rights. It brought opportunities for women and men to learn a building trade to develop local pride in the environment in which they lived. It could not have had the same effect within the private sector and sub contractors.

Second, the City Council as the largest employer in the city could measure and address institutional gender and race inequality because of its scale and size. The Positive Action project showed how exposing data about inequality was key to supporting Sheena Clarke's work as Chair of the project, and Jude Stoddart from the Employment Department.

Third, the face to face aspect of Isabella Stone[20] and her team's positive action research, along with that of the Paid Educational Leave team, boosted workers' confidence and belief that their work was valued. It was important social investment. Further

20. Isabella Stone left the Authority for a few years in February 1985 and was seconded back to the EOC to do a report on Equal Opportunities in Local Authorities (published 1988). She was able to use her figures from Sheffield, but also included Newcastle, Leeds and Greenwich. She returned to Sheffield and the Employment Department (DEED) to cover for Gill Greenwood and worked with the Low Pay Campaign, researched for case studies on Sheaf Markets with Angela Galvin, had a spell at Sheffield Hallam University, and was brought back into the Central Policy Unit in 1990 after the Women's Unit and Race Equality Unit had been formed.

comparative research using the same or similar methodology could reveal what has changed about women's opportunities and expectations amongst lower paid part-time women workers and raise their aspirations.

Fourth, all three projects used politically rooted adult education in their work. It is an underestimated feature of how cultural change can be successfully delivered. They brought class politics into step with equality politics in a clever and subtle way. The vociferous Tory opposition in the Council, and ensuing publicity helped to smooth the passage of positive action schemes on gender through the Labour Group and Party. As a result, the pledges within the manifestos of '82, '83 and '84 on equality of opportunity and how to bring it about became more specific and practical each year.

> (1982) 'Looking into the employment situation for women and ethnic minorities', moved on to
>
> (1983) 'Addressing Low Paid work and part-timers within the Council's workforce, and setting up a 1-year task force',
>
> (1984) 'developing job-sharing agreements, a minimum wage and pay-scales, and 'single status' for all Council workers, together with a women's micro-electronic training initiative and young women's plastering training project'.

The wider equality agenda grew roots within Sheffield politics, and became better understood and articulated. Richard Caborn, as an MEP, worked to put positive action at the core of the European Social Fund and other EU funding streams. The startling nature of the conclusions expressed in the publication of the Positive Action Project Final Report in October 1984 led to media interest and a Sheffield Low Pay Campaign being established which hosted a major Low Pay national conference, which concluded that:

> A national Minimum Wage would be a major step towards the eradication of low pay. However it needs to be introduced as part of a package which: tackles the concentration of women, black workers, young workers and people with disabilities in low paying jobs; Re-evaluates the status of manual and low-paying jobs; Reinforces the employment protection of those workers who are simply claiming their basic right to a living wage.

The Positive Action project was also a crucial prelude to a series of women's training initiatives which the Employment Department started to work on, whilst 2,000 beneficiaries of 'Take Ten' over the eight years of its operation, opened new opportunities for low paid workers mainly female, from ethnic minorities, or both, to progress in their careers within the authority or in other fields. The culture had changed. The following chapter describes how this influenced the wider conurbation.

CHAPTER 6

Politics in the City

Employment Challenge New Industries for Old

Three months after John Benington took up his post, he brought a report to the Committee setting out its aims.

Employment Department – An Initial Outline

> Sheffield is the first local authority in the UK (perhaps in Europe) to create an Employment Committee and an Employment Department.[1] Its aims are ambitious: to co-ordinate everything that the City Council can do:
>
> - To prevent further loss of jobs in the city.
> - To alleviate the worst effects of unemployment, and to encourage effective training for new skills and jobs;
> - To stimulate new investment, to create new kinds of employment, and to diversify job opportunities in the city;

1. The Greater London Council (GLC) also ensured that the economic and employment work was quite separate from their Planning Department. The May 1981 Labour Party manifesto implied that '*interventions in the arena of industry and employment would all be guided by the London Industrial Strategy. Now, as the Strategy goes into publication the GLC, the Enterprise Board (GLEB) and the Training Board are already backing around 600 employment, investment and training projects*'. Michael Ward, Foreword to London Industrial Strategy.

- To explore new forms of industrial democracy and co-operative control over work.

> The thrust of the Department's efforts must go into fieldwork rather than into headquarters management. The Department's most skilled staff will be in the field, leading the exploration and innovation themselves, rather than supervising less experienced junior staff from the headquarters. This kind of less hierarchical, more collective inter-disciplinary project-work is familiar in many research and development situations in industry, and in action-research.

The subsequent advertisement in the *New Statesman* in January 1982 describes these aims and the way they would be organised, asking for no fewer than 21 posts, from Principal Officers to shorthand typists. The council had agreed five broad areas of work, two basically relocated from the Planning Department and three major new programmes, with an initial staffing of 30.

Join a Team Developing
Radical Strategic Action Against Unemployment

- Industrial Development (promotion of trade, inward investment, industrial land and premises)
- Sheffield Enterprises (financial assistance and specialist advice to workers' co-operatives, small firms, and new job creation initiatives).
- Economic Development;
- Research;
- New Technology.

> Further specialists to join those already transferred from other departments, will work in small project teams which are being formed for each of the five programme areas.

The advertisement attracted an impressive range of applicants, many with strongly left-wing views. They included: Jude Stoddart from the Equal Opportunities Commission who became John Benington's Deputy Co-ordinator, with responsibility for Equal Opportunities; two former members of Lucas Aerospace shop stewards committee; young, bright research officers from around the country; academics with research experience; and former trade unionists. Others from within the Council's financial, administration, planning and legal teams were seconded to assist along with 50% of Paul Skelton's time as a Municipal Enterprise Officer. Within 3 months the department was in place with its initial funding allocation of £2.5m and basic staffing of 30, fifteen of whom were new appointments.

In its first year, the Employment Department's priority was to build its credibility within the authority and in particular outside it. Karen Escott,[2] a young researcher fresh from London School of Economics in her twenties, described why she responded to the advertisement:

Karen Escott

> It was 'different and exciting', and I liked the description of collective

2. Karen Escott worked for the City Council from 1982-1989 at the Centre for Public Services with Dexter Whitfield. She became a senior lecturer at Sheffield Hallam University and Deputy Head of the Natural and Built Environment Board. Karen now works as a volunteer at Citizens Advice Sheffield.

> working and action research that was not the sort of formal 'analysis' research I was doing in London.

She moved to Sheffield with her partner Jol Miskin. They were both politically active in London – she in the Labour Party; he in the 'Militant Tendency'. She described the novelty of her first experience at work.

> Days after I started working within the Research team, the Department was contacted by workers at Newton Chambers Engineering Works to say they were worried about a threat of job losses. A few days later I was having a face-to-face discussion with the shop stewards committee at the plant in Chapeltown about their situation, never having done anything like that before. It was direct and full of action, so different from desk-based research. We had to learn fast about how politics in Sheffield worked, with the influential Trades Council. As officers we were expected to involve many groups outside the Council in our research.

These groups included the unemployed; BAME communities and Sheffield Campaign Against Racism (SCAR), trade unions and shop stewards committees; co-operatives, through the Co-operative Development Group; voluntary and community associations including Sheffield's new Tenants' Federation and Sheffield Women's Network; Educational institutions – Sheffield University, Sheffield City Polytechnic, Further Education Colleges and Northern College worked closely with the department, as did also the MSC (Manpower Services Commission). This in itself constituted a large outreach project, albeit it did not really include Sheffield's business organisations, initially.

This significant influx of politically driven individuals employed within the public, voluntary and other sectors, started to change patterns of activity and emphasis within the labour movement. Many of the new officers were already active in their own trade unions and understood how to make use of the strong local trade unions and Labour movement in the city to help widen their influence and work with the wider industrial and general public. Their presence not only shook the local authority culture, it started to shift the balance of influence within the Labour and Trade Union movement from the manufacturing sector Amalgamated Engineering Union (AEU), Iron and Steel Trades Confederation (ISTC and the 'Confed'), to public and service sector unions, National Union of Public Employees (NUPE), Association of Scientific, Technical and Managerial Staff (ASTMS), National Association of Local Government Officers (NALGO) and the National Union of Teachers (NUT). Equal and Low Pay were more often on the agenda, even though continuing job losses in steel and engineering remained the first priority.

With its heavy emphasis on work, training and lifelong learning, the Employment Department helped to consolidate the Council's strategic programmes. It relied on detailed statistical research and measurement of impact, which from the beginning included gender analysis, so it further brought positive action into the mainstream with the important input of David Childs, the head of that team. Research always covered economic and social impact and the interaction between the two. The emphasis on action-based research, and a people-centred approach which allowed community involvement from the start on projects with economic and social justification, were its hallmarks.

1983 Parliamentary Elections

It could be said that these early years of the new strategy in South Yorkshire were evidence of political confidence bordering on arrogance. Loss of a political majority in the region was never considered. Neither Barnsley nor Rotherham had any Conservative Councillors and in Sheffield Labour

Labour Rules Sheffield OK!, indicative of Labour's political confidence in Sheffield in the 80s – the loss of a political majority was never considered. The graph demonstrates the support for Labour in Sheffield since 1973.

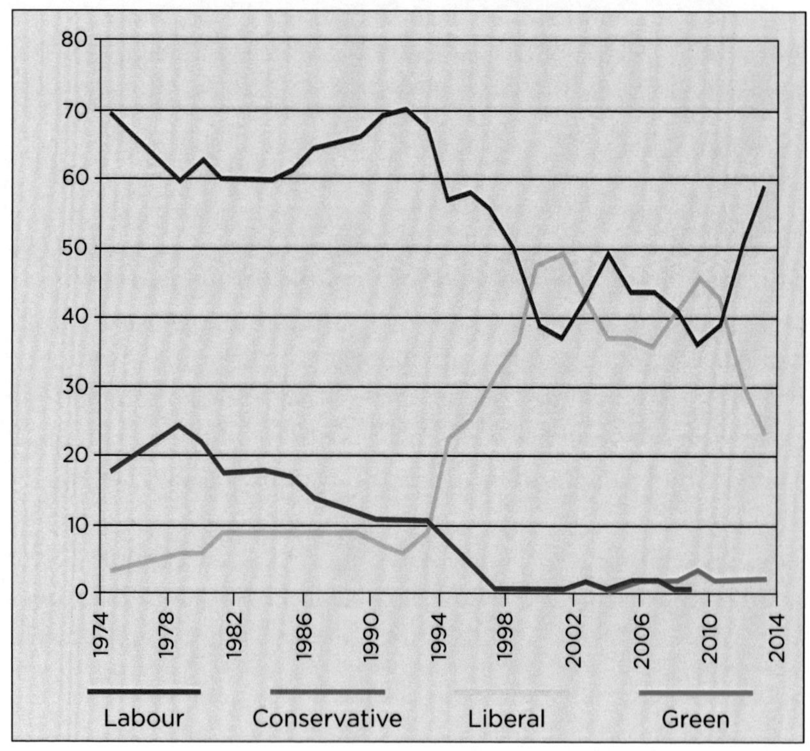

Bill Michie

held total control. A red flag flew on the Town Hall on the 1st May 1983. However a General Election approached, and two of the prominent Labour figures on the Council had ambitions to enter Parliament. The Brightside de-selection in 1974 had set a precedent that made mandatory selection of sitting MPs a feasible prospect. Richard Caborn, by now an MEP, was looking at Central constituency; Bill Michie, in charge of the Employment Committee, had designs on Heeley constituency, held by Frank Hooley MP. Both Richard and Bill had risen to prominence through the AEU, with close links to the Trades and

Labour Council, and reputations associated with the battle in Brightside. Richard, and Bill were both part of the Spring Bank camping group and knew that Sheffield Labour Party members were not too worried about de-selecting sitting MPs. In Central constituency, Fred Mulley retired with some dignity to make way for Richard Caborn. In Heeley the selection was more bitter. Dave Hague, another member of the AEU, was Bill Michie's agent for the Heeley selection battle which Michie won, de-selecting Frank Hooley, on a narrow vote.[3]

This event also impacted on the Employment Department. Bill Michie stood down as Chair of Employment around

Dave Hague (far left) a former member of the Snows workforce, supporter of Militant and Bill Michie's (second right) election agent, seen here at a meeting of the 'Mons' workers' co-operative. The Chair was John Smilie (second left).

3. I am grateful to Dave Hague for sharing with me the inside story of that battle.

Christmas 1982 to concentrate on his Parliamentary campaign. I was unwillingly removed from the position of Chair of the Works Committee and asked to take over his Committee. I was enjoying the challenges of Direct Labour, already described, and knew I had less experience with the media than Bill Michie. The Committee was getting high profile media coverage for all its new ideas and John Benington had an experienced team of highly motivated political activists from a variety of backgrounds. It felt a hard act to follow, and I questioned whether I was the novice and they my political mentors. However, the Employment Committee and Department had been created to lead the way on our political programme to which I was committed, and since numerous big projects and ideas for future work were well under way, I wanted to ensure they were successful. The position gave me confidence in my relatively new world of local politics.

Outside in the City, the organisations such as those mentioned above all supported the fresh approach and were undeterred by the Chamber of Commerce and media view that the Council was too dominated by socialist ideas. Some significant leaders of the business community, and as we have seen some senior officers inside the local authority, were unsettled by the speed of change, and the possibility that left-wing groups such as Militant might take control. The authority rejected this. Despite having appointed officers with a wider range of backgrounds and political opinions than had traditionally been the case, including some supporters of Militant, it found that they quickly became absorbed into the political culture of Sheffield. Earlier chapters have described how Sheffield defined its own identity in terms of employment as manufacturing in steel and engineering, a heavy industry and therefore distinctly male. Transforming this culture, at a time of crisis almost as traumatic for the city as

A mural of a steel worker in coloured brick in the old market area of Sheffield City Centre, and a depiction of buffer girls in a frieze on the walls of the Town Hall. Sheffield has long defined its identity in terms of its heavy industry.

World War 2, was the dominant aspiration of the City Council using its Employment Department as a catalyst. The whole local population was affected, so it was taken for granted that the public sector should take the initiative to achieve change.

Maybe forty years later, the Showroom Cinema publicised its intention to celebrate the 25th anniversary of the release of *The Full Monty*,[4] a film released in 1997, starring Robert Carlyle as Gary who had been made redundant from his steel works and with his former colleagues and son Nathan was trying to earn some money to keep the family going. It was set in Sheffield and had become internationally famous. They had invited Robert Carlyle and William Snape ('Nathan', now in his thirties) to talk

4. *The Full Monty*, directed by Peter Cattaneo won BAFTAs for Best Film and Best Actor in a Leading Role (Robert Carlysle), and was nominated for four Academy Awards (Oscars), winning Best Original Score.

about it afterwards. It was advertised on the website and word got around. But no-one, least of all the Showroom managers, expected the size of the public response. They had to move the screening to the largest of the four screens, and I was lucky to get one of the last tickets as I joined the long queue. I had expected to see people I knew from local politics in the past, but no. The place was jam-packed with ordinary Sheffielders who joined in with 'oohs' and 'aahs' as the pictures of the twin cooling towers were felled to make way for Meadowhall retail and leisure centre; the empty crumbling steel works; the dirty canal with a car in it; the clubs and dance halls; and of course the job centre brought back memories. It was a great fun evening that revived the hilarity and verve of the original film. Its popularity made me understand that, for the city at that time, an analogy with the post-war government was appropriate.

Officers and Councillors rose equally to the jobs challenge. They developed a two-strand approach. The first strand aimed to widen the range of the area's industrial base by developing new industries, new products, and ensuring that jobs and training were open to all in these projects. At a time when boys aspiring to serve an apprenticeship in one of the big firms were leaving school to find this no longer on offer, attractive alternatives were essential. The second strand introduced a feminist element and focused on industries with limited opportunities of jobs or training for women like housing, heating and building. Promoters were from the Women in Manual Trades group; the Tenants' Federation; young people and others outside the manufacturing and industrial structures of trade unions and political parties so far described in some detail, but with the full backing of the Union of Construction, Allied Trades and Technicians (UCATT) and the T&GWU. Both strands were essential, and together were effective in changing traditional definitions of work for the people of Sheffield, especially young people and women of working age.

At the heart of the Department's work, but relevant to both strands was the Employment Proposals Panel, empowered to offer financial grant aid to firms, co-operatives or other bodies outside the Council for initiatives which met these aims, and for which other finance was unavailable. Dr Peter Cromar,[5] an economist from Cambridge, undertook this area of work and Councillor George Mathews,[6] an AUEW senior shop steward from Ambrose Shardlow's large engineering works and vice-chair of the main Committee, chaired the panel. As was said at George's funeral:

> The work had to be meticulous, transparent and fair. Decisions whether to say 'yes' or 'no' to applications were often challenged. George and Peter's judgement was superb. George could recognise 'fools' and 'blarney' a mile off and respond with a definite 'NO' without ever being rude, whilst also recognising honesty and genuine need in others, going out of his way to help and support.

George Mathews

It is worth describing five or six examples from a range of policy strands and aims in more detail, as they expose how the methodology and people-centred approach outlined in John

5. Later Deputy Director, until he moved to Kirklees authority in 1987.

6. George Mathews, 1934-2020.

Benington's initial aims were put into action in a wide variety of projects. However, the number one priority was to listen to those now out of work and provide training and other support for them.[7]

A Centre Against Unemployment

One of my first tasks as the new Chair was to appoint someone to take on the development of outreach work with the unemployed, through the creation of a Centre. Unusually, the official was to be an employee of the Trades Council although the funding came from the Employment Department. The interviews took place at a small centre for the unemployed at the bottom of Snig Hill in the centre of the city. One applicant was Jol Miskin[8] a young man of 29 from London, where he had worked with the General Municipal and Boilermakers (GMB) in trade union studies education. He had arrived with his partner Karen Escott and was teaching at the Northern College. I was impressed by his infectious enthusiasm and by his emphasis on mature students and the potential of adult education. He had trade union experience and good credentials through Northern College, who were already developing short residential courses for the unemployed. We appointed him, despite warnings about his politics from the GMB at national level. He took on the work of developing Sheffield Coordinating Centre against Unemployment (SCCAU), a drop-in centre offering support, advice, coffee and adult education courses in the city centre. He described his early happy impressions of life in Sheffield, after

7. See Appendix 1, Sheffield City Centre map, page 314-315.
8. Jol Miskin retired from the Yorkshire Region of the WEA in 2015 after 40 years teaching.

Jol Miskin (far left) and Pat Coleman (second left), Director of Libraries, at the opening of a library at the Sheffield Co-Ordinating Centre for Unemployment on West Street in 1984.

London, heavily engaged with childcare, and thoroughly enjoying the family friendliness of the city. He became one of several individuals within the Employment Department who pressed the authority to give more priority to couples wanting to share their paid maternity leave. He joined the Labour Party whilst openly backing Militant, pleased to be part of Sheffield's well publicised left credentials and too busy to be interested in a take-over.

New Culture – New Industries

Paul Skelton and Bill Michie both liked pop music. They especially admired a clutch of up-and-coming Sheffield based bands, including The Human League, Heaven 17, Cabaret Voltaire and Comsat Angels. They talked with them and learned of their frustration that the only well-equipped sound recording studios available to them now that they were too famous and successful to work from each other's homes were in London, and expensive. Why, they asked, could there not be top quality music studios in the city with top rate equipment which they could use, and which might inspire youngsters to follow their lead.

They put their minds to opening up wider career and training choices to young girls as well as boys which could be accessed without post-16 educational qualifications.

Popular music and film were markedly different from engineering apprenticeships, but through these leisure industries it was possible to engage with all young people including many from Afro Caribbean communities. Councillor Dave Morgan, himself one of the younger members of the Labour Group, was enthusiastic about this work. As described earlier in Brixton and many towns and cities in Lancashire, racism was causing discontent in mixed race communities, leading to riots amongst unemployed black youngsters. Sheffield, in contrast, organised a large march in solidarity with this discontent encouraged by the Council, with Dave Morgan playing a leading role in mustering support amongst trade unions and working closely with its local community organisers.

With Paul Skelton's housing and community development background from his work at Coventry, Bill Michie's enthusiasm and some excellent imaginative ideas from architects Tatlow Stancer, the co-operative builders mentioned earlier, it was suggested that the empty shell of a former car showroom was an ideal structure in which to place a sound-proof music studio slung within the space in such a way that vibration would be kept to a minimum. Two huge buildings on Shoreham Street, built in the thirties as car showrooms known as Autoways and Kennings, which had closed in the 1970s, were acquired by the local authority because of their central location. It was close to the Sheffield Midland Station on one side near where the River Sheaf flows into the Don, and Pond Street bus station on another. Now the area lies within 100 yards of the international scale swimming

Red Tape Studios, housed in the converted 'Autoways' building on Shoreham Street, was opened by Neil Kinnock in 1986.

complex, Ponds Forge, three or four Art Galleries and Museums, the Crucible and Lyceum Theatres, and is surrounded by the buildings of Sheffield Hallam University.

A detailed report outlining the feasibility and costs for the installation of four recording studios in the Autoways building, two geared to training sessions and two of professional quality for The Human League, went to Committee in 1982. It stressed how the buzz and excitement for young musicians to practise and learn how to make music tapes in the same building as such pop idols as Phil Oakey[9] would make the proposal really popular. The recording studios offering new industries and training for young unemployed people were initially greeted with ribald opposition both by the Conservatives in the council chamber and the private sector generally. Provocatively we named them 'Red Tape' studios.

9. Lead singer of The Human League.

They were formally opened by Neil Kinnock in December 1986. They have proved very popular and are still in use for training purposes as I write.

Paul Skelton recently described a Town Hall Finance committee which one of the bands attended with the Finance Committee, chaired by Rev. Alan Billings, to discuss the capital, costs and timescales. The four young, long haired musicians, dressed in colourful long cloaks, appeared bemused. A normal style of meeting was out of the question. But as the capital estimates were outlined and the group considered how much money they would offer the project, the mood changed. The project was approved; and the architects' design worked well. Contractors and architects along with Paul Skelton kept in close touch with the local groups, using their practical experience, and technical advice. Although positive action was not defined within the scheme, inclusivity for all young people out of work was its core.

Meanwhile, Geoff Green, who lived then in Walkley, heard of a group of young aspiring film makers working from their own homes to produce independent films. They were part of a national movement known as the 'Independent Film Makers Association' and were encouraged by the publication of the Annan Report in 1977, commissioned by Roy Jenkins, Home Secretary in the Wilson government in 1974. This was a pre-cursor of talks which concluded with the establishment of Channel 4. In Sheffield, the Walkley group included Jenny Woodley, Colin Pons and Roz Brunt. They were keen to develop a small film studio where amateur film makers were able to take up training in a suitable atmosphere along with specialist enthusiasts. Filming and sound recording would fit together to offer a totally different Sheffield production skill. The novelty of the project appealed and there was still room in the former empty shell of 'Autoways'. Colin Pons was appointed to lead a project to establish 'Sheffield Independent Film' which opened in 1985, and was joined a year or two later by Sheffield Women's Film Co-operative. Sylvia Harvey, a recently retired professor of film from Hallam University, explained how she, Ian Wild and Colin Pons were particularly keen to establish the production element of popular music and of film making.

However 'film' did develop in a different way. Next door to Autoways was an even bigger former car showroom called Kennings, also derelict. I have an abiding memory of a visit to see how the Autoways' makeover as workspace for these film and artistic enterprises was taking shape. Paul Skelton in his municipal enterprise role pointed to the remaining original wall and doorway through to the next door Kennings building.

> 'Through there' he said quietly 'I think we could develop a superb independent cinema. I've been working up, together with the architects, an initial plan to share with you'.

He went on to describe its future potential and a possible programme of work, outline the capital costs, and even suggest the date he had in mind to bring the proposal to committee. The Showroom Cinema and its complex was launched in 1989 by Sir Richard Attenborough. It included four cinemas (with particularly comfortable seating), a café, meeting rooms, a childcare centre on the roof space, and an exhibition centre with small business spaces named the 'Workstation' next door. The Leadmill night club, Yorkshire Art Space and a photographic studio made up what has become known as the Cultural Industries Quarter (CIQ). Originally so controversial, the CIQ now attracts serious

This area of Sheffield City Centre is now known as the Cultural Industries Quarter (CIQ) and includes the Showroom Cinema and the former National Centre for Popular Music, which is now home to Sheffield Hallam University's Student Union.

national and international players in the film industry. In 2019 the internationally acclaimed 'Sheffield DocFest'[10] welcomed 3,489 individual industry delegates from 59 countries to Sheffield. and had 28,000 general public admissions. The festival screened nearly 200 films of all lengths, encompassing works from 40 countries around the world, 54% of which were co/directed by women. Colin Pons, Ian Wild its first manager, and Professor Sylvia Harvey are still familiar key organisers in and around the CIQ. Sylvia in particular regretted deeply that, despite persistent lobbying over the location of a Channel 4 facility in Yorkshire, the decision in 2019 had gone in favour of Leeds.

Today, cafes and bars are plentiful close to Sheffield Hallam University. Other well built former cutlery works have been transformed into part of the University Science Park with units

10. Annual Documentary Film Festival (www.DocFest.org)

for product development; another into Yorkshire Art Space, with a variety of workshops. Pictured is the building that was planned to be a National Centre for Popular Music. It was specially designed by architect Nigel Coates in the shape of four stainless steel drums as befitted the 'City of Steel', and mainly financed by the Lottery. Opened in 1989, it closed 18 months later. As a museum and leisure industry project, it failed, but the iconic building remains, acquired by Hallam University for its now busy students union.

For council officers the high public profile and novelty of the Municipal Enterprise concept meant that cross departmental contacts and support were essential. Close analysis was required of the financial potential and structure of each development, as scrutiny by the District Auditor was constant and every new idea had to be tested at departmental and Policy Committee level. Despite some hiccups and inter-department rivalry, as the National Centre for Popular Music (NCPM) was rescued by the University, the Employment Committee celebrated the decision by the Libraries Committee, backed by its director Pat Coleman, to relocate their Archives Division into the remaining space of Kennings car showroom, to put the final financial brick in place. Eventually, in the early nineties, even BBC Radio Sheffield re-located to the Cultural Industries

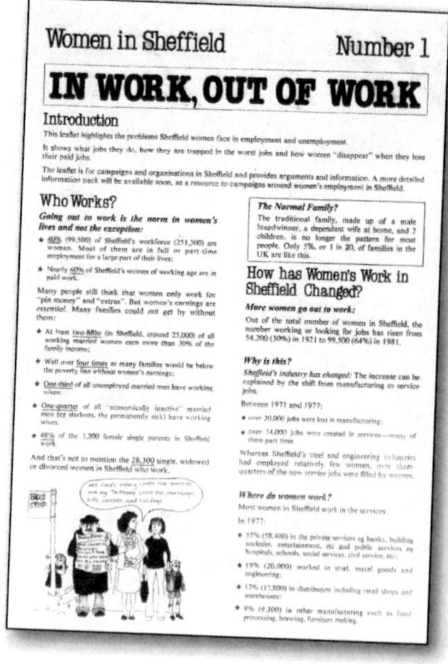

Women in Sheffield — Number 1

IN WORK, OUT OF WORK

Introduction

This leaflet highlights the problems Sheffield women face in employment and unemployment.

It shows what jobs they do, how they are trapped in the worst jobs and how women "disappear" when they lose their paid jobs.

The leaflet is for campaigns and organisations in Sheffield and provides arguments and information. A more detailed information pack will be available soon, as a resource to campaigns around women's employment in Sheffield.

Who Works?

Going out to work is the norm in women's lives and not the exception:

★ 40% (99,500) of Sheffield's workforce (251,300) are women. Most of them are in full or part-time employment for a large part of their lives;

★ Nearly 60% of Sheffield's women of working age are in paid work.

Many people still think that women only work for "pin money" and "extras". But women's earnings are *essential*. Many families could *not* get by without them:

★ At least two-fifths (in Sheffield, around 25,000) of all working married women earn more than 30% of the family income;

★ Well over four times as many families would be below the poverty line without women's earnings;

★ One-third of all unemployed married men have working wives;

★ One-quarter of all "economically inactive" married men (eg students, the permanently sick) have working wives.

★ 48% of the 3,200 female single parents in Sheffield work.

And that's not to mention the 28,300 single, widowed or divorced women in Sheffield who work.

The Normal Family?

The traditional family, made up of a male breadwinner, a dependant wife at home, and 2 children, is no longer the pattern for most people. Only 5%, or 1 in 20, of families in the UK are like this.

How has Women's Work in Sheffield Changed?

More women go out to work:

Out of the total number of women in Sheffield, the number working or looking for jobs has risen from 54,200 (30%) in 1921 to 99,500 (64%) in 1981.

Why is this?

Sheffield's industry has changed: The increase can be explained by the shift from manufacturing to service jobs.

Between 1971 and 1977:

★ over 20,000 jobs were lost in manufacturing;

★ over 14,000 jobs were created in services—many of them part time.

Whereas Sheffield's steel and engineering industries had employed relatively few women, over three quarters of the new service jobs were filled by women.

Where do women work?

Most women in Sheffield work in the services:

In 1977:

★ 55% (58,400) in the private services eg banks, building societies, entertainment, etc and public services eg hospitals, schools, social services, civil service, etc;

★ 19% (20,000) worked in steel, metal goods and engineering;

★ 17% (17,800) in distribution including retail shops and warehouses;

★ 9% (9,300) in other manufacturing such as food processing, brewing, furniture making.

Quarter. The area remains a lasting tribute to one of the key priorities spelt out clearly by Sheffield City Council to seek out and promote new and different industries that would take root in Sheffield.

Women and Manual Trades: Training

Of the three women mentioned in Chapter 3 who were active in the 70s, Sheena Clarke became a Councillor in 1982, oversaw the Positive Action project and research, chaired several committees on Women and Training and women in the Economy, and was active in establishing the central Women's Unit.

Rose Ardron was putting together monthly newsletters about women's work, along with Karen Escott, Gill Greenwood, Angela Kalisch and Caroline Poland within the team of women in the Employment Department. She was developing the proposal for the Women's Technology Training Workshop and the Young Women's Plastering Project. Ruth Nelson, another woman active in the Manual Trades Group, worked with the Council and its Shirecliffe FE College to open a women-only joinery workshop and became its lead tutor, when the furniture workshop opened in 1989. Anna Childs[11] switched from being an art student at Shirecliffe when the workshop opened to learn joinery and woodworking, then helped out as an assistant and went on to teach furniture making at the Sheffield College. Anna described recently how the applications were plentiful especially from working class and black women in the early days, and that most of the students had young children, so it was important that their child care needs were taken into account.

11. Anna Childs works as a tutor at Sheffield College.

Anna Childs and me sitting on the bench I made at the women's furniture course at Sheffield College.

She also described how:

> Because of the course they would discover they were much more intelligent than they had ever realised. It widened their horizons. Many went on to other jobs. They did the course because it was women only.

Anna also described, however, how the applications fell when total family income, not just the woman's income, was taken into account for those qualifying for reduced fees. Her view has been echoed by many. Sadly officialdom today still sees women's job opportunities as secondary as the benefits system fails to recognise the costs of childcare when applying for training or further education.

In 2006, after I stood down from Parliament, I became a student again at Sheffield College, on one of their women's furniture making courses.[12]

Roz Wollen was still seeking a career as a motor mechanic. The story of how she made use of an Employment Department grant (see above) is told by Liz Kettle of Women in Engineering, Science and Technology (WEST).

Go with Gwenda's! How a garage in Sheffield drove a generation of women onto better things

1985 was the year that Ford unveiled the third generation of its top of the range Granada. In Sunderland, Nissan was building Britain's biggest car factory; and 100 miles away in South Yorkshire, three feisty women took the plunge and decided to open their own garage. Unemployment had reached nearly 3 million in 1984. MSC training schemes were big, and two women, Roz Wollen and Annette Williams, had just passed TOPS motor vehicle training courses with flying colours. They were eager to get work as mechanics and applied for loads of jobs, with no success.

'We were so fired up! We had just completed these intensive nine-month courses at skills centres that were completely dominated by blokes, and we really wanted to get stuck in and work with bikes and cars.

12. Anna was my teacher at Sheffield College. My last project was this school bench for a community room near my home, made from the original wood from the former school opened in 1807 and closed in 1880 to become a 'reading room' for the village.

Because we were women nobody would take us seriously,' recalled Roz.

Roz, Ros and Annette at Gwenda's

The third woman, Ros Wall, was a skilled mechanic. She learnt about the workings of bicycles, motorbikes, and cars from her father as a girl, later spending happy hours stripping down engines with boyfriends.

They kept trying to get jobs. Roz and Annette went to Leeds to gain experience at a radical female-run garage called Spanners, and Roz also went to London for two weeks experience at the Big Ends women's garage down south. The three women loved motorbikes. They met to talk engines and models, and the idea of taking control of things and setting up their own garage took shape. Roz explained, *'We were getting more and more disillusioned. We tried to get apprenticeships, but these were set up for younger women and we were in our thirties. We knew we had to do something!'*

In this context Gwenda's Garage was born, a time when the concept of 'positive action' was well known but rarely acted upon. But in Sheffield enterprise grants were available and the three applied to the Council and after endless meetings and forms, negotiated six months free rent. Roz said, *'We were so chuffed. None of us had any money and now it was really going to happen. There was lots of energy. We were part of a feminist culture and felt we could do anything! We loved bikes and cars, but we loved the idea of empowering women even more.'*

The premises needed a lot of work. With friends they converted the building into a working garage, delighted when the three-phase electricity contained in metal conduits sailed through inspection and went live. When their newly fitted inspection ramp was in place, they stood looking at it as proudly as the directors of the soon-to-open Nissan plant in Sunderland. A collective ethos ran through the enterprise. It was set up as a legal partnership, but with no one person in charge. Ros, Roz and Annette were all paid the same rate. Then came the choice of a name; a women's name! Roz borrowed a copy of the *Guinness Guide to Feminine Achievements* from the library. They found a Gwenda Hawkes, who won medals for driving ambulances through dangerous territory during WWI. She had worked in an armaments factory and broken motor-car speed records to become the fastest ever female racing car driver at Brooklands. So 'Gwenda' was the woman for the job! Gwenda's Garage offered normal garage services, repairs, servicing, breakdown help, welding and chassis repair and body work.

But Ros, Roz and Annette were as interested in empowering women as in being mechanics. So, Gwenda's also taught DIY car maintenance classes, gave advice on buying second hand cars and information on adapting cars for disabled drivers. They took time to explain to their mainly female customers exactly what was wrong with their car and why something was not working in a deliberate attempt to demystify what went on under the bonnet.

They ran car maintenance training courses in community centres, and saw how women grew in confidence, by learning to strip down an engine or change a tyre for the first time, and knew they were onto something special. They carried on learning themselves. Roz and Annette gained more qualifications after long days in the garage, despite patronising by male tutors and classmates. Gwenda's thrived.

One day a smart looking man rolled up in front of the garage driving a Morgan, Gwenda's favourite car. He told them Gwenda was still alive, living on a small Greek island. He had sent her a newspaper cutting about the female-run garage in South Yorkshire. Very excited, they wrote to her, and she replied, wishing them 'good luck'! By 1989, Gwenda's had outgrown the workshop, the partners needed to re-evaluate the business model, and after much soul searching the three women agreed they could reach more people through teaching and other jobs. It had been an inspiring phase in their lives. They sold Gwenda's as a going concern in 1990. Sadly, Gwenda died the same year.

Roz's reflection on the story of Gwenda's Garage is typically clear and direct.

> Gwenda's really did make a difference. At that time, it was the only garage in England run entirely by women. We showed people that women can do things, be mechanics and set up a business. We did teach really useful vocational skills, but even more than that, we gave our students what we called the fourth dimension. And that's the confidence to do something that most women have been brought up to think they can't do, so-called men's jobs in engineering and

> technology. That confidence and those skills then go on to empower them in all sorts of other areas of their lives.

The Women in Manual Trades Group had become significant and respected – at least by the local Labour movement. A video put together by the national Women in Manual Trades group, *Building Our Futures,* inspired another young group in Sheffield to set up a 'Young Women's Plastering Training Project' with help from the Council. It ran from 1984-1987. Its final report describes some of the political reaction from media and parts of the business community. The merest mention of the name guaranteed howls of laughter in Tory circles, and Sheffield Tories even cited it at their 1984 Conservative Party Conference as a prime example of 'loony left' Councils wasting ratepayers money. Opposition at Council meetings became more vociferous whenever positive action for women in the labour market was mentioned. The Conservative lead Councillor for Employment was also a woman, Councillor Angela Knight.[13] During the meeting which included the initial launch of plans for the Women's Technology Training

13. Later a contemporary of mine in Parliament as the MP for Erewash (1992-1997).

Workshop (WTTW), the largest of such women-only training initiatives to date, she launched an attack. The report described the transformation of a former cutlery works, now disused, near the city centre into a major training centre, bringing together a young people's training initiative known as ITEC with one for disabled adults and the WTTW into a joint complex know as TRITECH. The timescale was to prepare to receive the first students the following year. Angela accused the report of failing to show any evidence that women wanted additional training in new technology for women only, asking, *'How many applications had we received?'* The answer was clearly none, since it was a proposal that had not been launched. *'How many did we expect?'*, she asked. The answer had to be *'We'll see but we believe it will be popular'*. She persisted, *'If you don't know the details, why waste ratepayers' money?'* The debate was reported in the *Star* newspaper. By the following Monday the Employment Department was receiving a flood of requests for application forms. These women-only training projects attracted funding from the European Social Fund (ESF) for students with childcare costs. The methodology used by the Employment Department was meticulous, in the same way as the Positive Action Project and Take Ten used face-to-face meetings to explain the work. Each applicant received a personal home visit to establish any childcare needs and give priority to those without post-16 qualifications, as the earlier Paid Educational Leave staff had done.

The main benefit from the ridicule and joking was that it helped make women's training projects in non-traditional trades acceptable in Sheffield's Labour movement, in addition to giving them added publicity for women in the city.

Housing, Heating, Lifts and Procurement

The Joint Works Group described in the previous chapter carried on its work and discussed many issues relevant to the construction industry. The last chapter described how Jane Darke had emphasised the need for a greater involvement of women in housing design policy.[14] The involvement of women from the tenants' movement was another facet of strengthening women's involvement in new industries.

The three post-war decades had seen millions spent on public sector-led new house building, often built by directly employed labour. By the 60s new build was more cost led. Tall flats or large maisonette blocks cost less per unit in land and building than a similar number of detached and semi-detached houses. Tower blocks were going up in every urban area, without the involvement of residents at the planning stages. In Sheffield, there was the development of massive blocks of flats close to the city centre built on a slope that gave clear views across the city centre over the Pond Street bus station and Park roundabout and which won architectural awards for building terraced streets 'in the sky'. They were called Hyde Park and Park Hill; terraces perhaps, but several floors up with bare stone stairways, which meant women struggled with push chairs. There were few lifts because they used the steep slope to access at ground level at the end of each 'terrace'. These flats never offered the same community cohesion as the former terraced housing, nor had tenants quite the same enthusiasm for them.

Pioneers of public housing in London boroughs such as Bermondsey had led the way through socialist Councils. Ada

14. See Chapter 5, page 154.

Salter, a devout Quaker and ethical socialist member of the Independent Labour Party (ILP), campaigned for housing that made space for children and gardens or balconies,[15] between the wars. She wrote a *Daily Herald* article, *Don't forget the Hidden London*, in 1934, which still seems relevant today and would have been music to the ears of tenants:

> Women can effect a great change in the social life of the Metropolis, if the common sense they manifest in managing their own homes is directed to the business of London government.

She argued that women were naturally humanitarian. They possessed a distinctive feature, motherhood, which gave them a humane outlook whether they had children or not:

> All over the world, women are crying out for fewer soldiers and more teachers, diminished expenditure on armaments and more comforts and convenience in the home, less of the trappings of war, and more of the beauty of design and construction … Women should therefore vote in the LCC elections for a more humane and kindly administration.[16]

Unlike these early developments in London, Park Hill and Hyde Park had given less thought to child centred details. Lifts in these and other tower blocks across the city were often out of order. A solution discussed in the Joint Works Group was to bring lift

---

15. Ada Salter, 1866-1942, councillor in Bermondsey, London. She had many humanitarian goals and is renowned for making settlement housing beautiful with play areas and gardens.

16. Taylor, G. (2016). *Ada Salter – Pioneer of Ethical Socialism*. Lawrence and Wishart.

maintenance in-house and expand the team by employing top quality lift engineers to establish and train up a new team using education powers and Shirecliffe College in order to maintain, refurbish or replace lifts as necessary. Tenants welcomed it and the scheme worked well. It seemed ridiculous that the new powers within the 1981 Planning and Land Act, designed to trim the influence of Direct Labour, stopped the in-house team from bidding for outside work, for example, from hotels or the Health Authority, whilst new competition rules made it compulsory that they had to win their own Council work in competition with outside private firms.

Both workforce and tenants with their memories and pride in their Council homes, were keen to preserve Direct Labour. They discussed how they could help in the Joint Works group which resulted in their preparing a small booklet outlining their plan for contract compliance. From this initiative the Council developed a Contracts Policy, which covered wider issues than housing. Compared with the private sector the Works Department recruited many more, mainly young people, to apprenticeships every year. The costs of their training put Direct Labour at a financial disadvantage when tendering for work. After discussion with the Council's legal and finance officers, a training requirement was written into all Council building contracts, requiring a ratio of 1:10 within a contractor's workforce. The Treasurer was thereby able to take training costs out of the tendering procedure to ease the competition and the Works Department balance sheet. This led to discussion of the poor gender balance in the apprentice intake. The Director of Works was persuaded to take on two girls a year, and Shirecliffe FE College agreed to include them in their publicity. The proposal was supported at a national level by George Brumwell, the general secretary of construction union UCATT, but it was a step too far to get the Treasurer to include a gender quota in its contract requirements.

Pat O'Neill, a senior officer from the Health and Safety Executive, used to attend the Joint Works Group as part of his efforts to help the Council include within its Countract Compliance document safe working practices as well as safety in its housing stock, alongside the more traditional contract conditions. It was not uncommon to hear from private builders speaking off the record that they knew they could not get away with poor quality work or untidy dangerous building sites, as taking a construction firm off the Council's approved list of contractors was a serious matter for them and it had happened following inspections.

Combined Heat and Power

A further problem with public sector housing involved a different area of Council operations, related to the energy industry and waste. It stemmed from district heating schemes which were poorly designed and often broke down. Flats at one end of the chain became stiflingly warm, while those at the other end were freezing cold. Partly as a result of complaints, a bigger project took shape to revolutionise heating throughout the Central Area of the City. The Cleansing Department, whose director was Keith Simmonite, was sensitive to the Council's new thinking in terms of enterprise and job creation, as was the chair of his Committee, Councillor Alf Meade. Meade, now well into his eighties, recalled, *'What made the difference for me was that I was an engineer. I liked to listen to people and then get on with the job.'*

Close to the Hyde Park/Park Hill flats complex was the city's large waste disposal and incineration plant, at Bernard Road, whose fumes were yet another bugbear for the tenants there. Alf Meade had listened and his solution, much used in Scandinavia as the cleanest and most efficient form of urban waste disposal, was commonly known as 'Combined Heat and Power'. Significant capital investment was required.

My interview with him was instructive as to how a very experienced politician, who had followed his Dad in representing the Hillsborough area of the city, but who was outside the inner group of 'Brightside mafia' councillors, had taken on a massive new project with intense conviction. He described how he often felt *'very much alone. I always knew where I wanted to go but how to get there? …'*

He admitted the Labour Party locally were strong on policy, but said, with a hint of bitterness, *'Some were just chasing their political careers. I just saw that it could be done. I didn't need any convincing.'*

He recalled clearly the CHP proposal. The first stage redesigned the incinerator, so that it worked at maximum efficiency, at high temperature and with emissions that were safe and non-toxic. The second stage introduced new technology which could capture the heat produced by incineration in such a way that it could be used to deliver heat to most of the buildings in the surrounding area; the third stage was to extend the complex so that it would heat most of the buildings in the city centre as well as the terraced streets in the sky. Finally, they would borrow new engineering technology being developed in Scandinavia to enable transformers to be put into tower block housing, which would produce enough electric power to lower the heating bills for poorer tenants. Dr

Peter Cromar went with a group of senior officers from a range of Council departments and tenants' representatives on a study visit to Malmö to investigate these developments. The first people to benefit from the new incinerator were the tenants of Hyde Park and Park Hill. They still had stone staircases to negotiate, but now had warm, reliable central heating.

The Labour Group respected Alf Meade's conviction and admired the way he doggedly got this major scheme under way. He in turn paid tribute to his key officer, Steve Brooks, an engineer who had transferred from the Works Department into Cleansing. Combined Heat and Power had the full support of the Employment Department (renamed DEED in 1984). Alf recognised this and explained how with other specialist officers in Treasury and the Legal and Administration departments they helped smooth the funding of the scheme. Alf was adamant that as they came to the more costly third phase, by the end of which in the mid 90s, both Universities, all the City Centre department stores, and the new Ponds Forge swimming complex and several more tower blocks were connected to Bernard Road, it was he, the engineer who had finalised the financial bid for funds. I asked, *'How did you get the Treasurer and Budget sub-committee to agree?'* He replied:

> It was when he saw the figures. He knew it would save money.

I also asked him where his political convictions had been developed, to which he answered: *'from my mother!'*

Wider Issues For the City

Another small scale example of a novel project related to housing with tenants' involvement and discussed at length in the Joint Works Group was the development by the newly formed MONS Co-operative enterprise, helped with a grant from the Employment Department,[17] of a domestic dehumidifier for houses that suffered from damp. Phil Asquith, a new appointment in the Product Development team, had already designed, as part of the Lucas Aerospace Alternative Plan, a dehumidifier product that used new technology and which he believed to be both useful and profitable.[18] The tenants agreed with the workforce at MONS that it might be a way of using their expertise as former workers in the steel industry to bring in new products that improved the existing environment and housing stock, whilst creating jobs through public and private sector purchasing.

Tenants and workers involved in these wide-ranging discussions in the Joint Works Group felt they had common goals and wanted to learn more about the politics behind the government's thinking and its drive towards greater competition and privatisation that threatened their livelihoods. They took advantage of the short weekend courses at Northern College to together learn more about aspects of housing and the building industry. The courses were backed by the full-time trade unionists of UCATT and the T&GWU. In the housing sector, for example, it enabled the Contracts and Purchasing Department to think in new ways and open doors to using new smaller firms and local

17. Snows; and Employment Proposals Panel.

18. Two former employees had been appointed to the Department as Product Development Officers.

This image was used as part of Sheffield City Council's campaign to improve the quality of the construction industry. It was produced through a Northern College course. (Sheffield City Council).

entrepreneurs. This work paved the way for the development of a national 'Homes and Jobs' campaign which brought together local authorities, Trades Unions in the construction industry and Tenants' Associations. Sadly, however, it was hard for the lower paid to resist the attractively large subsidies offered by the Thatcher government to families buying their council houses, and sales accelerated. Local authority rent income was reduced as a result, and they lost the capital value of the land whilst not receiving the proceeds from the sales, which went to central government. Councils were then blamed for deteriorating council house maintenance, and 'social housing' became represented as second best. Council estates were derogatively described as 'sink' housing and this undermined pride in a council home.

Two officers within DEED were responsible for close working with the race equality team in the Central Policy Unit of the Council on training and employment issues. Early in the 80s the Headquarters of the former Osborn steel works, one of the oldest large steel and engineering works in the city and an iconic building on the Wicker, were acquired by the Council. They worked closely with Sheffield and District Afro-Caribbean Community Association (SADACCA),[19] to design and oversee its transformation into the group's headquarters. The resulting success in raising the profile of the black community in the city stimulated demand for another project – this time a new building on a cleared site nearby for a new training centre known as the Afro-Caribbean Enterprise (ACE) Centre. The Asian community in the city worked with the race equality officer team in the authority to transform a derelict school in the Attercliffe/Lower Don Valley area into the Pakistan Muslim Centre.

The headquarters of SADACCA (Sheffield & District Afro Caribbean Community Association) housed in the iconic former Osborne steel works.

19. Founded in 1986 from the former West Indian Association to represent and support the 7,000 Afro-Caribbean residents in Sheffield.

Mike Bower

John Benington left the Employment Department in 1984 for a post with Warwick University, handing over to Dan Sequerra,[20] who led the Department until he went to work for Kirklees Council, and was followed as Director by Keith Hayman through the remaining years of the 80s. Its original ideals and 'collective' way of working remained. It championed the notion of co-operative development in the context of business, in conjunction with Sheffield's Co-operative Development Group (CDG), led by Mike Bower.[21] The focus on positive action to remove inequality wherever it was evident throughout the city as well as within the Council permeated all its activities.

Dan Sequerra and Deputy Director, Dr Peter Cromar, became well acquainted with the senior officers right across the local authority, but especially in the Administration and Legal, Treasury, and Planning Departments. Glyn Sherwyn from Treasury and Peter Cromar recently described how:

> The practice of working across departments, necessary to maximise the job impacts of so many varied initiatives, gave its projects and research papers status. Although it was a smallish team of around 50 staff at its height, the up-front political nature of its publications and the working style of co-operation with associations and groups

20. Dan Sequerra became director of DEED in 1985 before leaving to work in Kirklees. He died on 10th April 2018.

21. Mike Bower, a future leader of the city council.

David Granville and Kath Harding with their baby daughter.

outside the Council and across the city, boosted the confidence of public sector officers and elected members, as well as giving its work a particularly high public profile.

Its lessons are as relevant today as they were then. Many former employees of DEED describe the uniqueness of its culturally inclusive atmosphere and identity. Its press officer was Kath Harding who, together with her partner David Granville, had been employed by Collets bookshop on Charing Cross Road.[22] Kath recalled coming north for the job of DEED Press Officer in 1986 with no pre-conceptions of what Sheffield as a local authority were trying to do politically, but wanting to move from London. David followed, taking up a post in the central Publicity Department. They spoke of the open, friendly nature of the Department and its commitment to its vision of 'equality' which had gender, race, and disability awareness at its core. David Granville described how tension arose between the press coverage of the established Publicity Department and the more controversial and separate nature of the Employment Department press coverage which always seemed to hit the headlines. In 1990 they were the first couple working for the City Council to take advantage of a new guideline allowing maternity pay and leave

22. First opened in 1934 by Eva Collett Rechitt, 66 Charing Cross Road, and sadly closed February 9th 1997.

to be split between a couple. David became the house-husband when their baby girl was four months old and Kath returned to her job in Employment. He told me this with pride, reminding me how redrawing gender stereotyping in the labour market has to be two-way. It is as important for men to have a place within the caring professions – primary school-teaching, nursing, social work and in the home – as it is for women to be car mechanics and financiers and managers.

While media criticism continued, by 1984 the educational establishment were very helpful. Sheffield University and Sheffield Polytechnic worked with the newly appointed research team in the Employment Department on sector studies and other economic statistics that went to Council on a monthly basis. FE Colleges supported the new training opportunities for women and young people. Northern College not only helped with ideas and advice but also delivered the crucially important adult education back-up. Local private sector specialists offered their expertise. training, and advice for the sound recording at Red Tape studios and film developments. Eventually, in a substantial way, partnership was built with businesses in the private sector (see Chapter 9, The Politics of Partnership).

Planning remained separate. Linked more closely with land use than labour markets, it had its own speciality, and undertook concurrently many important economic developments of its own in conjunction with the Employment Department. In other authorities Economic Development more often was a unit within the Planning Department. One exception was the Greater London Council (GLC) which, like Sheffield, developed its Industry and Employment Committee separately from Land and Planning. Between the separate departments there were overlaps, tensions and doubtless some jealousy. But the political rationale for insisting that economic factors must be related to social impact to give them justification, stands the test of time. This book celebrates the people-centred uniqueness described by former employees of DEED.

Sheffield was not alone. Hundreds of people attended Robin Murray's memorial in the Round Chapel in Bethnal Green on 17th June 2017. He was appointed to the GLC as Chief Economic Advisor in 1981 working with Michael Ward, the Chair of Industry and Employment. Robin was an inspiring personality with a brilliant mind who frequently visited Northern College, and close networking between GLC officers and the team in DEED was also frequent.

Networking between the GLC and Sheffield was frequent. The London Industrial Strategy, completed in December 1986, has been described as *'the most comprehensive plan ever put together for a major conurbation and one of the most impressive works on development ever written'.*

Professor Marj Mayo recently described the way it had been put together.

> The London Industrial Strategy was the product of collaborative research, sector by sector, 24 of them, drawing on the work of the relevant teams at the GLC and GLEB (Greater London Enterprise Board). Robin Murray provided the creative leadership for this massive undertaking, stimulating debates along the way, an iterative and inclusive approach.

It showed how locally driven economic policy rooted in the ideas and aspirations of communities can create social and economic improvement. Social reform drives economic prosperity when its goals of well-being, tolerance and equality are well embedded within it. Michael Wards Foreword to the book spells it out:

> When the history of Britain's experiment with monetarism comes to be written, the contrast between unmet needs and vast human and financial waste will be the theme.
>
> The financial waste of London's unemployment is now two and half billion pounds a year in benefits and lost taxation alone. To include the value of lost output, this figure could be more than doubled.
>
> The human waste is the loss of precious skills of our unemployed engineers, builders, carers and curers. It is also the waste of those who have never worked and may never do so.
>
> The needs confront us every day: housing and hospital waiting lists increasing; roads, bridges and sewers crumbling; poverty and decay. Our strategy is to use wasted resources to meet needs. Elected, publicly accountable authorities must intervene to replace the anarchy of the market economy with justice and fairness,
>
> The health of our economy depends above all on rebuilding a viable economic base. The uniqueness of the London Industrial Strategy is that we show how this can be done

> in the interests of the people who live and work in London, and in ways which involve working people in the process of planning and restructuring. The strategies for each sector have been developed in conjunction with employers, trades unions and consumer groups.
>
> Our experience of implementation has been the single most important contribution to this strategy. The success of GLEB's investment programme commands enormous interest around the world. We now have groups of people who know what our objective of 'restructuring industry in the interests of labour' means in practice, because they have done it. Our staff know how we can begin to tackle discrimination in employment opportunities against women and black people. We are running dozens of projects, exemplifying what can be done.[23]

Eventually financial pressures bit harder after the miners' strike and, in 1991, DEED was disbanded and merged back into Planning's overall control. It was ten years old. It was a little victory for Mrs Thatcher and the District Auditor, but short-lived as her downfall loomed.

---

23. *London Industrial Strategy.* Foreword by Michael Ward, Deputy Leader and Chair, Industry and Employment Committee. Published by Greater London Council, 1985. Michael Ward is also the author of a biography of Beatrice Webb published by the Smith Institute in 2011.

CHAPTER 7

Women and Conflict
The Miners' Strike and Further Afield

Returning to 1983, and South Yorkshire, national politics influenced the local scene in other ways. In 1983, after Thatcher's shattering election victory over a divided Labour Party, she took on South Yorkshire in a quite different way. Although her plans included challenging Labour in its local government heartlands, she wanted first to show she could diminish the power of trade unions. The Labour movement in South Yorkshire outside Sheffield was, as described in Chapter 2, dominated by coalmining and the two trade unions National Union of Mineworkers (NUM) and National Association of Coal Overseers and Deputies (NACODS), controlled and funded by men and women in mining communities. Top of her agenda was to plan and orchestrate an industrial dispute that would destroy the NUM strike and weaken the influence of Trade Unions. Opening the attack, Thatcher appointed Ian McGregor chair of the National Coal Board (NCB) in 1983 partly because of his record of cutting thousands of jobs whilst the chairman of British Steel. He promised and delivered unwavering support. Mining was chosen partly because she believed it crucial politically to claim victory over a Trade Union with such a vivid history of struggle. It became highly personalised by Thatcher and Scargill's similar styles of leadership. Arthur Scargill's rhetoric and character made it easier for Thatcher to treat the issue not as an industrial dispute within the energy sector, but as a war. After all, she had just won a war in the Falklands. Both leaders emphasised the absolute need to win. Pit closures threatened whole families in mining communities. Technology in wind and solar power was in its early stages as were concerns over climate change and the Green lobby. Although the National Union of Mineworkers backed research into clean coal technology, a future energy policy based on wind, water, nuclear and solar, rather than fossil fuels, was not then given serious thought by her government, which limited the scope for a negotiated settlement.

Coalfield Communities

The headquarters of the Yorkshire NUM were in the middle of Barnsley. Arthur Scargill and his wife, Ann, lived at Worsborough a couple of miles away, close to Northern College at Wentworth Castle. South Yorkshire lay at the heart of the ensuing battle. As in other coalfields, Yorkshire landowners had grown wealthy in the 19th century by exploiting the minerals underneath their estates. The more land in their ownership the greater the potential wealth.[1] In stark contrast, housing for mine workers clustered around the pit heads was dense, traditionally rented from the mine owner or, since nationalisation, from the National Coal Board. Before the War, only those working in the pit had the right to rent a house. Sons went off to work down the pit as early as possible to lessen the stress and anxiety of women and family, since a second employee halved the chance of a pit accident or

1. Bailey, C. (2007). *Black Diamonds – The Rise and Fall of an English Dynasty.* Penguin. (The family being the Fitzwilliams from another stately home in South Yorkshire, Wentworth Woodhouse.)

illness taking away not only the sole bread winner, but the right to the house as well. A vivid description of such an impact from the 1920s was spelt out by Frank Rodgers of Chapeltown, born there three miles away from our home in Grenoside:

> Evelyn was the youngest of six children in the Rodgers family of Arundel Road in Chapeltown. She was only two when her father, Frederick, died suddenly at the age of 45, in 1923. He had worked the steam pumps in the local coal pits. From then on the family lived in hungry poverty until older sisters and brothers could leave school at 14 and earn some money. Our mother, Alice, applied in her destitution for Parish Relief. She was told to put her plea to the Board of Guardians of the Poor at Grenoside Workhouse. The guardians would not allow her any relief but told her she should put the children in the Workhouse and she herself should find a live-in job as a domestic servant.
>
> Alice refused to give up her children to the Workhouse. She told us, stifling her sobs, that 'we would eat grass first'. These words stuck ever since in our childish minds. The Rodgers family then scraped a living by taking in washing, the little brothers delivering newspapers, and the big sisters helping other families who were in work, with cleaning and scrubbing, looking after small children and running errands.[2]

2. *Life Long Labour – A Local History Chronicle of Life in South Yorkshire.* Frank Rodgers. 1916-2012. Edited Helen Jackson. Grenoside and District History Group.

Frank's family were at least not deprived of the house they lived in, but such experiences gave coalfield communities a unique close-knit loyalty well described in countless stories, pictures, memorials and films such as *Brassed Off* (1996) or *Billy Elliott* (2000, and later opened as a stage musical in 2005 at Victoria Palace Theatre).

In 1983, an interesting book was published by Margaret Holderness, born in the 1920s and the daughter of a miner, *The Changing Role of Women in South Yorkshire, 1960-1980.* It is based on her research as a mature student at Hillcroft College, from 1977-79.[3] She knew her community well, and in its Introduction she talks about how her experience of the role of women was not shared by her student colleagues.

> I was continually reminded of the wide gap in understanding, between the women of the South and their Northern counterparts … In vain I reiterated again and again, that, despite the obvious differences in background, the northern women were strong, significant and as important in their own way. Family and men-folk came first, but this in no way detracted from the northern women's important role.

This drove her to embark on her research, which included interviews with women from four mining communities. Her conclusions are ambiguous, as she received many statements from the women she interviewed that their men came first, but she was surprised how interested they were in politics and how strongly

3. A residential College of Adult Education in Sudbury, founded as a women's equivalent to Ruskin in 1920 and merged with Richmond FE College in 2017.

they felt that things were changing. She exposed an excellent women's campaign, against the long-established culture that prevented women from being members of Working Men's Clubs, still prevalent in the 1970s and 80s although, now in 2020, it is no longer the case. Her book and its conclusions, which she published in 1983, were to be tested to the limit in the years that followed.

Every mining family in South and West Yorkshire felt the pit closure programme was an attack on themselves, and on their communities and way of life. Among other confrontations, the real and frightening battle of Orgreave was horrifying and unforgettable. Miners and their families were faced with trumped up and often serious charges leading to wrongful prison sentences, some as yet still unresolved.

However, it is as important that we do not forget the battles and suffering of the pit communities in 1984/85 as it is to be wary of populist memories of coal mining that verge on the sentimental. The idea of the pithead's winding wheel dropping men, women and, in the past, even boys and girls into dark, dangerous and terrifying tunnels of the mine can seem out of place today. I was reminded of this a few years ago. I took four of our grandchildren to the National Coal Mining Museum near Barnsley in the school holidays. The guide, who fitted them out with helmet, safety gear and a torch, insisted that each had an identity disc. He had worked down the pit and went through the safety drill explaining how in the event of an accident or power failure each item was essential – especially the disc – to ensure that rescuers would know exactly how many people were underground. We were ushered into the cage the doors of which shut with a clang, and then dropped at an alarming speed down to the coal face.

It was not unlike one of the scarier rides at Blackpool Pleasure Beach, the venue for a previous trip. Yet it was different and 'real'. My four boys went very quiet. One of the other children started twirling the torch that hung from his neck around his fingers and was reprimanded sharply by our guide. It was a reminder that this was no pretend experience; we were being shown the start of his every working day. Now in their early twenties they recall the experience, aware of their own future in a rapidly warming global climate due to the burning of fossil fuels which their forbears fought so hard to continue.

So what was the legacy of the dramatic year of activity in the context of this study? One view is that accepted definitions of the left-wing solidarity of the working class were defeated and Margaret Thatcher and her right-wing ideology emerged victorious. But this view is partial, and mistaken.

By the beginning of 1985 after nine months of the strike, cracks were evident within the NUM. Some of the Nottinghamshire miners were returning to work and bitterness between them and the Yorkshire NUM pickets was increasing. During the strike, the intensity of the effort made it hard to expose divisions about the leadership of what was happening politically in order not to appear treacherous, but unease and questions were being expressed as the strike wore on. The endless televised violent confrontations had less impact. The personalised depiction of the dispute begged the question of whether it was turning the heads of both protagonists. Whether there was justification in blaming the leadership style of Scargill is still debated since the driving force behind the increasing violence seemed, in Yorkshire at least, to come from government and Prime Minister Thatcher with her strident voice and no interest in compromise. Both shared some guilt in prolonging the confrontation: Arthur seemed to relish his populist power of oratory more than seeking a solution. Questions were asked about his lavish office on the top floor of the NUM's Sheffield offices.[4] The trickle back to work grew, and the general public were questioning what it was all for and starting to switch off.

The NUM's former Headquarters in Sheffield

In contrast, there was both admiration and sympathy for the role played by women within the coalfield communities who stood together to campaign, whilst managing their own financial predicament, both as a group and within their families. Their slogan 'WOMEN AGAINST PIT CLOSURES NUM' and the little emblem, a pithead with a wheel at the top looking almost like a halo, appeared to be a celebration of the mining industry. However, listening to the women involved, as they took to public platforms it went wider, rooted in and driven by loyalty and pride in their communities. Their belief in collective power through their trade union, to help maintain their living standards

4. Former Water Works building in Barkers Pool, put in the hands of NUM with council support.

was inextricably linked to their sense of community. It provoked a universal empathy that went beyond Barnsley, South Yorkshire and the UK, and crossed class, gender, age and ethnicity. Locally it was unforgettably inclusive and memorable, and appeared to bring together Sheffield with the rest of South Yorkshire, as perhaps nothing else could have done. The introduction to a contemporary book spells this out:

> It was the vast support campaign in which Barnsley Women against Pit Closures played an important part, that helped sustain the miners throughout 'their' bitter fight. This book records how and why we worked so hard.[5]

The word 'their' is significant. Coal mining was about men. Women were the support staff, albeit mainly in the offices where they were also on strike. This echoes one of Margaret Holderness's conclusions in 1983.

> … that the supportive role of women in mining communities is still crucial and an integral part of the mining industry, but has changed from being subordinate to 'alongside'.

In Sheffield, away from the pit villages, the Labour Party, at ward and constituency level, along with many other groups in the wider Labour movement twinned up with individual pits. Frequent visits to deliver donations were made to the particular food kitchens, miners' welfare halls and community centres, and handed over in cash or kind to the organisers, invariably women. All funds raised, which were considerable, went directly

---

5. *Women Against Pit Closures. Barnsley Women*. Vol. 2 (1985).

through this network. Strong friendships and alliances were built.

Another book, *We are Women, We are Strong*, by Sheffield Women Against Pit Closures, printed by Sheffield Women's Print Co-operative, published in July 1987 describes their formation:

> On 25th March 1984 a few women active within the Communist Party set about organising support for the miners and their fight for jobs. We understood the implications of the miners' strike, a strike not for wages or mere economic gain, but a strike provoked and planned by the Tory government … A leaflet was produced … and a meeting was convened to form a broad-based women's support group and as a result the Sheffield Women Against Pit Closures was formed … The women came from a multiplicity of backgrounds, including teachers, housewives, local authority workers, engineers, pensioners, students, Quakers and churches, bus drivers and some miner's wives – though less dominant than in the Barnsley group. All were united in the desire to see a successful conclusion to the strike, a future for the mining families and the preservation of the coal industry.

Its Preface describes the preparation of the booklet:

> A group from Sheffield Women against Pit Closures went to Northern College, together with the Barnsley group on two occasions to work together to compile this book. Several sections are transcribed from tape recordings

> made during discussions in various workshops, covering different aspects of women's involvement in the strike. The other sections are members' own written work

The wealth of thoughtful statements by the women involved indicate that a new understanding of politics was developing, more focused on the strength of whole working class communities, than the personalised battles shown on television of picket lines, police, and Leaders' declarations.

These women held the WAPC together until the end of the strike, and set up Pit Camps outside Houghton Main colliery in Yorkshire and other pits around the country to draw attention to the closures that happened in the early 90s. Caroline Poland, Debbie Mathews and Flis Callow from Sheffield Women Against Pit Closures, were closely involved with the group from the beginning of the strike to the pit camp at Houghton Main in 1992, one of the last South Yorkshire pits to close. Both Caroline and Flis had partners on strike. Their recent publication, *You Can't Kill the Spirit*, published by Northern Creative Print Solutions in 2018, includes a remarkable array of pictures depicting and celebrating the political and gender significance of the WAPC as an historic protest. For those involved, like Debbie Mathews,

who at the time worked at Sheffield Coordinating Centre Against Unemployment (SCCAU), the success of the day-to-day working of the pit camp left a vivid impression. She now works for Manor Employment Project heading a community economic and social development based in Sheffield and describes how:

> They may have destroyed the coal mining industry but they haven't killed the spirit of the communities. I see that day in day out – people supporting each other in poverty or difficulty, getting ready for the next challenge.

Frances O'Grady[6] in her Foreword to the book writes:

> We all know women who never would have dreamed of speaking publicly, organising kitchens, staging protests, joining picket lines, or marching on 10 Downing street. But they found the courage to do so. And in the

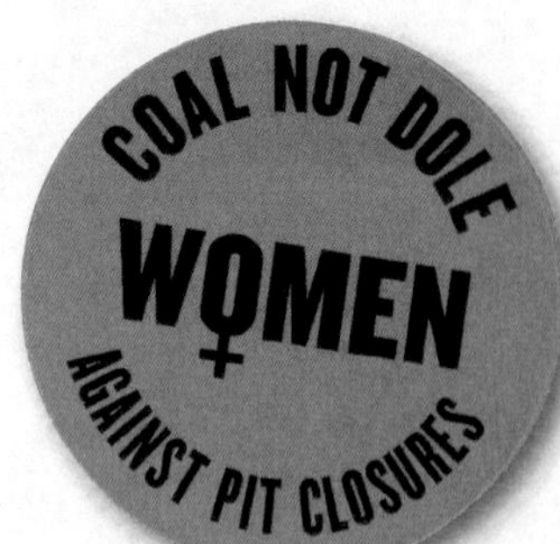

6. Frances O'Grady, General Secretary of the TUC.

> process, they discovered they were not just wives and supporters, but powerful leaders too. As Women against Pit Closures rightly said, working class women would never be the same again.

It was ironic that a woman Prime Minister made matters worse. The women's cry of 'Maggie, Maggie, Maggie! Out, Out, OUT' had a bitter resonance. During the miners' strike women gave recognition to the role of community in political struggle which has stood the test of time. The prefix 'working class' to community defines the coming together of the two threads in socialist solidarity. Thirty years later it was still commonly used in Brexit debates in reference to constituencies gained by the Tories in the 2019 General Election.

I'LL BE THERE
APRIL 28th
UNWELCOMING THATCHER
Thatcher Unwelcoming Committee
Sponsored by Sheffield Trades Council & District Labour Party

Miners demonstrate as Margaret Thatcher visits Sheffield's Cutlers Hall (above). This 'welcome' sticker (left) was handed out at the time.

Northern College: Political Adult Education

Northern College, became a central learning resource and social location during the strike. Its policy of free child care made a big difference to women from the pit villages. Many of the cleaners, catering and office workers at the College were themselves women from pit villages. The whole institution embraced the campaign. South Yorkshire may have been unique in having the support of an educational institution like Northern College so close at hand, but more generally the tradition of workers education in mining areas across South Wales, Lancashire and the Potteries came into its own. The educational impact was especially inspiring as women went on to embrace new opportunities after the strike. John Grayson and Malcolm Ball describe how, from 1980 to 1984, between 25% and 32% of students at Northern College were women. By 1998 the proportion had reached 47%.

> A very important factor was the influence of the miners' strike of 1984-85. During this period the College became the centre for the women against pit closures movement … and attracted a growing number of women who had been active in the coalfields support groups during the strike, many of whom, transformed by the experience of the strike, gained the confidence to enrol on the two-year diploma course, tutored by Dr. Jean McCrindle.[7] An important expression of these changes in participation witnessed a growing demand from women for their own curriculum,

7. Dr. Jean McCrindle. The papers of Jean McCrindle about women and the miners strike are now available on the Women's Library@LSE online catalogue.

> which led in 1990 to the creation of a one year diploma course in Women's Studies. This in turn saw the proportion of women on diploma places reach 57%.[8]

By 1998/9, of 227 women from the coalfield areas who joined residential short courses, 61% were from socio-economic groups C, D and E, and were either unwaged or unemployed and 62.9% had no previous educational qualifications.

A heightened political atmosphere triggers the urge and appreciation for adult education, but equally can quite quickly be forgotten by future generations that did not experience the struggle. After the strike, the Coalfield Communities Campaign was established. This also had its base in Barnsley. European funding for areas designated as 'Objective 2 or 1' funding targeted former coalfield communities, so South Yorkshire's share was significant. I spoke with Linda McAvan[9] to discover the degree to which the early years of Coalfield Communities Campaign recognised the role played during the strike by women and whether special efforts were made to support women into training or other work to make up for jobs lost through pit closures.

Linda worked for the CCC before she stood for election. Her office was in Wath, a village once with a large coal mine. I was left with the impression that apart from some new community centres opening, a significant element of the economic regeneration of the area was investment in physical infrastructure.

---

8. *Northern College: 25 Years of Adult Learning*. Chapter 11, edited by Malcolm Ball and Bill Hampton. Published by NIACE, 2004.
9. Linda McAvan was a Member of the European Parliament who was elected in a by-election following the resignation of Norman West in 1998. She served until her resignation in April 2019.

A woman shields herself as a policeman on horseback with a raised baton approaches, Orgreave, 18th June 1984.

Environmental reclamation of derelict land took place, which transformed the former towns and villages but into something very different. A new dual carriageway linking Barnsley more closely with Rotherham and Doncaster, with associated firms established with financial support, was constructed through the countryside.

I had recently enquired whether there was any prioritisation of women's projects, only to be told that he *'didn't think the men would like that!'*.

It was disappointing to find few detailed statistics or solid studies of the gender impact of the strike itself or of the impact of EU funding afterwards. Its most important legacy may well turn out to be the Northern College itself and an archived history of its

Sheffield's 'Women of Steel' a sculpture by Martin Jennings unveiled in 2016.

dramatic heyday with miners' banners arrayed down its 'long gallery'.

Those in political power and influence know well that the presence of women and children make a protest more powerful. Others tasked with the day to day work of administration can easily fail to quantify the impact. Political establishments, civil servants and public sector administrators at the time failed to analyse the social and economic impact of political protest and conflict from a gender perspective. The women who finished the building of Waterloo Bridge, or worked in Sheffield steel production during WW2, are seldom remembered for what the experience meant to them in their own learning, education or career. The history of the miners' strike shows that the more intense a political struggle, the more significant the role of women can become. It can give a cause universal appeal, through the way it throws the spotlight on families, communities, injustice and the reality of people's lives, which the media can promote. But history perhaps also shows how quickly it can be forgotten.

Nicaragua

Clearly the 1984/85 miners' dispute is of a different scale from the Sandinista revolution in Nicaragua, led by Daniel Ortega in the early '80s. It also is different from the peace process after the violence of the troubles in the north of Ireland, although the scale of the region is similar – a little more than South Yorkshire and less than Greater Manchester or the West Midlands. South Africa, much further away, is different again, but all four have stimulated solidarity campaigns from a number of those on the left-wing of

UK politics. The leading WAPC women's recollections recently exposed how many of them saw links between their stories and the role of women in conflict situations elsewhere which are worth exploring.

I was inspired in part by 'Women Against Pit Closures', but mainly from talking with women in the Chilean community, whose stories had been a major factor in the City Council's decision to twin with the town of Esteli in Nicaragua. I joined a women's study tour at the invitation of the Nicaragua solidarity movement in 1987. I took with me a letter from David Blunkett to the Mayor of Esteli, about the fresh water project the City Council had agreed to support in one of the poorer communities of Esteli, Nicaragua's second largest city.

We met a series of women representatives from many organisations, working on the land, in health and education. Relevant to the subject of this book was a meeting with the women's section of the Nicaraguan equivalent of the TUC. Our guide from the agricultural workers' trade union described how they were developing both greater recognition of women's rights and involvement, and strengthened trade union influence and workers' rights. I recorded:

She said that after the Triumph[10] when women's problems became an issue, they first decided to do a study of the position of women workers in the agricultural industry. This became like an interesting two- to three-year action research project. It was organised so that the process of the study, interviewing in person women in every workplace, became part of the solution, because people started thinking hard about the issue.

A beautiful picture used as a symbol for the struggle.

Then they had two choices of how to take action: either focus on the main issues that arose from listening to the women – about child care, the dual role of work and housework, abortion and contraception, and campaign vigorously on

---

10. This was how revolutionary protagonists referred to the day in 1979 when the former right wing government was overthrown by the FSLN (Sandinista National Liberation Front) forcing its President Somoza into exile. Daniel Ortega became Leader of the FSLN and was elected President in 1984 winning 60% of the vote. His dismissive comment about women is perhaps an indication of how his autocratic behaviour has increased during his second period as President of Nicaragua. Additional reading. Melrose, D. (1985). *Nicaragua: The Threat of a Good Example.* OXFAM.

> them, or to use the more traditional trade union concerns of wages, bonus, health and safety, and raise the specific needs of women within each context. They specifically chose the second so as to take everyone – all classes, men and women, along with them.

It seemed to me to be a model of how to mainstream women's issues and turn them to universal benefit.

Another conversation, with Myra our guide and Martha, from a community development organisation, revealed how educational pictorial advice boards displayed in health clinics and nurseries, directed especially at women with little schooling had dramatically increased, on the one hand, women and children's health and diet and, on the other, their literacy and desire for education.

> She [Martha] talked about her work with commitment and enthusiasm. She said a lot about the type of adult education she believed in. How to use the life experience of women in the basic education process of literacy and numeracy; how to develop their confidence by drawing them into the work processes and organisation, and how eventually, long term, they would participate in the non-women decisions other than child care, health and education and join in political policy making.

It sounded very like Keith's approach to adult education in his short courses for women. On a personal level, my perception of feminism was given an international focus, making me more aware of the relevance of my exciting five years striving to achieve better economic, health and educational equality. My commitment to gender politics within a socialist framework was also given greater depth. I recorded:

> Maybe our view was coloured by the fact that we were all women, and our face to face discussions were almost exclusively with women's organisations. However, we had been shocked when Ortega's response to a question from a man at one of his open air 'face the public' mass meetings, asking Ortega in what ways did he feel women should be involved in the 'struggle' was that their first duty was to rear a family! No support for abortion rights there!

Northern Ireland

Ten years after my visit to Nicaragua I was asked by Mo Mowlam, the day after she was appointed the Secretary of State for Northern Ireland in May '97, to be her Parliamentary Private Secretary (PPS). I had known Mo before I became an MP, from her work at Northern College. I jumped at the opportunity. I well remember her first conversation with me, the following day.

> We can't do this, Helen, without the support of the women, so as well as doing the normal PPS job in Parliament I would like you to spend part of your time in Northern Ireland working and meeting with the women of Northern Ireland and their organisations to maintain and strengthen their support for what we are hoping to achieve through the Peace Process.

I totally agreed with Mo's approach to boosting women's role, which she described in her autobiography.

> If you are inclusive from the beginning, then change is easier to deliver. With women all issues are women's issues, and just trying to get them tagged on to policy announcements doesn't really help anybody. I concluded that to have a Women's Ministry is good window dressing, good to build the morale of women, but doesn't help get women any closer to power. I think the best model is to have a team of people or a unit in No.10 so that every time the Prime Minister breathes on a policy issue, the unit is there, to get decent legislation in place including a delivery mechanism to ensure that a policy like equal pay is actually happening – not to mention a mechanism to take men with you. Until attitudes begin to shift equality will continue to be elusive. To take men with you is important if women are to achieve real change.[11]

In fact women had a pivotal input over the critical first two years of the Peace Process under Mo's leadership. She supported the founding of the Northern Ireland Women's Coalition (NIWC) as an elected political party in order to ensure that women had a voice in the first formal talks and discussions. The timetable was extremely tight for the two governments – Bertie Ahern in Dublin and Tony Blair in London – to agree joint proposals to put to the talks in Belfast, and win sufficient support for them from the people and parties north and south of the border, to

11. Mowlam, M. (2002). *Momentum: The Struggle for Peace, Politics and the People.* Hodder and Stoughton.

The author with Mo Mowlam and Julie Berrisford (far right) at a women's conference in Sheffield, 1995.

sign the Good Friday agreement, and hold two referendums. At the same time paramilitary groups were persuaded to decommission their weapons, since any serious violence could derail the process. It required courage to make links between the Protestant and Catholic working-class communities. It took tireless concentrated work by others in peace and reconciliation movements, often unsung, but making all the difference; such as Alan and Janet Quilley,[12] for example, whose reconciliation

12. Leaders of the Quaker movement in Belfast.

sessions included tea and cake in their front sitting room, breaking the ice between former violent paramilitaries, recently released from prison which, inch by inch, brought the end to continuing violence a little closer.

The intensity of the challenge of both task and timeframe brought international support; from Europe, Monika Wulf-Mathies, the EU Commissioner in charge of the Peace and Reconciliation grant programme, worked with Mo to fund community support and adult education; Inez McCormack, a Unison Trade Unionist and superb educationist, delivered inspiring women's courses across the cultural divide; from the USA, Hillary Clinton developed close working relations with Mo, the two NIWC representatives, Monica McWilliams and Pearl Sagar, and with Mary Robinson, the Irish President. Hillary Clinton developed 'Vital Voices', an international organisation that aimed to celebrate the role of women in peace building. Northern Ireland was one of her first examples; Finland and South Africa supplied independent observers to verify weapons decommissioning.[13,14]

Matters moved very swiftly indeed. Momentum was one of Mowlam's favourite pleas, and she depended on the international stage to deliver it.

South Africa

UNIFEM published a booklet in 2000, *Women at the Peace Table – Making a Difference* by Sanam Naraghi Anderlini, in which

13. Martti Ahtisaari, Finnish President and later Nobel Peace Prize Laureate active in the United Nations.
14. Cyril Ramaphosa, ANC activist and former head of South Africa's TUC, and now South Africa's President.

she researched and celebrated a range of post-conflict situations, including South Africa, Northern Ireland, Guatemala, Liberia, Palestine, Georgia and Cambodia, about how women had helped the reconciliation process. Cheryl Carolus,[15] who became the South African Ambassador to the UK in 1998, maintains in her contribution that while acknowledging the danger of stereotyping women as 'nurturers':

> … the fact that the women were nurturing and caring became hugely positive attributes. The process became one of listening to what other people were saying, listening to their fears even if you disagreed with them. People came out feeling that their concerns were being dealt with. It wasn't just posturing.

Reflecting on Mo's Mowlam's influence in the Northern Ireland peace process for this book I recognised that, although she was always sceptical about attributing any of her own skills to gender alone, she acknowledged one of her contributions was to look beyond the façade. *'You have to ask why do they need to shout?'* she is quoted as saying, referring to the male-majority political leaders.

> If you are trying to make peace the blame culture doesn't work. You have to look at what ways you can build trust and confidence to make progress. I believe you can only do this if you give people a sense of hope. Then the fear and distrust begin to

15. Cheryl Carolus, born 1958 in Western Cape, South Africa. Currently Executive Chair of Peotona Group Holdings, a wholly women-owned company powered by a vision to leverage sustainable opportunities for individuals and communities.

Freedom Charter – Drawn up by the ANC

adopted by a Congress of the People at Kliptown, South Africa 26th June 1955.

'There shall be work and security'

All who work shall be free to form trade unions, to elect their officers and make wage agreements with their employers.

The state shall recognise the right and duty of all to work, and to draw full unemployment benefits.

Men and women of all races shall receive equal pay for equal work.

There shall be a 40 hour working week, a national minimum wage, paid annual leave, sick leave for all workers, and maternity leave on full pay for all working mothers.

Miners, domestic workers, farm workers and civil servants shall have the same rights as all others who work.

Child labour, compound labour, the tot system, contract labour, shall be abolished.

Taken from South Africa's 'Freedom Charter'.

> decline. The aggression declines too … There are people who shout a lot, and because it is mainly men, people associate it with male behaviour. I don't think women would necessarily behave in the same way. Its abusive, unfair and difficult to cope with.

In my contribution to the Carolus book I described how the women in the community felt that their housing, education and childcare were the important things: that although there was public acknowledgment of the importance of constitutional and political issues, these were abstract for many people. The women gave a human face to the conflict and highlighted the personal consequences of the violence. Outside the Maze Prison they told us:

> There we were, all queuing up together with the same things in our bags to give our menfolk. There they were, locked up in their separate wings for the same reason, trying to kill each other. It seems ridiculous now.

From both communities, women were able to laugh together by drawing attention to these tangible factors and succeeded in showing that the quality of life in Northern Ireland highlighted the issues that mattered.

As Mo suggested we have to maintain a gender perspective, *'by breathing it into every area of policy'*. Violence and conflict undoubtedly have an international perspective. I explore these links further in the concluding chapter.

CHAPTER 8

Rate Capping and Local Government Finance 'Furthering Socialism in a Cold Climate'

Having dealt with the NUM Margaret Thatcher turned her attention to reducing the powers of Labour controlled, local authorities. Sixty-five days after the miners went back to work on May 7th 1985, Labour unity broke down at a chaotic 'special' Council meeting, as described by the *Sheffield Morning Telegraph* the following day:[1]

> **RATE DEFIANCE CUT TO SHREDS –**
> **Rival Factions End Labour's Firm Stand**
>
> Council Leader David Blunkett became a helpless bystander as rival factions of the 61 strong Labour group voted with the opposition parties in a tempestuous special council meeting.

Rates Act

The powers within the Rates Act passed in July 1984, a year earlier, were draconian. They did away with the idea of independent local authorities, democratically elected on a

1. Article by David Holmes, *Sheffield Morning Telegraph*, 8th May 1985.

regular basis. The Rates Act made little mention of electors, nor accountability to voters, nor of preparatory policy presented to voters in a manifesto. It also abolished the GLC and other regional Metropolitan authorities. It was a high-handed, undemocratic proposal of historic significance from which local government has never since recovered.

As described in previous chapters, neither South Yorkshire County Council nor Sheffield City Council had tried to disguise the nature of nor reason for rate increases. Their Labour majorities had increased as a result. Therein lay a problem for the Thatcher government. In 1983, the government increased its parliamentary majority but so also did those authorities such as Sheffield and South Yorkshire that had increased their rates to fund jobs and services. The government knew the potential opposition from Labour-run authorities would be very high, especially in London, where the GLC had also popularised local authority initiative. Nor was opposition only heard from Labour.

The Rates Bill had a stormy passage through Parliament considering the Tory overall majority. Its second reading debate in January 1984 included nearly as many Tory as Labour backbench

	Con	Lab	Lib	Other
1973	13	82	1	4
1977	31	62	2	5
1981	14	82	3	1

South Yorkshire County Council election results. In 1977, only South Yorkshire and Tyne and Wear retained a Labour majority.

MPs opposed to the legislation. Led by former Prime Minister, Ted Heath, the arguments from both Tory and Labour MPs were strong:

> It has always been Conservative philosophy that one of our main purposes in politics is to balance power existing in our society. The Bill weighs it heavily on the side of central government. My right Hon. Friend the PM said this afternoon that it had long been accepted that the local authorities knew best. With that I agree strongly. If they know best how they wish to carry on those services, they should be enabled to raise the resources they need for those purposes.
>
> Nor can I accept the view that because the House is responsible for financial matters and national taxation, it should therefore take over responsibility for the rate taxation of local authorities.

Stan Crowther,[2] Labour MP and former Rotherham councillor, insisted that: *'overspending is when an authority is spending more than it intended to spend. According to ministers it will now mean authorities spending more that the minister intended them to spend'.* Geoffrey Rippon (Tory) described the Bill as: *'One of the most deplorable bills that has been brought to the House all the time I have been a member'.* Renée Short, Labour MP for Wolverhampton, declared that: *'to sweep away the budgetary freedom of local*

2. Labour Member of Parliament for Rotherham from the 1976 by-election until his retirement in 1992. His successor, Jimmy Boyce, was from Sheffield, a councillor and member of the Employment Committee.

authorities merely because their ideas about the uses of that freedom are different from those of this government is dangerous and scandalous.'

Twenty-four Tories rebelled and 11 abstained. Thatcher and Patrick Jenkin, the recently appointed Secretary of State for the Environment, had a timetabling problem with Parliamentary procedure, since they were determined to prevent Metropolitan elections, due early the following year, to the GLC and other regions such as South Yorkshire, West Yorkshire, West Midlands, Tyneside and Merseyside from taking place. They knew that popular antagonism to the government was immense with the miners' dispute at its height. There was no time for the Bill to be considered by a standing committee and then the House of Lords. So, it was rushed through with minimum scrutiny and received royal assent in June '84.

Labour Movement Response

A year before the chaotic Council meeting headlined above, I had taken on the position, along with a council colleague, Cllr. Tony Tigwell, of jointly chairing an anti-rate-capping campaign committee. We worked hard: he with community groups, I with trade unions to strengthen popular support for our potential refusal to comply with the legislation, when it came to setting a budget and rate for the 1985/6 financial year.

A month after the Act finally received royal assent, over the weekend of 7th-8th July 1984, Sheffield hosted a major national conference, 'Forging the Links', of mainly Labour local authorities. Its attendance outstripped expectations. David Blunkett's paper for the conference, stressed: *'collective action, achieving government retreat, and not martyrdom is the objective'.*

Despite the invitations going out to many moderate Labour Councils not associated with the left wing politics of Sheffield, the meeting did not endorse the official Party line, as most of the media had expected, but adopted an attitude of non-compliance, with many councillors willing to break the law.

One aspect of the Rates Act which particularly enraged councillors at the conference was not just that the freedom to set their own rate was being challenged, but that if a council asked for a reassessment of its cap, they were required to supply any information the Secretary of State requested about the detail of their budget proposals, and to give him the power to impose, *'such requirement relating to its expenditure of financial management as he thinks appropriate'*. Refusal to do so also counted as non-compliance with the same penalties of surcharge and removal from office. Only ten years before it had seemed like a civic honour to become a senior councillor or alderman. The idea that they were to be stripped of all financial independence was felt, like the pit closures in South Yorkshire, not simply to be a personal rebuff to them as civic dignitaries, but a belittling of the democratic rights of the people.

In Sheffield most Labour councillors thought that the significance of a strong enough defiance by major Labour controlled local authorities in large cities would force the government to make concessions and that they had to take it right to the brink. Sheffield Councillors in the main believed they had made the decision to stand for election in order to make a contribution to their communities. The potential outcome of breaking the law was well understood. Locally elected members found guilty of defying the rate-cap imposed by central government by setting an illegal rate for the year '85/'86 could be individually surcharged and removed from office. Some councillors put their mortgages in the names of partners, others realised they might be putting their jobs at risk but stuck with the line of defiance, whilst others made it clear they were unwilling to act illegally. Councillors at this time were not entitled to a wage or payment. They could claim personal expenses at a rate linked to meetings attended. There was in law a special responsibility allowance available for chairs of committees, which at the annual meeting of the Sheffield Labour Group of councillors we regularly denied ourselves, because it seemed invidious to then go on to elect on an open vote who should chair which committee. It was another example of adopting a collective principle to maintain a style of co-operative solidarity.

The 'Forging the Links' conference meant that Sheffield became a leading player along with the GLC of a national movement. David Blunkett was a national figure. He was the first non-Parliamentary member to have been elected to the constituency section of Labour's NEC. He knew the new leader of the party Neil Kinnock well, and was a familiar face and voice at both local and national Labour Party conferences, where Sheffield's reputation was at its height, for delivering a left wing programme of activities, and suffering some of the worst violence of the coal dispute.

However an opportunity was missed at the Labour Party's annual conference held in Brighton, six weeks after Sheffield's 'Forging the Links' event, when the NUM President Arthur Scargill launched an acrimonious personal attack on Neil Kinnock. The debate became loud and vitriolic, dominated by emotional speeches about the miners with David Blunkett defending Kinnock's leadership. Scargill tried to make it a left/right issue. The atmosphere became personal and bitter, drowning out proper discussion of the threat facing local authorities and their elected

David Blunkett campaigning in Sheffield.

members. The tone left no room to describe local authority successes in winning public support for their equality projects described earlier, nor to debate the wider threat for the general public which The Rates Act presented. Instead the shouting made it hard to have serious discussion of how change had been brought about without bitterness, but with outcomes supported by growing majorities, that included Militant on the left and business and entrepreneurs as well. The description earlier of how 'Militant' in Sheffield, for example, had been neutralised by incorporating activists into a wider political drive around inspiring initiatives was eclipsed'. The outcome was the adoption of an official line that was opposed to non-compliance with the Rates Act on grounds of illegality. The opportunity to unite the organisation around practical programmes to deliver a fairer society was lost in the uproar. Divisions about the miner's strike hit the headlines.

Sheffield Anti-ratecapping Campaign

After the Brighton conference in September 1984, campaigning in Sheffield resumed. Cllr Tony Tigwell and I organised local meetings about the potential impact rate-capping could have on jobs and services not only in the council but the whole local economy. We produced badges, leaflets, and put a slogan 'Against Rate-capping for the Right Reasons' along the sides of buses. DEED and the Council increased its publicity as part of the campaign against the legislation.

David Blunkett made the case in his foreword to *Putting You in the Picture*, one of the Council leaflets, praising the efforts of the Council to:

> … maintain services and protect jobs, when all around us other councils are cutting theirs. Our policies focus on the needs of the underprivileged, women and young people and are starting to work well and deliver community cohesion in poorest neighbourhoods.

Blunkett described how they:

> … helped create a sense of local pride so strong that it cut across Party loyalties.

yet accepted that as well in the past, there was:

> … a certain complacency, a tendency to take the electorate for granted, doing things for them rather than with them.
>
> Since 1980 we began to take a more critical look at ourselves – at our weaknesses as well as our strengths. Since then in the face of enormous pressure from a government that wants council to do less and less, we have moved forward. Steadily

> and systematically, we have built on all the best of the past and shown how a local council with popular support can make real economic and social progress for its citizens.

The Audit Commission had not found fault with Sheffield's financial management. In the same booklet Blunkett quoted how it had *'praised Sheffield's FE colleges for the way they have responded to unemployment and the needs of young people'*.[3]

A set of graphs illustrate this convincingly and were achieved despite constant reductions in the government's rate support grant contribution.

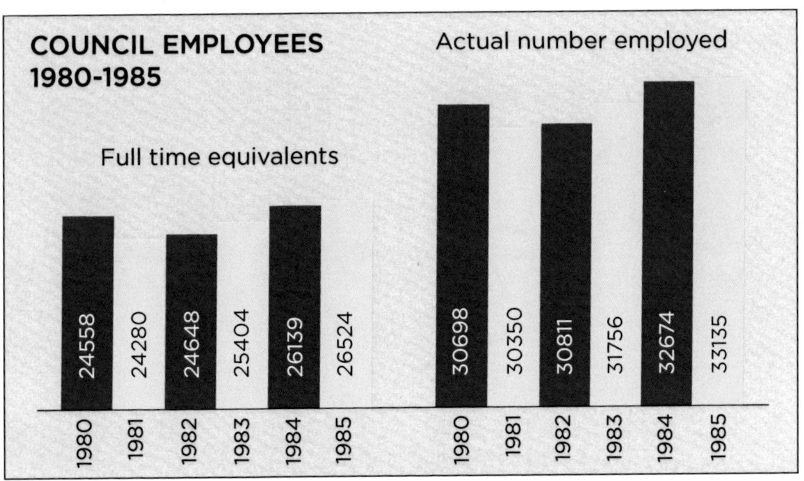

COUNCIL EMPLOYEES highlights the priority given to innovation in product development, training opportunities for women and young people, and examples of where outsourcing had been successfully resisted through better management, and where services had been brought in-house to improve efficiency. It shows

3. *Putting You in The Picture*. Sheffield City Council, 1986.

how the increased number of part time workers, many in low status low paid jobs, would be entitled to the low pay supplement.

HOUSING INVESTMENT shows how housing investment has improved overall and celebrates the fact that more apprentices are trained by the Works Department than by all the city's private builders put together!

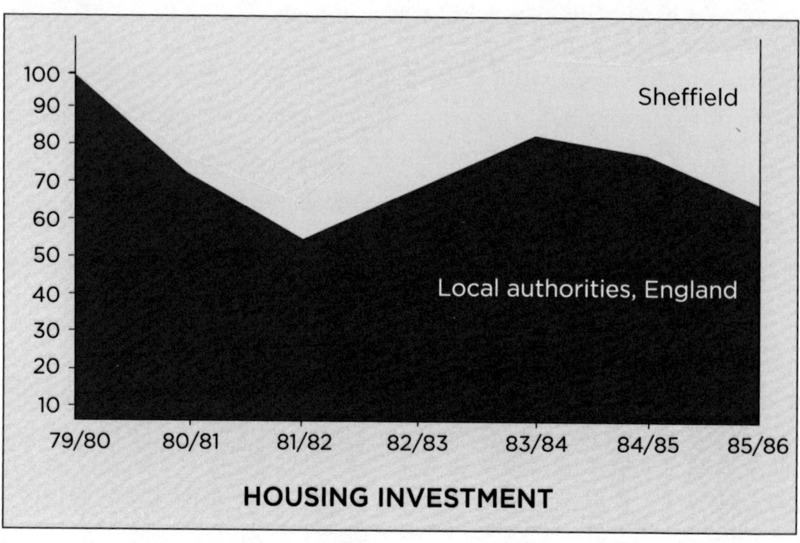

HOME HELPS AND WARDENS illustrates the expansion of home helps – again part time worker making a difference.

GRANTS TO VOLUNTARY GROUPS showing the increase of grant aid to voluntary organisations, mentions the priority given to poorer neighbourhoods but not the direct link between them and high ethnic minority populations, nor the fact that a majority of voluntary groups were run by women. A gender and race impact assessment of all Council operations had not yet been normalised.

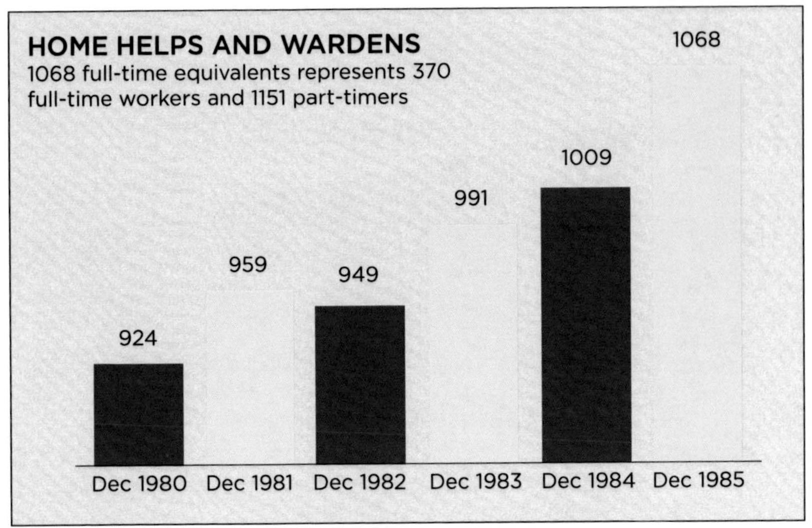

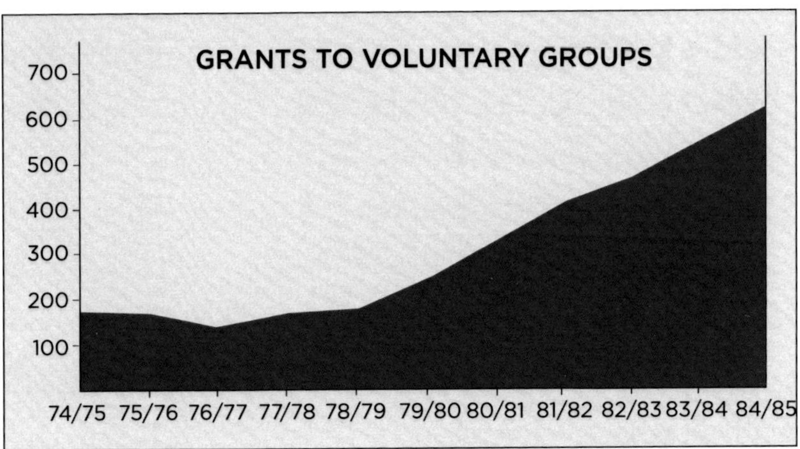

PUPIL TEACHER RATIO focuses on how for 'four years in a row Her Majesty's Inspectors of Schools have placed Sheffield in the very top league of local authorities providing acceptable services', and how disadvantage has been addressed through a significant drop in the pupil teacher ratio and celebrates the rising proportion of 3-5 year olds in nurseries. 1978/80 - 28%; 1985 - 36%

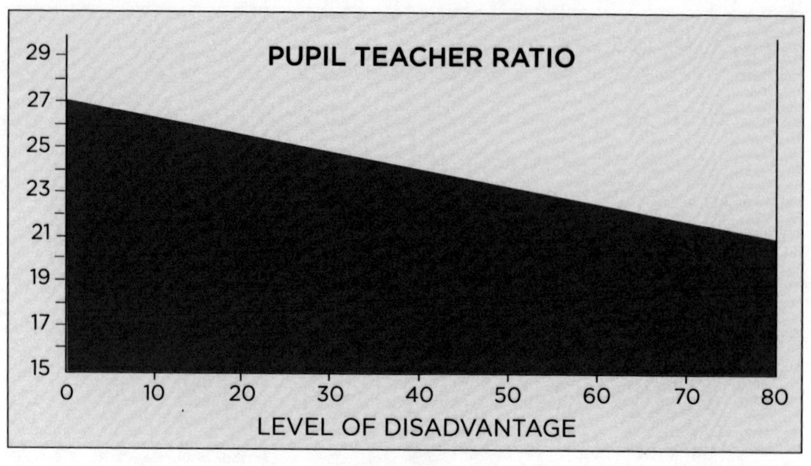

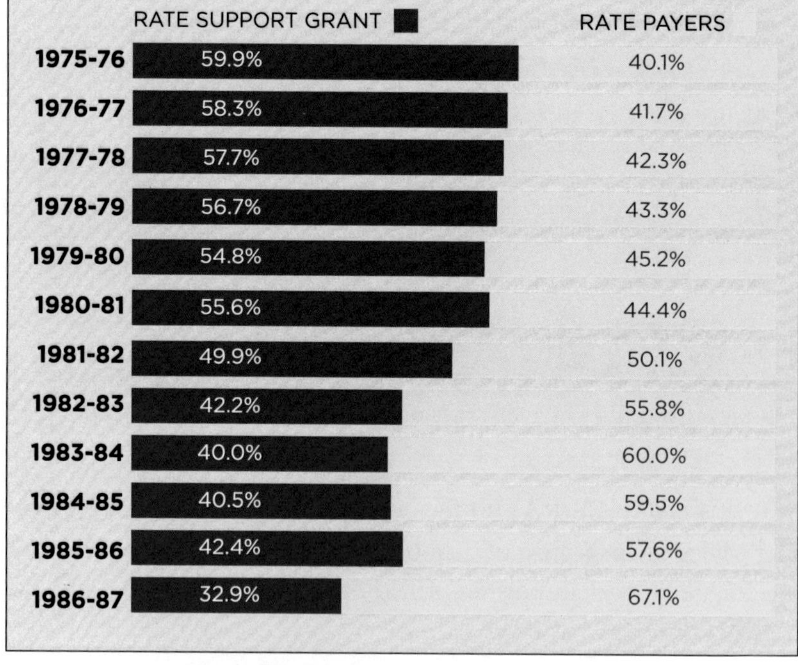

Share of Sheffield City Council's expenditure met by rate payers and rate support grant between 1975-1987.

These points were set out in detail to contrast them with evidence of the year by year reduction the government had made to local government in rate support grant (RSG),

This is clearly exemplified in terms of Sheffield's share of RSG over the same period. The contemporary book, *Democracy in Crisis: The Town Halls Respond,* published in 1987 by Hogarth Press co-authored by David Blunkett and Keith Jackson, has fuller details of the comprehensive way many of these achievements were delivered.

Rate-capping – Chronology of Events

The Council's initial rate-setting meeting was held on 4th April 1985. A crowd of 15,000 supporters had joined a demonstration outside the City Hall. *The Star* described it as, *'one of the biggest demonstrations in the city in recent years'.* Sheffield, along with several other Councils around the country, was reluctant to set a rate that would mean massive cuts to jobs and services and proposed a budget resolution along these lines. The Conservative group responded with an amendment which proposed £22 million savings, amongst which *The Star* listed:

> An end to the Employment Department
>
> Schools doing their own repairs rather than the Works Department
>
> No more payments to drop-in centres for the unemployed
>
> No more financial contributions to Northern College
>
> Plastic sack refuse collection instead of dustbins

The possible privatisation of Cleansing Services

The sale of 7,000 acres of surplus land

The Tories were overwhelmingly defeated, but because of the legal uncertainty no positive resolution was proposed by the Labour group and no budget or rate was set. It was instead postponed for a month until 7th May.

Blunkett and Billings had attended the district party meeting the evening before and had suggested a possible legal way out, that might avoid rate-capping. But the District Labour Party resolved that Councillors should remain defiant and *'refuse to set a rate until the government made financial concessions to enable them to do so without cutting jobs and services'.* So, the Council debate opened the next day by Alan Billings outlining plans for a budget of £250m, well above the maximum set by the government.

To return to David Holmes' report of the 'tempestuous' special Council meeting a month later on May 7th.

Eighteen Labour rebels argued that the council should obey the law and set a rate and balanced budget accordingly. They were supported by 17 Tory councillors and would have won the vote on that amendment had the 9 Liberals not abstained. It was defeated by only 3 votes. There followed a long, fruitless debate. The Liberals wanted to use the opportunity to gain more influence with positions of responsibility in the Council and access to all budget meetings. Their manoeuvring appeared petty considering how seriously the opening speeches had described the significance of the political decision. It indicated an inability to recognise the bigger political picture. Eventually a second amendment, almost identical, but this time supported by Labour rebels and both opposition parties was carried.

The Labour Group retired into private session, where a fallback position, to set a legal rate, but maintain a 'deficit' budget, was narrowly agreed (29:27) and Council resumed. This amendment proposed by David and Alan was also defeated after an emotional debate.

Holmes commented:

> Claims that Labour divisions could remain honourable and friendly appeared strained as left-wingers held back tears and pledged they would continue the fight outside the council chamber with trade unionists.

22 of the Labour left voted against Councillor Blunkett's amendment with the opposition parties producing a Labour defeat by 48 votes to 36.

Re-reading the list of 'How they voted' I was struck by the fact that only one of the 14 Spring Bank friends who were elected councillors, voted for the initial rebel amendment, whilst 13 remained solid. Three weeks later we were licking our wounds by Ullswater.

As Joint Chair of the campaign committee I was trying not to take the defeat personally. How had it all gone so wrong one month later? Questions abounded! It was obvious but too simple to put all the blame – or credit – on Margaret Thatcher and her cabinet, but why had Council colleagues not held the line?

Were we all too demoralised after the miners' defeat and their return to work to care anymore?

Were 15,000 on the streets not enough? The crowd filled the space around the City Hall, but it was hardly a popular uprising.

Were our arguments about maintaining local democracy too academic? The slogan on the buses did little to publicise or celebrate the council's performance on equality, training, health, transport or culture that voters had supported at election time.

Were our colleagues so concerned by the continuing local media opposition that they were unable to defend the Labour group agreement, even though a few months before, vitriolic attacks in the council chamber on projects such as the Women's Technology Training Workshop, or the recording studios described in previous chapters, had strengthened Labour solidarity?

Had the national media and official Labour Party opposition to non-compliance with government legislation and thereby breaking the law, scared them and their families?

Perhaps the main reason was general exhaustion and demoralisation. Council members believed that a further fight would inevitably end in defeat.

At the end of July 1985 Sheffield was named as one of the potential designated authorities to be 'capped'. It was the largest of the provincial cities to be threatened, since Liverpool had pre-empted the collective action of Labour authorities, and gone it alone, by setting an illegal rate early rather than postponing the decision. Its councillors led by Derek Hatton and Tony Mulhearn, had already been surcharged and barred from office. The 1985 annual conference witnessed another even louder and more emotional debate about members of the Militant Tendency, which yet again overshadowed any celebration of local authority's achievements on low pay, training and economic development initiatives which Sheffield, the GLC and other authorities were delivering. The leaders of Militant were finally expelled from the Labour Party at the subsequent conference.

I remember vividly the high tension both of the final traumatic council meeting and the year-long campaign Tony Tigwell and I were involved with, concurrent with the final months of the coal dispute and culminating in the street demonstration in the run-up to the final rate-capping 'retreat'. The experience taught me many political lessons, some of which I explore below, some in the next chapter, the Politics of Partnership, and others more generally in the concluding chapter.

Political Outcomes

It certainly was a ruthless political victory. With the miners on the front line defeated, Thatcher chose her moment to strengthen legislation already planned by Michael Heseltine and others during the early years of her premiership to put the brake on public sector initiative. The slogans and unemployment figures displayed on the GLC headquarters across the river from Parliament kept her awake at night. They threatened free market ideology. Being an elected local representative has never since held the same authority, independence or pride. Victorian Town Halls stand as empty shells of the past. Local government, very often driven by committed politicians on the left, was the victim of its own success.

However, we can see today that the Rates Bill, the rushed extremity of which had not been supported by many of Thatcher's Parliamentary colleagues, was also the beginning of her downfall. William Waldegrave, the Secretary of State in her first term, had adopted a more conciliatory way of delivering changes to local government. These had imposed a financial squeeze but proposed a steadier pace towards compulsion. It had been rejected by the PM and Waldegrave had been replaced by Patrick Jenkin. Michael Heseltine, the architect of earlier community development projects in cities, and of two Local Government Finance Bills (1 and 2), was unsettled. At his second attempt to cut local government income, he first abolished their power to levy a supplementary rate and secondly had found:

> A well designed weapon to punish individual 'high-spending' Councils. The penalty system was a cruelly simple device. Authorities would be given their grant related expenditure assessment level and their spending target as before, but now spending over target led to a withdrawal of grant at a progressively increasing rate. Grant was not merely withheld after spending reached a certain level, it was progressively reduced for every pound spent.[4]

Local authorities began 1982 with hope that the government's unpopularity could be exploited as the parliamentary term started to run out. Margaret Thatcher's standing in the public opinion polls had plummeted, but support for the Falklands War stopped all that, and the Conservatives were returned to power with an increased majority though fewer votes than in 1979.

Thatcher may have thought that rendering local government demoralised and debilitated would be easier than defeating the miners or winning the war over the Falklands. In the end she achieved a permanent weakening of local government, but also the beginning of the end of her own premiership.

---

4. Blunkett, D., Jackson, K. (1987). *Democracy in Crisis: The Town Halls Respond.* Hogarth Press, pp154.

Not since the Thatcher era has being an elected representative held the same authority, independence and pride. Grandiose Victorian Town Halls, such as Burslem's (pictured here alongside the statue of Henry Doulton), stand as empty reminders.

There were other political outcomes. Rate-capping and the associated legislation made local government a far more central feature in national politics. It also brought local authorities together to strengthen their collective political influence.

Over the rate-capping year of debates the District Auditor made frequent visits to Sheffield for off the record briefings with the Treasurer and our Chair of finance, Rev. Alan Billings and Howard Knight, assuring them his aim was to assist us achieve our objectives. The Department of the Environment probably knew as much, or more, about our budget planning than most of the Labour group of councillors. Information gleaned in this way would have helped civil servants responsible for implementing the Rates Act make their decisions as fool-proof as possible. The Audit Commission was established under the Local Government Act of 1982 to *'oversee the effectiveness, efficiency and economy'* of local councils and appoint auditors to all local authorities. However, it did not always side with the government. Its Chairman, Steve Banham, had declared in 1985 that:

> The best local government is superb and private enterprise could never improve on it, with Sheffield a shining example.[5]

Aspects of campaigning held salutary lessons for activists and politicians. For example, the importance of public demonstrations may be more limited than they think. At the time we had been surprised and pleased that 15,000 people marched to the Town Hall, with their trade union and community banners but looking back it was irrelevant. Ten times the number or a quarter of the city's population might have been significant but even 2 million people did not stop the Iraq War. Fewer than a million people on the streets is a social occasion, rather than politically relevant.

Another lesson from the campaign was perhaps that we used the wrong imagery. In Sheffield enough money had been directed to the publicity against rate-capping to fund an outside body to help us explain to the public our opposition. We shortlisted three organisations to advise us. One group worked for the Local Government Information Unit (LGIU).[6] Its language of the left was familiar. It could have been drafted by the Council's own Employment Department; a second was more elaborate and

---

5. The Audit Commission Report of 1985.

6. The LGIU was a David Blunkett initiative formed in 1983, funded by the GLC and local authoriies. It was Chaired by Blunkett and led by Judy Mallaber, who later became MP for Amber Valley.

expensive, the third impressed us with the simplicity of its pitch. They had done background research and understood the political nature of the campaign. They said:

> We understand that you don't want the Rates Act to succeed because you are proud of what you do and are unwilling to reduce your spending on the jobs and services it provides.

'*Quite right*', we replied.

> In that case your slogan needs to be very simple and appear inexpensive so that rate payers don't think you are wasting their money. We suggest you keep it black and white. You believe strongly and deeply that what you are doing is right. Use that word and emphasise your conviction with a 'tick'.

Their concluding recommendation was memorable and left us convinced. It went something like this:

> Our research shows that you have a strong and loyal electorate, so don't worry too much about the people who you know will support you. It's the others you should target, so that even those who don't agree with you can say with sincerity, 'I understand what they are doing even though I don't agree'. That way you will convince those in the middle that you honestly believe in what you are doing, and they will follow your lead.

Their suggestion for our slogan, 'Against Rate-capping for the Right Reasons. Tick' was agreed and shortly after appeared on buses across the region. Much later we heard the publicity firm had been occasionally used by the Conservatives. Was the word 'Right' placed there to emphasise a different point?

The Financial Impact of Rate-capping

One undeniable impact of the Rates Act and its associated legislation was financial. It challenged the whole concept of local government's financial independence by turning the legal and financial screws down so tight that no regional or local public authority has since had the same degree of influence to frustrate government intentions.

Dr Peter Cromar, who controlled the Employment Department's budget in close consultation with Treasury, recently commented on the degree to which he thought the greater impact of rate-capping on local authorities was financial. His comments clearly indicated that was not the case.

> The skill was to find a different way around most restrictions by using new avenues of funding or legal powers to avoid direct cuts, but this required great clarity in terms of describing goals and designing a project's planning and implementation with careful monitoring so that results were well audited and understood. It was a question of bringing discipline into budgeting with a clear social purpose as the outcome.

Julie Muscroft joined the Treasury team around this time before moving on. She echoed the views of Peter Cromar, describing the job as one of the best experiences she had ever had in terms of exploring new ways of funding what the Council wanted to achieve.[7]

At the time and since, innumerable analyses have shown how those who make most use of universal publicly funded services that are easily affordable are those at the lower end of the income bracket. Equally, evidence abounds that women and ethnic minorities make up the majority in that category. The charts above illustrate how the rate support grant income from government had been declining since 1978, leading to Blunkett's comment that the authority had been '*running to stand still*'. Funding from rates were increasingly needed to maintain a level of service rather than reform, improve or make them more accessible. The Council and its Employment Department celebrated its actions and success through constant publicity, often helped not hindered by local media reaction. The change to a defensive approach made it less effective and politically harder to retain support.

There were constant attempts throughout the next couple of years to constrain local government resources further. Each attempt affected the potential of the authority to use flexible ways to protect the services with key equal opportunity objectives at their core. Cllr the Rev. Alan Billings brought a Report dated 21st March 1986 to the Labour Group of Councillors entitled *Furthering Socialism in a Cold Climate*. Those involved remember it well. It was for discussion, before going to the Sheffield District Labour Party for their endorsement. It opened by stating the obvious:

7. Julie Muscroft worked for Sheffield City Council from 1987-1993 and is now Chief Monitoring Officer in the Legal and Administration Department of Kirklees Council.

> Drawing up the Revenue Budget for 1986/87 has been a very difficult exercise.

It then sets out some basic assumptions:

> … that we would agree to the net expenditure figure imposed by government of £215m to comply with the law, escape further grant penalties and receive maximum grant; that we assumed that the base budget for each department was the same, apart from including additional teaching posts, and home helps to reflect demographic trends. This, including inflation, totalled £283m expenditure.

It also suggested that all fees and income from charges including rents would rise but by no more than inflation. In addition:

> We would budget for an additional contingency provision of £9m to protect our priorities:
>
> £5m to help support bus fares; £1.9m for our low pay agreement; £3.2m to increase housing repairs (and jobs); £0.4m to add an additional 180 polytechnic students.
>
> Our total requirement therefore totalled £322m.

The strategy would be to maximise grant income and avoid rate-capping in '87/'88 by reducing net expenditure by £52.5m to around £269m in order that:

> The £52.5m would be met largely by £31m 'deferred purchase'; capitalisation of expenditure currently met from revenue

> £7.5m by extending leasing
>
> £1m by deferring the low pay supplement to the following year but agreement with the trade unions would be needed;
>
> £9m from departmental savings that would affect staff numbers and capacity; would leaving £1.6m to be met from reserves.

The overall aim would be to:

> Protect, preserve, and in the prioritised areas, improve the services the City Council provides for the people of Sheffield.

Billings ended by claiming that:

> It is clear that the Labour Group has found both the political will as well as the financial means to preserve and extend socialist commitments even in a cold financial climate.

Just four months later after much agonising debate, a note from the City Treasurer was circulated to Chief Officers explaining that Sheffield had been one of five authorities outside London along with three others from the North East as well as Brighton and four more London boroughs to be rate capped. It went on to describe how in response the government now proposed to control deferred purchase and other capital financing arrangements even more tightly.

Statement by the Secretary of State on 22 July 1986

3.1 The Secretary of State has announced that, from midnight on 22 July, [i.e. the same day] any contracts or other arrangements entered into to defer capital expenditure to a later year will be prevented from avoiding the Government's capital expenditure controls. There will be possible future exemptions for single projects where it is desirable to spread the incidence of capital expenditure over a number of years.

3.2 It is unclear whether contracts already entered into by the City Council will avoid the new controls and clarification of the Government's intentions are being sought.

3.3 A further announcement will be made by the Secretary of State in due course.

The Council duly noted the new regime and entered into a cat and mouse game of finding ways of maintaining services around the constraints imposed. It was thrown onto the defensive. No longer was there the same scope to address new projects and ideas from councillors or officers aligned to manifesto commitments and priorities. It had to develop projects according to where partnership funding opportunities might be found.

South Yorkshire Abolition; Transport

The most resented element of Thatcher's financial and legal constraints on local government in South Yorkshire that was, and still is, vividly remembered, was implementation of the Transport

Act on 15th September 1986 that outlawed the possibility of maintaining South Yorkshire's cheap fares. Bus passengers saw their fares treble overnight as its policy made subsidy illegal. Led by representations from the Road Transport Federation the legislation simply put private competitive principles before public benefit in every area of existing public transport whether tram, rail or bus and restricted virtually all local financial autonomy over public transport. The legislation said that the Transport Support Grant would be retained but only for capital expenditure, and be received through Block Grant, which of course was controlled by government.

Ian Saunderson at Leeds University has produced a useful article from his research of the impact.

> Passenger Transport Authorities (PTAs) had to prepare three year plans analysing options for the development of public transport services, and providing justified proposals for service levels, fares and subsidies, indicating the benefits accruing from such subsidies. Subsidies could not be paid by the PTA except on the basis of an approved three-year plan and in the light of guidance from the Secretary of State, based on his scrutiny of the plan.[8]

Removing the local/regional powers to address how best to plan and operate one public transport system for the wider labour market, damaged social and economic opportunities within the whole area.

8. Ian Saunderson, Leeds University, 1988.

Peter Sephton,[9] Chief Executive of the SYPTE in the 80s, is quoted by Scott Hellewell countering the decision of the government:

> Some still regard South Yorkshire's Transport as the aspirations of the 'loony left'. These people generally live outside the area. Of those who experience these trials and tribulations at first hand, hardly anyone will criticise the underlying aim – a higher quality of life through a higher quality of public transport.[10]

He spoke for an increasing number of local private sector business leaders whose reservations about refusing to talk or work with the local authority were growing. The era of partnership on many levels was taking shape. The next chapter looks at how the political culture within local government adapted to the new financial climate, and the impact of this on its work and services.

A large advertisng hoarding used as part of the campaign against the Transport Act.

9 Peter Sephton, later Chairman of Sheffield City Centre Residents' Action Group (SCCRAG, now renamed Changing Sheffield), led the employee buy-out of SYT from SYCC to form Mainline Group.

10. Scott Hellewell. Introduction, page 7 (ibid 1996).

CHAPTER 9

The Politics Of Partnership

Throughout 1986 there were thoughtful debates within the Sheffield Labour movement. The rate-capping trauma and raft of aggressive legislation provoked a variety of responses. No longer was the movement so sure of itself. Nor did it have the same confidence to initiate projects which translated equality policy into action. Some Council members were defeatist, believing resistance to the government was hopeless; others defiant, eager to find ways around the legal and financial constraints. A majority felt unjustly penalised. The phrase 'cranes on the skyline' emerged as a key aspiration to show pride in the city and keep some dignity. It was a way of rebuilding confidence, but the bold emphasis on people-led progress towards a fairer society, driven by the belief that what was good for social progress and equal opportunity would help the local economy thrive and vice versa, became more hesitant and muted.

The Department for Economic Development attempted to maintain the theme and by the '87 general election had published well over fifty research pamphlets and leaflets about a wide range of specialist sectors and more general issues. Each asserted the belief that an active local government regime would not only bring better health, education and community cohesion, but also benefit the private sector directly through land deals, grant aid for small start-up businesses and purchasing power, and indirectly through the increased spending power of the general public. Staff included the department's own Press Officer, Librarian, and Graphic Designer, to manage publicity, publications, design, and distribution. Its public profile was high. The department was located in Palatine Chambers, a building across the road from the front entrance of the Town Hall, which helped its own perception, and that of many others, that it was different and independent from the Central Policy Unit, headed by the chief executive or the Planning Department. A research team, headed by Mick Paddon, another of its first employees, worked closely with the two universities and came into contact with many in the private sector who appreciated and often agreed with its conclusions.

Regeneration – Planning and Building Led

Some Sheffield companies believed privately that partnership rather than enmity between public and private was needed because the stranglehold of rate-capping and constraints on capital expenditure depleted the authority's scope for development projects, many of which they appreciated and were well under way. For example, Sheffield Science Park had the strong backing of the future Sheffield Hallam University, whose Chair at the time, Bill Owen, was working hard with John Stoddart, its Chancellor, to establish Sheffield City Polytechic as a fully fledged University. Historians noted that nearly a century earlier in 1904 the people of Sheffield raised £50,000 by penny donations from local steel and factory workers and residents for education and training in the city.[1] Phase 1 of the Science Park was to be located

1. Sheffield Hallam University was designated a University in 1992. Its main building is known as the Owen Building.

in a former cutlery works, the Cooper Building, a handsome example of Sheffield's cutlery industry, right next to the future university's Main Building, named after Bill Owen. The project, led by the Product Development team in DEED aimed to provide accommodation for new start-ups using innovation and new technology. As with other projects the planning was done in close liaison with the SMEs or co-operatives concerned.

Another example using the same methodology was Aizlewood's Mill in the Kelham Island area which was renovated in liaison with the Co-operative Development Group (CDG) to become its centre with space for several co-operative enterprises. Councillor Mike Bower[2] was also the Manager of the CDG. He proposed that this fine but derelict building, which he cycled past on his way to the Town Hall every day, should be acquired by Council for £1.00, with the intention of employing Tatlow Stancer[3] to undertake the renovation work.

Aizlewood's Mill

2. Mike Bower former journalist who had chaired the Education Committee following Peter Horton's tenure, and became leader of the Council in 1992 when Clive Betts went into Parliament.

3. Architects of Autoways/Kennings.

Bessemer converter at the Kelham Island Industrial Museum

The Planning Department meanwhile, were working on the Canal Basin and neighbouring Neepsend, which historically had formed the heart of 19th century industrial Sheffield, where barges loaded and unloaded raw materials for the growing steel industry and other goods to and from the East coast ports on the Humber estuary, and where the two Victorian railway stations had in the 19th century linked the city with Manchester, London and Birmingham. 'Kelham Island', formed in 1180 when a 'goit'[4] was created to carry water from the River Don to the town's Corn Mill near Lady's Bridge, and gave its name to an area of Sheffield with many small iron, steel and engineering works and workshops. An industrial museum called Kelham Island was opened in 1982 and later the neighbouring property became a brewery near the 'Fat Cat' public house, known at the time for its huge selection of hand-

The Fat Cat, Kelham Island.

4. Goit – the channel from a stream to turn a water wheel or mill race.

pulled beers. Other former cutlery and engineering premises such as Globe Works, and the empty former Royal Infirmary were renovated as office accommodation for private firms. Today, Kelham Island and Neepsend are lively areas expanded to house a growing number of university students and have recently increased in property value to become a very popular place to live near the city centre.

Empty derelict buildings close to the city centre were not special to Sheffield. They were a feature of most northern industrial cities across Yorkshire, Lancashire, the Midlands and in the North East. They needed substantial long-term capital investment. Just as Secretary of State for Environment, Michael Heseltine had made publicity out of his work regenerating the former docks around the City of Liverpool, for which he was made a 'Freeman of the City', during his years as Minister of State for the Environment in the early years of the Thatcher government, Birmingham and Manchester were upgrading their inner city canal areas and buildings whilst the GLC were working on the London Docklands.

Sheffield Chamber of Commerce

Land and buildings regeneration across the country met little or no opposition from Chambers of Commerce. However, in 1986 Sheffield was still being presented as 'loony left' by the Sheffield Chamber of Commerce, which had for years grumbled that the left-wing image of the city was 'holding back development'.[5] Bitterness still dominated the political debate, spilt over into Council meetings, and made headlines in the media, even though

5. *Sheffield Star*, and article by Peter Lee in the *Yorkshire Post*. 25.04.85.

the only real quibble seemed to be the end-use, as with Aizelwood Mill, or the way in which sites were developed and managed in close collaboration with less advantaged groups and communities, whether young women plasterers, new co-operatives, or ethnic minority youngsters with guitars. The Chamber was derisive about building a new relationship with the City Council. The tensions are well described in a recent book by Sir Norman Adsetts.[6] Born in Sheffield in 1931, Norman attended King Edward VII's secondary school where he obtained a scholarship to The Queen's College, Oxford to read bio-chemistry. He changed his chosen subject to Philosophy, Politics and Economics (PPE) having decided to do his National Service before his degree. He showed an early interest in public life describing his attendance at a week of lectures in London staged by the Council for World Citizenship, a United Nations initiative, where he saw the singer Al Jolson on film. He went on to describe one of his early friends from national service as a *'miner and black faced comedian singing Al Jolson songs in the clubs of South Yorkshire'*. In 1985 he was a self-made, well respected and successful businessman, Chief Executive of 'Sheffield Insulations Group', whose head office was in the former barracks building in the ward I represented. In his book he describes his reaction when he was invited to join the Chamber of Commerce's 'Council'.

> After attending only one meeting I had no difficulty in deciding on the first priority for the Chamber of Commerce. In order to fulfil its primary duty to support the interests of industry and commerce in Sheffield there must be a constructive working relationship with the

6. Adsetts, N. (2017). *A Man of Sheffield: the Adsetts Story*. RMC Press.

Sir Norman Adsetts

> City Council to help address the condition of Sheffield – and this required effective communication.

His first area of interest was the city's image. He described how he asked Richard Field, Chief executive of Dyson Refractories, and a new president of the Chamber of Commerce, recently appointed Chair of the new Training and Enterprise Council (TEC)[7], *'What can I do to help in your year of office?'*, and Richard Field replied *'Do something about the image of Sheffield'*.

> After a preliminary meeting with city council representatives in November 1986 … an Image Working Party was formed, but not before meeting in secret with a few early 'believers' in partnership from the chamber of commerce and the city council, knowing there was no clear majority for this approach in either body.

My first conversation with him took place at his request in my office in Palatine Chambers at one of these 'secret' meetings. We had agreed that its location in DEED was tactful. I listened to his plea that partnership and coordination with the public sector

---

7. Established during 1990/91 throughout the country as independent, local, employer-led councils, to take over responsibility for running the training and enterprise programmes previously organised by the Department of Employment's Training Agency, which effectively transferred local training policy away from local authorities to private sector government appointee control.

was a better way forward than the existing rows and negativity and found that he was mindful of and admired the verve and active enthusiasm amongst so many officers within the council and the employment department for exploring every opportunity for training and jobs. As we discussed our own backgrounds and approach we found that he and my brother Chris Price had been in the same year at Queens in Oxford and had been friends. Norman said that he felt it was time for the private sector and local authority to join forces. I saw him as someone I could work with and agreed. Maybe the Oxford link helped or even the carefully chosen black and white tones of the anti rate-capping campaign.

While the 'Image Working Party' commenced work under his chairmanship along with Chamber and Council representatives, the Employment committee proposed the creation of a new body, Sheffield Economic Regeneration Committee (SERC), to be chaired jointly by myself and Norman Adsetts. Both he and Richard Field became regular attendees along with University, Polytechnic, Trades Council, tenants and community representatives. One of its first joint initiatives was to commission Coopers and Lybrand to research and report on the state and potential for redevelopment of the Lower Don Valley

World Student Games

Meanwhile, the Labour group on Sheffield council, urged on by the Trades and Labour Council, maintained their commitment to developing left wing policies despite the split over rate-capping. They wanted action and 'cranes on the skyline' just as the private sector did. The determination to stay in the driving

Peter Price

seat and be seen as the agents for change was overwhelming. The Chair of the Recreation committee, Councillor Peter Price, a stalwart of Spring Bank camps, responded to his own bitter disappointment that the anti-ratecapping campaign had failed by suggesting that Sheffield should bid to be the UK city to host the World Student Games in 1991. The combination of revenue spending reductions, and capital cut-backs made it hard to deliver on-going, let alone new building projects, so he presented the idea as a bold, defiant proposal. The idea was discussed at length in the Labour group, as some colleagues hadn't really heard of the World Student Games and had reservations about 'mortgaging the future' with such a huge expense while others including many in the employment department felt unhappy about the prospect of job losses in engineering to make way for sporting facilities. There were no elements of the proposal that focused especially on positive action for women or deprived communities. One paper for discussion, prepared by Mike Bower and myself, was entitled *The Games – An Unglossy View*. This compared costs initially estimated at £115m with mainstream commitments like tertiary education, further Elderly Persons Support Units (EPSUs) or housing development and questioned its priority. It criticised the vague nature of financing.

> We have found a legal solution to how this sum can be borrowed outside capital controls – from an Australian bank. We will pay it back in debt charges at £10.5m a year over 40 years.

> The various financial companies and trusts have got business representatives on their management boards, but none from a trade union, nor from the voluntary sector. Minutes of the Games company will not be presented to a Council committee. Conditions for council involvement are weak. Once agreed we could hardly withdraw!

With no other financing options for 'cranes on the skyline', Councillor Peter Price gained the support of Councillor Peter Horton a former Lord Mayor and Chair of Education, who was not amongst the group of councillors who had supported defiant action over rate-capping. He argued strongly, along with Peter Price, that the drive for Cultural Industries could be enhanced with the addition of sport being linked with proposals to restore the derelict Lyceum theatre in order to complement the growing popularity of the world snooker championships which, since 1977, had been held in the Crucible Theatre in the Round. It would also give funding to refurbish the ageing City Hall. So despite the prospect of capital costs having to be met through deferred purchase it was agreed to make a bid to host the WSG

Sheffield's Lyceum Theatre

to give a boost to the city. The decision helped to re-unite the Labour group in the run up to the imminent general election for which David Blunkett was selected to take over from Joan Maynard as MP in the safe Labour seat of Sheffield Brightside. Backing in the name of partnership was sought successfully with the private sector, through the Chamber of Commerce, and a 'partnership' group went off together in smart new blazers to argue with enthusiasm for the money.

Labour Movement and Partnership

A few months later, on June 11th 1987, Labour again lost heavily to the Tories at the Parliamentary elections, in which the Tory majority was 102, whilst Labour increased its share of the vote in Scotland and the north and maintained its popularity at a local level in South Yorkshire.[8] Sheffield lost its Council Leader, David Blunkett, once he was elected to Parliament and Clive Betts became the leader of the Council.[9] I remained Chair of Employment and Economic Development. 'Partnership' was now the flavour of the month and together with officers in DEED we continued working on our existing projects through financial partnerships on many fronts, a far cry from my intensely political year 1984-85 as the joint Chair of the anti-rate-capping campaign. Explaining to the Sheffield District Trades and Labour Council why we were advocating teaming up with the private sector and how this would affect our support for co-operatives, trade unions, women and ethnic minorities, against all of which the Tory opposition in the City Council were still vociferous,

8. See page 164.

9. See page 18, Clive Betts.

was an unenviable task. *'Why waste valuable time winning their support?'*, they asked. The answer was hard and pragmatic. Together with Clive, we prepared a short paper, *The Politics of Partnership*, about how to square the circle of this policy shift. We wrote:

> The report of the Employment Select Committee on Employment makes frightening reading. 20% of the population now exist on or below the official poverty level; are dependent on state benefit for their continuing livelihood, and are increasingly strapped in to a poverty trap.
>
> There are two obvious responses in the Party to the subject coming to the fore.
>
> First, that the government's present market led economic policy is so bad for ordinary people that the correct response to ever increasing demands for 'private led' should be to steer clear, stay away, and have nothing to do with the private sector, neither its dinner parties, its offers of help and advice, nor its money. Instead to concentrate on criticism and hope that voters next time will agree that a different policy is needed.
>
> Second, that partnership is good per se, that economic development, cranes on the skyline, new grand buildings, hyper-stores and leisure complexes are a contribution in themselves to a better life. That simply by being involved in the developments, a certain economic credibility rubs off on the players in the 'partnership'.

Neither are totally correct.

The first approach convinces no-one that there is in existence a useful and different commercial or industrial strategy to that of the present regime. It makes it more difficult to have links with organised workers in an industrial sector. It becomes impossible to gather essential know-how about products; production services; technology; the required skills of tomorrow and training needs within different sectors. It makes it very hard to persuade even one employer of labour, however disenchanted with the present regime, that a labour government's policy would give them better long term benefits than Margaret Thatcher's buzz words of 'market', 'inner city regeneration' and 'enterprise'.

The danger of the second is that endorsing the talk of economic 'boom' or 'miracle' simply gives credibility to the present government's free market policy. For example, Meadowhall has displaced 500 jobs in two steel foundries.[10] Some of the displaced workers will find jobs on the construction phase of the leisure centre and the demolition of their plants, but if so these will not be new jobs, nor will that particular private sector investment have gone to benefit the local economy.

10. Meadowhall is a major retail and leisure complex built on the site of Hadfield's East Hecla Works. It was the second largest shopping centre in the UK when it opened in 1990 and remains the largest in Yorkshire.

Our recommendations briefly summarised were:

- To shift the bottom line from the ***who*** of decision making to the ***what and how***.
- To maintain as a basic objective, full employment, and sharing the benefits of regeneration, insisting also on equal opportunities, local labour, public accessibility to all papers and minutes.
- To add an essential requirement that proposals have been discussed with trade unions, community and ethnic minority organisations.
- To maintain in-house an ongoing base of sound social and economic research and policy development – not an economic exercise alone – so that agreed physical developments can spawn further projects which fit in with an overall integrated strategy.

We concluded, somewhat weakly that:

> Capitalism is not designed to distribute wealth fairly. All along in dealing with the private sector we are trying to make the best of the situation. The efforts of people in the Labour movement engaged in this process should not be judged against perfect solutions. They should be measured against realistic goals of trying to achieve investment in the city, turning that investment into jobs so that at least some of the wealth from the development process is shared as equitably as possible amongst the local community.

The Labour movement, reluctantly, went along with the paper. In fact politicians were readjusting their aspirations as Labour members of local authorities, having been forced onto the defensive, through government legislation which reduced their powers. As Chair of the Employment Committee, together with officers within DEED, I became heavily involved in developing these and other partnerships, not simply with the private sector but with other local authorities across the UK, using Urban Programme, European 'Objective 2' funds and any other sources of match funding to generate and maximise capital contributions for projects that had the Council's backing. Through S.E.R.C and the Image Working Party another body, Sheffield Partnerships, was formed. In addition to the Lower Don Valley study by Coopers and Lybrand other projects were taking off, which were brought together into a marketing 'Sheffield Vision' document called *Partnership in Action*, to be launched at the Mansion House by Norman Adsetts. We discussed these years recently from our different experiences – he with Chamber of Commerce, CBI, and local business leaders and I with trades unions, Labour local authorities, tenants and the unemployed – but both seeking funds and financial assistance for local action. The first point we made to Sheffield Trades and Labour movement about concentrating on the 'action' rather than on 'who takes the credit', was what we had in common. Norman and his wife, Eve, expanded on the description of an encounter they had with Margaret Thatcher as he launched Sheffield Vision in 1988.

> When she came upon the grouping in which I was standing with Eve and a small number of people from Sheffield, her first question was blunt: *'Are you the man who believes in talking to the Council in Sheffield?'* When I said I was doing just that, she moved closer, placed a firm hand on my forearm, and in an accusing voice said, *'You can't*

> *trust them'* … I gave her a few examples of progress and she replied with a question. *'Who will get the credit?'* I replied that I had not thought about that, but that the point of partnership was that we could all share it.

Eve emphasised just how hard she had gripped Norman's arm! Norman admitted he found himself trembling.

'Who was going to take the credit for inner city regeneration' was Thatcher's top concern at that time. Of secondary concern was that projects should minimise regulation and costs to the private sector. Of no concern was whether projects were designed to ensure that social benefits, such as training facilities, childcare, easy access for the disabled, drop-in centres for unemployed, affordable housing, job opportunities, or well being for women and run-down communities were in-built.

Thatcher had clearly been bruised by the uncertainty and rebellion of her Party colleagues during the passage of the Rates Act, as they saw the continuing popularity of local government in areas like South Yorkshire and especially in London. The continuing electoral success of Labour in local government in London and elsewhere was a real irritant. This may have been the reason behind her fateful decision to embark on the wholesale redrawing of local taxation, by replacing the centuries old land and property rates which at least had an element of fairness through its link with the size and valuation of the property concerned, with a new 'Community Charge', or 'Poll Tax' as it was immediately labelled, a flat-rate tax on each adult, regardless of their income or wealth. The duke and the dustman paid the same. A large family in a small house could see their local taxation increase tenfold while a wealthy widower living in a mansion would get a massive bonus. In the US, payment of a poll tax qualified an individual's right to vote, with the effect of disenfranchising poorer citizens. It was widely recognised as one of the most regressive forms of taxation. The slogan 'Can't Pay, Won't Pay' is the title of a recent book about the history of the poll tax by Simon Hannah,[11] which makes the point that the Labour Party did not come out forcefully against the poll tax. They were themselves still bruised by the intensity of the argument over rate-capping and reluctant to go illegal again. However, by 1989 it brought large crowds onto the streets in protest, starting in Scotland where it was first introduced. The cost of its implementation was a nightmare, which fell on already cash strapped local councils. Individuals and where they live constantly change, whereas a property at least remains where it is, within its same local authority area. Many in Thatcher's cabinet were concerned. Patten, Portillo and Heseltine as well as the general public saw its unfairness and the impossibility and extra expense of collecting it.

Urban Programme to Urban Development Corporations

The combination of rate-capping and new restraints on local authority capital spending had impacted on the style and efficiency of economic development. 'Urban Programme' funding was first established in 1968 under the Home Office and developed through the Inner Cities Act in 1978.[12] It left local authorities fairly free to determine priorities and use the criteria established by the Home Office programme of Community Development

---

11. Hannah, S. (2020). *Can't Pay, Won't Pay – The Fight to Stop the Poll Tax*. Pluto Press.

12. See David Blunkett's comment on page 126.

Projects like Coventry Workshop to give priority to employment projects that were open to community consultation and benefitted those most likely to be out of work. It had been used to help finance many of the positive action projects already described. But for the very reasons that it worked well it came under government fire, because these powers, left at local level meant that the Thatcher government did not get the credit.

Former officers from the City Treasury and DEED have described to me how cuts and then abolition of the Urban Programme made planning ahead full of uncertainty. Within the Central Policy Unit of the council, Phil Nuttall, an experienced officer responsible for the Urban Programme, worked closely with finance colleagues in Treasury. He would be in touch with every Council department advising whether a proposal involving capital expenditure might qualify for Urban Programme funding. He aimed to have ready a series of possible projects of various sizes from a range of departments. He would then always have something ready to fit into each funding round, allowing the authority's own capital programme to go further.

After 1987, Urban Programme funds were diverted into Enterprise Zones, which were specifically known as Area Based Initiatives (ABIs) – land not people-led – geographically determined by the Department of the Environment with a business led culture and little local authority influence. Another idea, 'City Challenge', used more of the UP funding stream. It took a competitive approach, making authorities bid for funds against each other. The link between 'social' and 'economic' was taken out as well as the link with local communities. They would be led by central government appointments and given direct grant aid.

Larger schemes were launched as 'Urban Development Corporations' (UDCs). Their Chairmen and Chief Executives were vetted and appointed by government, which also determined the budget. They operated in a limited designated area, i.e. land not people led. Local authority powers of planning and compulsory purchase were taken over by the UDC. They had a short term life of 5-7 years, so there was a requirement for quick and visible success.

London's East End where the GLC were actively involving communities well before its abolition was re-designated Docklands Development Corporation in the first batch of UDCs. The second batch included areas in Trafford, the Black Country, Cardiff and Teesside. Despite the funding assembled through SERC to commission Coopers and Lybrand to plan a strategy for the Lower Don Valley, Sheffield was designated a UDC in the third batch. All the preliminary work was in favour of different objectives and style of management. From being a major initiative of the new partnership working in the city, it became another bitter aggravation strongly opposed by the local authority on the grounds that regeneration was already underway.

I had the task of negotiating an 'agreement' that satisfied the City Council, the government and our partners in the private sector. Re-reading this recently I can remember the detail in which we tried to incorporate into the Agreement the points on partnership made at the District Labour Party. For example, after insisting on public access to the deliberations of the UDC, a final bullet point was reluctantly agreed:

> As part of the UDC's commitment to work to aims at the long-term regeneration of the City, it accepts

the role of the Council to be closely consulted and involved in the construction of its corporate Plan. Matters for consultation will include:

- Land assembly and site preparation
- A focus on industrial development
- Analysis of transportation requirements
- Protection of existing businesses and economic activity
- Targetting employment to local people and disadvantaged groups.

The additions were minimal. No mention of positive action to remedy discrimination against women in the labour market, only a brief nod towards any social impact monitoring; a very basic commitment to *'consider itself to have the same responsibilities under section 11 of the Race Relations Act as those organisations to which this section applies'*, and to trade unions *'measures will also be taken by the UDC to ensure consultation with the community, trade unions and employers'*.

In comparison with the bold aims of the Employment Department the contrast is stark. Our negotiations took place in the employment department with civil servants from the Department of the Environment present. The council was offered two rather than one place on the board, but in practice the clauses and words were in name only.

After I left local government and before entering Parliament in 1992, I worked on an analysis of urban regeneration funding streams over the eighties, analysing the cost and community benefit of each. On the whole my research showed that as local authorities reduced their lead role in economic development, impact in terms of social benefit reduced. Land based projects were less effective.

> The Urban Programme emphasised positive action. 20% of all projects (in Sheffield) have

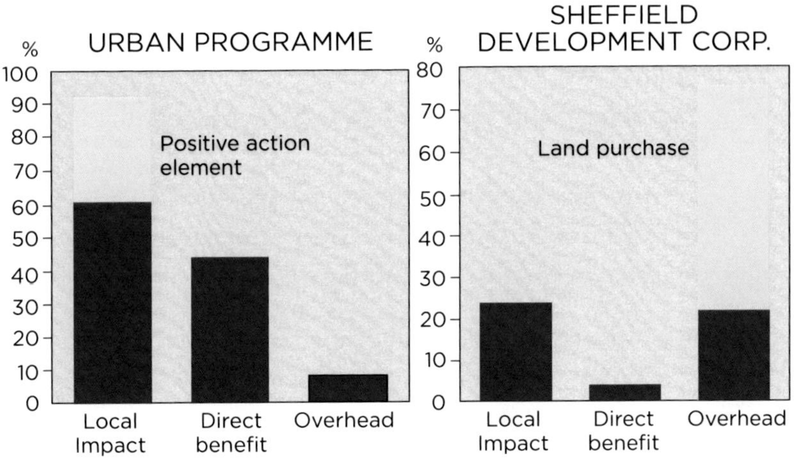

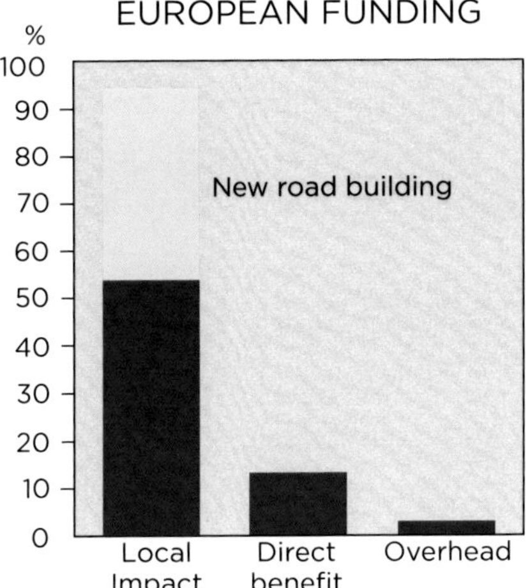

From 'Challenging City Gimmicks', by Jackson, H. (1992). Fabian Review; Vol 104: No. 2.

> specific impact on Sheffield's black community. 4% are targeted at women, and 37% arise out of bids from the voluntary sector, under community management.
>
> Moreover there is always a substantial list of valuable projects in the reserve list, such as a technology transfer centre, community centres to offer advice and child care, culture and leisure industry developments, further phases of Afro-Caribbean and Pakistan enterprise centres, and further resources for small firm assistance or city centre environmental improvements. The Urban Programme therefore could easily and usefully deliver an increase in funding.

South Yorkshire was designated an 'Integrated Development Area' by the European Community in 1988. DEED appointed an officer with special responsibility for European funds to help find ways of securing the continuation of our projects. EC funds covering up to 50% of the overall costs, were used to maintain many of the local authority positive action initiatives already described to improve job and training opportunities for women and ethnic minority communities. Indeed projects with clearly defined social as well as economic objectives fitted well with European criteria.

The least effective (see chart) was the Urban Development Corporation model.

Joint Authority Work

As described earlier, the rate-capping legislation brought like-minded authorities together. Sheffield's initiative in calling them together had been pivotal. With the notable exception of the GLC and some of the London boroughs, the voice of local government as expressed by the Council leaders was essentially male. Pat Hollis,[13] the leader of Norwich City Council, stood out.

> Patricia Hollis was one of the greats in Labour politics. A brilliant intellect combined with charm and a keen political mind meant she was a wonderful local council leader, a fine minister, and an outstanding member of the House of Lords.[14]

Pat Hollis

Aspiration to equal opportunities for women and ethnic minority communities characterised left wing Councils, but not always as a top priority. Most significant was the role played consistently by the GLC, which had championed and taken pride in breaking new ground in economic development with a social purpose. Now they had been abolished it was important to collaborate more closely with all local authorities to argue the case for public

---

13. Patricia Hollis (1941-2018), author of *Ladies Elect – Women in Local Government, 1865-1914*, which she dedicated to 'Mabel Clarkson, Norwich's first women councillor and all the women councillors who have followed her'. It is one of the most comprehensive historical studies of women in public life.

14. Lady Hollis of Heigham obituary. *The Guardian*, 18.10.2018.

sector-led economic and social development, because we knew it could work.

Joint authority partnership working was the main means of integrating the work of local government. The Association of Metropolitan Authorities (AMA) was set up as part of local government reorganisation in 1974.[15] Dominated by large urban and regional conurbations mainly under Labour control, this body was vocal in its opposition to the Thatcher government, but could not claim to represent local government as a whole since the Association of County Councils (ACC) was mainly made up of Tory controlled authorities, and District councils had their own Association, the ADC.[16]

We have seen in the previous chapter how the Local Government Information Unit (LGIU), initially funded largely from the GLC, and was able to work and campaign at a national level with greater independence. It was based in London.

One of its plans was to establish another joint body focused sharply on local government's role in delivering social and economic regeneration, using the lessons learnt through the publication of the *London Industrial Strategy*[17] completed days before the GLC's abolition came into effect. This led to the formation of a Centre for Local Economic Strategies (CLES) in 1986. The five key proponents of the body were, besides David Blunkett from Sheffield and Graham Stringer the Leader of Manchester City Council, Mike Ward and Ken Livingstone from

---

15. See Chapter 2.

16. The three groups were amalgamated into the Association of Local Authorities – ALA – in 1997.

17. Cf Robin Murray and Michael Ward, see page 199.

the GLC, Geoff Edge of the West Midlands, and Keva Coombes of Merseyside, all three of which faced imminent abolition. Its initial funding came mainly from winding-up money from the GLC and other Regional authorities, enhanced by contributions from other local authorities keen to back the initiative.

After considerable discussion it was agreed to base CLES outside London to have a stronger north/south voice. Graham Stringer, the Leader of Manchester City Council, agreed to host its offices. This was a significant decision. It gave this new body, CLES, specificity and a degree of authenticity. Northern industrial cities were experiencing similar problems of unemployment, dereliction and poverty. From its base in Manchester CLES generated and encompassed a different, wider agenda than the Greater London Council, whilst retaining the GLC's comprehensive social agenda in all its work. Michael Ward was its first Chair and I his deputy. We appointed as its first Director two women as a job sharing arrangement, Marjorie Mayo[18] and Irene Bruegel,[19] both from London. CLES had its office close to Manchester city centre and Town Hall, and developed an action-based research focus using evidence from local authority members across the UK to develop policy, publish reports and arrange joint authority events on different industrial and social aspects of the labour market. Along with the staff we tried to keep alive the inspiration around municipal enterprise in its widest sense.

CLES grew rapidly. A year later Michael Ward took over as Director, and I became its Chair. It was welcomed by regional and

18. Marjorie Mayo, Emeritus Professor of Community Development at Goldsmiths University. Specialist in Learning for Citizenship.

19. Irene Bruegel (1945-2008), South Bank University, becoming Professor of Urban Policy in 2000. She retired in December 2006.

city authorities alike, bringing in St Helens, Liverpool, Hull, North Tyneside, Norwich, Sandwell, Harlow, Thameside (Swindon) and Glasgow to name a few. Through its work, local authorities of many political persuasions could gain support and publicity, despite the financial cuts they were experiencing across the board that made it harder to celebrate and exemplify how implementing economic development projects in a way that maximised social benefits for women, the unemployed and those living in poor communities was crucial both to their success and popularity. John Shutt[20] moved from leading the municipal enterprise team at Sheffield to work for CLES. He recently described how:

> It sought to respond to key changes in the labour market, and the rise of new sectors in the economy, promoting the importance of the local authority role in setting out the case for locally based and regional strategies, soundly researched often with national and European or international initiatives to combat industrial change.
>
> It recognised that the national and international economy was changing away from manufacturing towards new sectors, including the cultural industries, well exemplified in Sheffield, and the green economy.
>
> Early reports included work on the Poll Tax and its impact for local authorities, with a conference in Glasgow; work on Urban Development Corporations, led by Bob Colenutt[21] and funded

---

20. John Shutt, Professor at Leeds Metropolitan University and now at Northumbria University.

21. Involved with the Docklands development area.

> by five local authorities: Sheffield City Council, South Glamorgan County Council, Sandwell MBC, Avon County Council and North Tyneside MBC; Training and Enterprise Councils; local authorities and Energy Planning;
>
> Over the years it adapted and survived, and still plays a key role in debates about the future of local and regional economies, showing them working together to challenge central government and pioneer new forms of economic intervention to guide and change their local economies and challenge inequalities.

CLES was quick to recognise the importance of building links with Brussels. An interesting transport related project entitled the 'Green Links to Europe' had support from Dublin City Council and Bremen in northern Germany as well as Lancashire, Liverpool, Wakefield, Humberside, Hull and Great Grimsby. It recommended re-opening the Woodhead tunnel for rail freight between Sheffield and Manchester and had encouragement from John Prescott MP. Their website[22] now boasts of *over 300 publications spanning 40 years of research.*

Other joint local government groupings included one focused on Combined Heat and Power, which promoted Alf Meade's contribution to that debate. Another, mentioned previously, which generated detailed discussion in the 'Joint Works Group' in the early eighties and continued into these later years of 'partnership', was the 'Homes and Jobs' campaign.[23]

---

22. www.cles.org

23. See Chapter 6.

Both the GLC and Sheffield had developed significant Contract Compliance reforms which influenced how public sector purchasing power could be used to promote its policies of employment creation, equal opportunities and training. GLC put a number of gender related clauses into their contract conditions, whilst Sheffield initiated those on safe working practices. Funded by the two big construction trade unions, UCATT through its general secretary George Brumwell, and T&GWU through its senior officer Jack Dromey, and supported with a secretariat from the National Tenants Federation, Marianne Hood[24] and a number of local authorities, a national 'Homes and Jobs' campaigning organisation was created, which I chaired. It operated at a national level in pursuit of the principles of better housing, more consultation with tenants, high levels of training including support for women in manual trades, and safer working practices in the construction industry. Marianne, myself as a city councillor and Ann Stewart, active in the tenants' movement in Birmingham, were key activists, lobbying through publicity and meetings at national TU and political conferences.

24. She remained the organiser of a tenants' movement, renamed Tenants Participation and Advisory Service (TPAS).

Yet another grouping was linked to the Campaign for Nuclear Disarmament (CND), promoting Nuclear-Free Cities, founded in Manchester and similar to more recent groups campaigning for Cities of Sanctuary recognising the plight of refugees in which Sheffield has maintained its reputation for being in the lead.

Joint partnership work with other local authorities was inspiring as I met new people from around the country, where there was a common political agenda. I travelled to and from Manchester frustrated at the centuries of failure to link up better the industrial areas to the east and west of the Pennines. Sheffield took leading positions in these organisations and helped strengthen the defence against the legislative assault, as well as being a powerful lobby within the national Labour Party's policy-making groups and conferences. John Prescott was a promoter of decentralisation to local and regional authorities, and a supporter of CLES. He convened a group which included local authority members as he put together his thoughts, presenting local authority projects as pilots in developing future national policy on Housing, Transport, Energy, Gender and Race.[25]

In Sheffield we welcomed Jo Richardson MP[26] to open the women's joinery workshop, at Shirecliffe F.E. College, promoting it as an excellent example of what could be done.

---

25. Published in 1996, *Renewing the Regions* recommended the creation of a network of Regional Development Agencies, or RDAs, which would bring together local authorities, voluntary organisations and businesses to work in partnership on regional economic strategy and regeneration.

26. Jo Richardson,1923-1994. She was a central figure of the feminist left and helped to expand women's rights in Britain (Wilson, E. 'Feminist Fundamentalism: The Shifting Politics of Sex and Censorship'. In Segal, L. and McIntosh, M. (1992). *Sex Exposed: Sexuality and the Pornography Debate*. Virago.)

Finally, the Council was reluctant to abandon its international twinning links because of financial cuts. By the late eighties these included steel industry cities in Germany (Bochum); China (Anshan, a huge steel producing city in Liaoning province, three times the size of Sheffield); Russia (Donetsk, then in the Soviet Union now in Ukraine), Esteli (Nicaragua), and in Kenya an educational project. The Chamber of Commerce enjoyed participating in these visits, and stepped in to fund the large joint delegation to China in 1990.

Later Eighties

The Politics of Partnership changed me and my politics. I found myself again, as in 1981/2, working in a largely male environment, not the Works Department this time but Sheffield's private sector. I am more conscious now than I was at the time that I was often the only woman closely involved. Six years later I was better equipped quickly to recognise male colleagues with whom I felt that I was treated as an equal, listened to with respect and with whom I could debate and discuss issues fully. For example, I never had the impression that Norman Adsetts found it in any way awkward working with a woman. Another good example was our work on 'Homes and Jobs' and the construction industry with George Brumwell of UCATT or Jack Dromey of TGWU. As a member of the Lower Don Valley Urban Development Corporation however, I always felt my opinions were received with some disdain, because my colleagues assumed I would not understand much about business, land-use, finance, or golf. I had to insert the word 'social' as well as 'economic' before 'benefit' into their draft papers, and patiently explain why. Suggestions for 'positive action', poverty or equality impact monitoring might be greeted with a smile, but not taken seriously. They understood why women's training opportunities benefitted the individual, but had no belief that this would also bring new life and skills to the economy, individual companies and the labour market generally. I was one of two Council representatives along with David Skinner, who had chaired the Planning Committee and was now in the process of changing career.[27]

The Employment Department with its 60:40 gender balance in favour of women, driven by equality policies and a friendly culture was both my office and comfort zone. I was one of two women as I travelled to China with the twenty strong Chamber of Commerce sponsored visit in 1990. Seeing steam railway engines still at work in the goods yards of Anshan steel works, together with coal-fired furnaces creating smoke-filled skies, was a shock. We had meetings with a number of Chinese women in senior positions in their delegations, and I remember a conversation with one of our hosts as she explained how the one child policy was not necessarily bad for women, since she valued her high education and her precious daughter, but had time to build her own career in industry. As in Nicaragua, I was reminded that the participation of women in society, the labour market and politics has a hugely diverse international dimension.

Life at home in Grenoside was different. The Chilean families had moved on. Our older two children had left for University. My parents, born 1901 and 1903, needed increasing support. They moved in with us in 1985. We had a small lift and additional toilet installed to enable them to live in self-contained accommodation upstairs. I was approaching 50. I shelved earlier thoughts I had

---

27. See page 124.

entertained of shifting into a different profession like accountancy or law, and automatically took on a role of being my parents' main carer – I was, after all, the only daughter in our family.

Keith and I had less time together. He had worked at Northern College for ten years when a job came up as Principal of Fircroft adult education residential college in Birmingham. He was duly appointed to start the following year in 1988. This time I didn't go with him. I was caring for my parents and engrossed in political work in Sheffield and around the country. Our lives were gently moving apart geographically and socially. My father, Stanley Price, died shortly after he and my mother, Kitty, celebrated their diamond wedding on 3rd October 1988. I was at a Labour Party conference in Blackpool at the time and hurried back to comfort my mother. She moved me to tears the following morning as her thoughts went back to her life before Stanley asked her to marry him. She had been trained as one of the early Health Visitor professionals at Battersea Polytechnic, after leaving Croydon High School with very good results shortly after WWI, and set out on a brief working career in Bishop Auckland. It was as if she was asking me, her daughter, what to do with her life now he was no longer there. Who to care for next had been central to her existence. She was a woman, and for her caring lay at the root of women's work. In her fifties, with her sons no longer at home, she had returned to paid work as a health visitor. I was aware of the struggle she had to persuade the health authorities in Hertfordshire that her training and qualification from the 1920s together with her volunteering in the community and during the war years, and as President of the Yorkshire WI (Womens Institute), were sufficient to qualify her to be appointed. These working years, though short, as my father returned to a new job back in Yorkshire had given her purpose and satisfaction. Kitty then got a place at Leeds College of Art to develop her new interest and enjoyed many years painting, looking after Stanley as he moved into retirement, and taking a huge interest in their growing number of grandchildren.

Without Stanley, her dementia worsened and she died on 19th February 1991, in a residential home. I lived with a guilt I still feel that I continued my work and political activities rather than caring for her to the end, full-time at home. I was, like so many people – most of them women – experiencing quietly that it is hard and often impossible to work both inside and outside the home. These changes in my personal life sharpened my rapidly increasing gender awareness. I felt myself to be a more mature and independent woman living on my own, with a stimulating and purposeful work agenda and a range of political colleagues around the country. I was driven increasingly to analyse political and financial issues with a women's focus and started to believe in myself as a feminist.

Around this time our Member of Parliament, Martin Flannery, announced that he had decided to retire at the next election. He had never felt very comfortable with additions of the towns of Chapeltown and Stocksbridge and the villages in between to the new Hillsborough constituency in 1983.

One day at a constituency event, we were chatting about his retirement and who might replace him, when Sylvia Parry, a Labour Party member from Stocksbridge, said to me *'Well I don't know why you aren't standing, Helen. You've got the experience and we could do with a woman candidate!'* I explained to her that I was well turned fifty, laughed, and replied that I had never considered it myself. *'Well, that's what I think'*, she answered, somewhat brusquely. At home I thought about her suggestion and my response. The following week, back at the town hall in the members' room I casually mentioned the possibility of putting my name forward to a group of younger male colleagues, who were members of the employment committee, chatting over a cup of coffee. I remember vividly their shocked silence and then their horrified response: *'But we never realised Helen that you were interested!'* I had clearly interrupted their conversation about the same issue. Why ever not, I kept thinking. Then of course realised it was because I was a woman. Also that it was because I was a woman I had taken so long even to consider the possibility of becoming an MP. My brother had been elected to Parliament many years before, why on earth had I never considered it.[28] Again, it was because I was a woman that even close friends and colleagues in the spring bank holiday camping crowd had never suggested it. In particular I realised that I had not been considered for the very reason that Hillsborough was considered to be a safe Labour seat, and therefore very desirable, despite the slim majority of 1,546 won by Flannery in 1983.

My brother, Christopher Price, MP for Birmingham Perry Barr and later Lewisham West.

28. Christopher Price (1932-2015), Member of Parliament for Perry Bar in Birmingham from 1966-1970, and Parliamentary Private Secretary to Tony Crosland. He returned to Parliament as MP for Lewisham West from 1974-83 and became Chair of the Education Select Committee.

Once I had decided to stand as a candidate for selection, and let members in the constituency know, I found I had more support than I thought and a lot more determination to win within me than I had expected. A dour working class Scot from Dundee, Charlie McDonald, a science lecturer at the University, offered to organise my campaign. He was assiduous in keeping a record of every single member's voting intentions and came to all my meetings. He, along with Angela his wife and their three young children, were a massive help. Keith and the family were very supportive, although not around at home, and my mother would give me a knowing smile of encouragement from her life in the care home that she knew what I was up to and wished me well.

I was late in making the decision and found that others, including Clive Betts, were also keen to stand in one of the safe Sheffield seats. One of the young councillors I had interrupted in the members' room that day, also lived in the constituency and had high hopes. He was backed by Martin Flannery. Clive transferred his campaigning to Attercliffe constituency. I embarked on the gruelling programme of speaking at each branch Labour Party and trade union meetings to get as many nominations as I could. My opponent cleverly brought along a crowd of his supporters to the constituency women's branch meeting, so I lost that nomination. However, word got around and it was generally considered to have been 'foul play' on his part. I decided with Charlie's and others' advice, not to go on too much about being a woman in the text of my statement in order not to antagonise the majority of members who were men. I relied on my picture and my personal presence to emphasise I was a women, and drafted (and practised) my speech so that my political beliefs in fairness, equality and grass roots involvement were clearly spelt out and hoped that my reputation in the city would help. I was delighted to receive a letter of encouragement from Jo Richardson. My political work with tenants and workers in the Homes and Jobs campaign also meant I had the enthusiastic support of local UCATT members, and, to the surprise of many, the Sheffield T&GWU. I squeaked through the final constituency selection meeting with just less than 51% of the final vote.

The actual election was simple and enjoyable after all that. My political platform centred around the slogan 'Hillsborough – Clean, Green and Safe'. We designed a small exhibition and presentation, and I travelled around the community centres in the constituency able to meet many community activists, mostly women, who were not scared off by the formality of a party political hustings meeting. I met some other first-time women candidates during the campaign, at training meetings organised by the national Party, but only found out after the election that of 138 women candidates fielded, 37 were elected, 14 of whom were standing for the first time. Only two of us, Rachel Squires from 'Dunfermline West' in Scotland and myself had managed to get ourselves selected to fight a Labour-held seat. The other 12 had been 'Labour gains' in key seats. A Labour Party analysis of *The General Election and Women*, dated June 1st 1992, noted that:

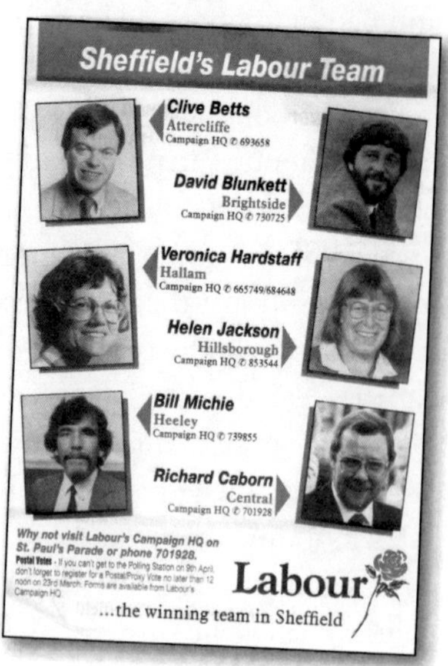

My election leaflet from 1992.

The author in typical countryside of Hillsborough Constituency.

> Generally women candidates did better than male candidates. The average swing to Labour in all seats was 2.09%, whereas in seats with a woman candidate it was 2.7%. In key seats the average swing to Labour was 3.55%, [note: roughly the same as mine] with a woman candidate 4%.

The same document concluded that *'had a swing of 3% been a nationwide average, Labour would have won the election'*. Therefore:

> An appeal to women voters must be central to all our campaigning activities. This work must be consistent over the lifetime of the Parliament.'

The scene was set for all women shortlists and quotas, approved by the Labour Party conference in 1993.

CHAPTER 10

The Way Forward

My conclusions look to the future not the past. They relate to topical themes and lessons from this study, what worked well in delivering change in a local democracy and what did not. At their core is my aim of suggesting how to bring social benefit, including greater equality and peaceful outcomes into economic, financial, and budgeting policies, relevant to women and men of various political outlooks and cultures internationally. They take on more urgency as the world looks forward warily to a future potentially more frightening because of climate change and the coronavirus health pandemic.

Global Solutions to Meet Global Needs

History is best understood within a context of international movements and comparators, an approach I have tried to apply in this study. The emergence of 'Me Too' within feminist thinking, and Black Lives Matter have added to climate and health in putting big issues that affect all our futures on the international agenda, helped by social media and new technology that is revolutionising the speed of communication.

From 1972-1992 devolution of powers to local and regional government, following the Redcliffe Maud report, was followed by years of increasing centralisation after 1986. Aside from devolution of considerable powers and some independence under the Blair government, to Scotland, Wales and Northern Ireland, this has never been reversed for English local government. As this book describes, European funding was a useful boost for positive action projects, whether through political education in Northern Ireland or local training programmes in South Yorkshire, which fitted well with its objectives. As local financial autonomy in the public sector was curtailed and metropolitan regional authorities abolished, it was noticeably harder to benefit from international funding streams such as the European Social Fund (ESF) or European Regional Development Fund (ERDF) compared, for example, with Germany, where regional authorities were much stronger. Once management and prioritisation of regeneration funding was more centrally controlled, its flexibility was weakened. It became more focused on remedial work to physical infrastructure than on supporting people and thereby less cost effective in terms of social need. It remains to be seen what effect leaving the European Union may have on income and wealth inequality in the UK. It appears that, for example and for the same reasons, Germany's handling of measures to alleviate the Covid pandemic has led to a lower death rate than in Britain.

This is a good time to call into question the whole basis of national identity based on borders and nation-to-nation trading and other deals, in favour of a changing hierarchy that encourages diverse regions to collaborate across national borders to use resources from a range of international regional bodies such as the European Union and the United Nations, or the Bretton Woods institutions and other finance bodies such as regional development banks.

Five years into this current study, in 1975, the United Nations called its first world conference on the status of women in Mexico. Twenty years later in 1995, the fourth UN Status of Women conference was held in China. The resulting Beijing Declaration and 'Platform for Action' was adopted unanimously by 189 countries. It did three things: exposed gender inequalities statistically; set strategic objectives; and, most important, put forward a platform of actions for the advancement of women and achievement of gender equality in twelve critical areas. The atmosphere was positive and assumed progress was inevitable. Twenty five years later the goals have not been met. Experience of gender inequality is prevalent across cultures and national boundaries; Beijing assumptions about the inevitability of progress may have encouraged complacency. However, the scale of the global data about the unequal status of women set out in the Beijing Platform for Action is itself recognition that fairness is the right way forward for the world in each of these areas of unequal treatment.

New ideas are coming to the fore from the United Nations which are designed to operate through regional and local bodies as well as the national state. For example, the United Nations Capital Development Fund (UNCDF) has demonstrated that chaneling aid money (which is relatively small in relation to the global economy)[1] achieves better value for money in terms of building peace, reducing poverty and working towards

1. Overseas development assistance accounts for less than $200bn in an overall global economy of $trillions. For a review see: *Staying the Course. 25 Years of Local Development Finance at United Nations Capital Development Fund.* UNCDF, 2021 (forthcoming). For an example with regards to the Covid Pandemic see: *Covid 19 Emergency Response – Local Government Finance Guidance Note for Immediate Action.* UNCDF 2020 https://www.uncdf.org/article/5477/guidance-note-covid19-local-governments.

environmental sustainability, when managed through city mayors or regional bodies than through the more traditional route of national governments or NGOs. In addition this route is more likely to enable scale up and replication by national institutions and avoids the risk of the initiative drying up once the external financing ends. Its research suggests that because local or regional government is more accustomed to operating through communities it can lead to a more sustainable environment for change, in part by including the positive role played by women.

This was something we heard frequently when I was in Parliament and involved with the cross party South Africa and Africa Parliamentary groups of MPs. In November 2004 I helped put together a submission entitled *Gender, African Development and the Commission for Africa...*

> The following suggestions place gender at the centre of African development. This does not imply that development initiatives should exclusively target women; rather that women face an overwhelming burden as a direct result of their gender, and that an improvement in women's lives and increased participation in public life would result in the improved livelihoods of women, men, and children.
>
> The submission mentioned five areas where solutions to problems can be found and better delivered by careful attention to gender: *Local Democracy and Good Governance*; *Women, Violence and Conflict*; *Health; Local Economies and Trade*; *Education*. These are issues which we feel the Commission for Africa may want to build into the case they make for extra

> support and resources being put into projects that really deliver on the ground.[2]

Data Collection and Monitoring

The Beijing Platform for Action outlines the importance of careful collection of relevant evidence on which to build policy. Isabella Stone's Positive Action Research in 1982[3] is an excellent example of the difference such data can make, the reasons for collecting it and the remedies that can result. Stones' analysis of the effects of gender, race and disability in the workforce helped Sheffield City Council address the 'double discrimination' faced by black and women employees. Its widespread publication of her statistics led to demands for a better deal for low paid workers, and her face to face interviews with low paid women brought about well targeted training opportunities to redress inequality long term. It opened the way for a Low Pay supplement to be agreed with local unions in 1985 and for Sheffield to be the location for a national Low Pay conference in 1986, which endorsed a universal minimum wage that eventually reached the statute book 15 years later in the early years of a Labour government. However, a gender gap still exists in many areas of work, and 35 years later the Fawcett Society still campaigns for open access to all wage rates to expose and reduce its extent.

---

2. Including signatories: Helen Jackson, Vera Baird, Tony Baldry, Hugh Bayley, Anne Brooke, Valerie Davey, Sue Doughty, Julia Drown, Alan Howarth, Beverley Hughes, Baroness Anita Gale, Sally Keebler, Tony Lloyd, Anne McKechin, Julie Morgan, Baroness Lindsay Northover, Sandra Osborne, Ernie Ross, Joan Ruddock, Baroness Glenys Thornton, Jenny Tongue, Baroness Pola Uddin, Baroness Janet Whittaker, Tony Worthington and Derek Wyatt, together with MEPs Glenys Kinnock and Linda McAvan.

3. See note Chapter 5.

Such research, exposed the links between these characteristics upon people's everyday lives. Poverty affects life expectancy and health across communities, as well as educational opportunity and political influence. Everywhere, most adults living below the poverty threshold are women, and in the UK many of these are from Black or Asian households. Data opens the way to reforms across the range of public services to counter the impact of wealth inequality and poverty, but only if their outcomes are monitored,

The UK ten yearly census provides vital comparative data by locality. Local authorities, the NHS and other public authorities are well placed to make use of further data collection in between census years. They have the detailed local knowledge of areas vulnerable to poverty from which to devise and model ways to redress disadvantage. If levels of pay and equality assessments became as normal a feature of annual reports as end of year accounts open to public scrutiny, the true picture of gender and racial disadvantage would be apparent and easier to monitor. Charities, corporations and private sector firms should provide similar data.

Collection, measurement and publication are the first requirements; monitoring is the second, equally essential to assess how successful and effective are measures to redress the severe ill effects of inequality. One-off reports are less useful than regular monitoring. Nationally and locally, government should be urged to work across a range of sectors to share good and bad examples of employment practices and spread new ideas.

Recognising Social Benefit

Strong political backing is required to establish that achieving maximum long term collective benefit for all of society does most for those who have least, but the first requirement is to recognise the role of society itself in creating that collective benefit. Margaret Thatcher raised the stakes against this approach in her 1987 article in *Woman's Own* when she wrote:

> They are casting their problems at society. And, you know there's no such thing as society. There are individual men and women and there are families. And no government can do anything except through people and people must look after themselves first. It is our duty to look after ourselves and then also to look after our neighbours.

Thatcher chose to direct her statement at women, in effect dismissing the previous decade in which legislation by Labour governments to address low pay, gender, disability and racial discrimination reduced the gap between rich and poor to its narrowest since 1945.[4] She used the image of the shopping trolley to emphasise how women make decisions for the family. She ignored those women without enough money to put anything in the trolley and allowed government to deny responsibility for general inequality. She exposed a continuing gulf between political ideology on the left and right still evident today. Forty years ago it explained Thatcher's intense dislike of local government initiative, which exemplified how fairness

4. Thane, P. (2018). *Divided Kingdom: A History of Britain, 1900 to the Present.* Cambridge University Press.

and equal access built in to public projects delivered outcomes that were recognised as effective and popular, even amongst many of her natural allies in business. Echoes of this view still blind the current government to the facts that women rely more than men on public services, including buses, child and social care, libraries, parks, play centres and welfare benefits, and they also form the majority of workers in the public sector and are amongst the lowest paid. Faced with vitriolic opposition rather than backing from national government, the local state in South Yorkshire developed a powerful sense of independence. This study has shown how public sector-led initiatives across a range of policy areas were piloted and implemented. From social care to heating schemes, training and education to low pay, public transport to new technology, they all incorporated positive action towards those with lowest incomes and eased the gender, race and class-based income and wealth gap, which people 'looking after themselves' could not have achieved. Also, the speed and enthusiasm with which these policies were activated would not have been feasible if managed centrally.

Public transport gave this book its title. Today bus passengers come from less well-off families and the majority are women. They gained most from low or free fares. In the 1970s passenger numbers steadily increased, enabling the bus fleet to expand, benefitting more families, widening the labour market, and adding job and training opportunities, while delivering environmental improvements in air quality when vehicles kept to low emission targets.

The fire tragedy at Grenfell Tower in London, costing lives and community security, shone a frightening light on the danger to safety standards of cutting costs. Local action with tenants' associations, many led by women, identified the inconvenience of lift break-downs in tower blocks. Investment in a relatively small team of in-house lift engineers saved money and improved the lives of tenants as well as the quality of the housing stock. The value of funding representatives from working class estates to join a residential course about housing policy with building workers, or an overseas group visit to learn about combined heat and power in Malmö, or to include training and good working conditions in procurement rules, cannot be quantified only in classical economic terms, but must add the wider goal of social benefit. Such initiatives strengthened the links between managers, labour force, and residents which assisted service delivery in ways that saved money and improved their quality. A cost-benefit analysis is hard to calculate, but as described here its extent was clear to those involved.

Another initiative allowed the flexibility to use in-house or contracted out staff enabling it to support new co-operative or small and medium-sized enterprises to boost local employment and training. On this basis the Council responded to a suggestion from the Co-operative Development Group to organise a study visit, including some of the workers in co-operatives, to Mondragon in the Basque country to observe how their regional bank, the 'Caja Laboral', had supported and developed small scale co-operative enterprises in a number of industrial sectors. This book shows how business and the private sector can and will co-operate with expertise in the public sector at a local level with ease, enthusiasm and effectiveness when the goal is collective social benefit.

In 1926, Sheffield, the first Labour controlled authority in Britain, argued that the main reason for using Direct Labour was

Sheffield's City Hall has long been the meeting place for local demonstrations and political marches.

financial; that it saved rate payers money and delivered what the public wanted. The leaders described the City Hall as a *'splendid contribution to Sheffield's city life...'*, which had created 120,000 'man days' of work for men who would otherwise have been in receipt of unemployment benefit, or public assistance relief. In the 1980s the Council was the largest employer in the city, with more than 30,000 on its books. Using Direct Labour made it possible to offer the workforce access to educational leave and in-house training, in order to help the authority boost skills whilst saving services and jobs during uncertain times. Adult education became a means of important investment in employment conditions and personnel support contributing to social benefit. It is time to review how the benefits of using directly employed labour can be brought about by public authorities.

Breaking up corporations through outsourcing, consultancies and sub-contracting makes such in-house benefits impossible, creating job insecurity and zero-hour contracts without sick or holiday pay which hit the low paid hardest. It has become known as the 'gig' economy, so called because a work contract lasts no longer than a 'gig' or night out, saving employers making national insurance contributions to HMRC, but in so doing cutting investment in essential services of health and education. Women and men who clean toilets, streets, make sandwiches or deliver them no longer 'work for the Council or NHS' with the status and security that implies, but do the same essential work often at night on poor or non-existent contracts. Those engaged on the other activities within or around those grandiose buildings do not even know their names, background or potential. They are simply the cleaner, or the caterer, of low status, maybe contracted to work through the internet and unable to identify with any certainty who they work for.

Clarity and Openness – Solidarity

Local public authorities understand the importance of community as a key resource more profoundly than national governments. Their strength relies on three key ingredients. First, conveying with clarity the goals the authority is trying to achieve; second, a belief in community development, which welcomes their representatives into discussions about how to do this most effectively; and third, openness in sharing goals with the wider public, through the media, print and social, through adult education and public meetings. As Sheffield's new leader, David Blunkett brought clarity into the message that a fair and equal society was the goal. He called for every employee of the city council, from cleaners and manual workers to white-collar and salaried officers, to be ambassadors for its reforms.

There were echoes of the post-war government in the way officers as well as elected members and employees joined in the mission. South Yorkshire's Labour movement, trade unions and Labour Party organised collectively as a body and consistently won secure majorities. The movement had an international dimension, which widened its vision, scale and positivity. It believed it could rid the world of unfairness, brutality, wars and *'Give peace a chance'* as John Lennon sang.[5] It delivered energy to socialising and campaigning, bringing friendship and kindness into activities which gave politics a very human face. This helped it avoid disruption by splinter groups such as the SDP on the one hand or Militant on the other because unity was paramount. Due to 'living our politics', a factor often under-estimated in winning elections, voters became supportive.

A constant theme of this book has been the role of senior paid officers, newly recruited to the authority, who understood, following the manner of their appointments, that their backing came with requirements to share a commitment to its goals. Complaints from opposition parties about the closeness between newly appointed officers and the trade union and Labour movement fell on deaf ears amongst the general public, and only served to add clarity to the council's programme and increase its popularity. People could see what they had voted for being turned into action. It is hard to imagine how South Yorkshire's buses could have been managed successfully by believers in competition between bus companies looking to profit from free market

5. John Lennon was murdered in New York on 8th December 1980.

deregulation. Voters notice hypocrisy quickly; those who argue for comprehensives and send their children to public school; public transport executives who never ride on a bus or train; health experts who celebrate the NHS but use private health care; government advisers who make rules against travel during the pandemic, but don't abide by them.

Paid officers at local and national level try to draw a distinction between their role and that of elected members stating, *'You determine the policy but leave us to manage the detail of carrying it out'*. The television series *Yes, Minister* cleverly spelt out the reality and contradictions that can follow. Politicians need to take note of operational detail if they intend to transform the culture of an institution. They are, therefore, likely to have more regard for officials who value their political goals. Consistency of message is assured, which as we have seen through the recent pandemic increases public trust in democracy. Despite senior public servants' desire to guard their political neutrality and capacity to ask awkward questions of ideologically driven politicians, they should not be excluded from making their political allegiances clear. Academics and researchers are needed to deliver political change and programmes for action, as this book makes clear and government, whether local or national, should not be deprived of their essential expertise. Maybe the deeper problem for those committed to transformational change designed to deliver a more equal society is that many professional groups are insufficiently aware of their own class, gender or racial bias, which can limit their understanding of the need for change. Greater openness about this issue is desirable.

Opening up policy making and manifestos to institutions and individuals outside a tight party political establishment enriched the process of policy development in Sheffield which Howard Capelin found 'liberating'. The call to build equality into the work and evaluation of every department went to all employees and since women and ethnic minority residents made up the majority of lower paid staff, councillors and senior officers alike, men as well as women, became more aware of how class, gender and race inequality were closely linked. A political outcome is that building such awareness throws the spotlight on the importance of whole communities, so that when discussing urgent issues, such as the job losses then, or the health crisis now, policy makers better recognise gender, disability and race in their deliberations. Providing training opportunities for women always raises wider issues about childcare and care of the old and vulnerable. It stimulated the creation of a city-wide Health Care strategy group. It remains an important means of mainstreaming equality into every policy area.

Lifelong Education

Education is not just for children. There is an urgent need to reinstate the right to lifelong access to education and training in this fast-moving world of new communication technology. The wider meaning of comprehensive education for all, cradle to grave, envisaged by Harold Wilson in the foundation of the Open University, and previously delivered through the trade unions and the Workers' Educational Association (WEA), has international relevance. If gender equality is ever to become central to socialism, men like Edward Carpenter, George Caborn, Bill Owen or Rodney Bickerstaffe, who may not have called themselves feminists, should be recognised as such, since they supported gender equality, and had the courage to challenge established norms to enable women to have rights to education, over their bodies, and to property ownership, universal suffrage, and equal pay. A feminist message is especially effective when it has vocal backing from men. This book outlines how adult education targeted at women, lifted levels of literacy in Nicaragua; how, sponsored by the ANC, it raised the status of women in the townships of South Africa;[6] how European funding of adult education played an important role in boosting the confidence of women in Northern Ireland's sectarian communities enabling them to play a major part in bringing peace and reconciliation in the Peace Process. It is an underestimated influence upon securing a more peaceful society after conflict or crisis.

South Yorkshire was fortunate to have Northern College, the residential college opened to students in 1978 with a 50:50 gender balance of students written into its founding constitution. There was a crèche and bedrooms were redesigned so that students' children could stay overnight. The short course programme was used by immigrant communities across South Yorkshire; by tenants to develop women's participation in community leadership; by the unemployed and in Sheffield's paid educational leave programme for council employees. It became a crucial resource for women in the pit communities during the miners' strike. It gave all short course students curricula geared to their work experience, and the period of residence stimulated aspiration to join long course programmes that could lead to further college and university opportunities.

Linking recording and film facilities with training for youngsters, many from black, often Caribbean, communities, developed new talents and boosted jobs in a new industry. Caring needs

---

6. ANC 'Freedom Charter', see page 227.

were recognised when recruiting women students to the new information technology centre, or the furniture making workshop at Shirecliffe Further Education College. Grant aided women's businesses, like Gwenda's Garage, found that they could combine their business roles with car repair training for women in the community. Adult education should be seen as crucial investment in social benefit. In the UK generally access is in danger of becoming an optional extra only for the middle class who can afford significant fees. It needs new champions to make it an essential part of any well-defined policy to redress inequality in poorer communities.

Work, Welfare and a Caring Economy

The theme of work and its significance in people's lives runs through the twenty years of this study. The dramatic rise in unemployment due to steel and engineering plant closure mainly affected men, who saw work as their purpose in life, essential to feed their families, and often felt ashamed to be out of work. Many of the public shared this view. Books and films have described this vividly, including *The Full Monty* (1997) described earlier (Chapter 6), and the films of Ken Loach throughout his career. The Department of Work and Pensions, which also covers social security and benefits for those not in work, describes a full-time job as being the main route out of poverty. However, it relies basically on male definitions of work and implies that part-timers, mostly female, are not really seen as having a proper job. It also overlooks how much full-time work is underpaid and insecure in the 'gig economy', causing, not eliminating, poverty. This approach allows DWP to measure unemployment rates in full-time equivalents, rather than people. This book describes the difference that can make. Despite the Labour government giving part-time workers equal rights with full timers in 2000, they are still often passed over for promotion, and although their income is equally important for the family budget, they often need additional time to manage other work like childcare or other family care, commonly unpaid.[7] This largely explains why the gender pay gap increases with age. Gender pay differentials for young men and women as they graduate scarcely exist, but then widens steadily throughout their working lives and into retirement.[8] The Women's Budget Group have recently pointed out that investment in care can create many more jobs than an equivalent investment in roads or construction, and they argue that care should lie at the heart of economic decision making.[9] Time off to care for sick children or elderly relatives reduces family income, adding to stress. The Covid crisis has rightly forced on the public more recognition of the key importance of carers whether in the home, care homes, or hospitals as key workers, which emphasizes the need to give greater recognition to caring roles in all settings.

Challenging work stereotypes exposes other roots of pay and status inequality explored here. The Gwenda's Garage story showed how training for girls and women lifted their expectations and job opportunities. It demonstrates how opening up new opportunities for men and women to retrain in all areas of the labour market leads to greater recognition of the breadth of the social and economic value of work across race, disability and gender groups. The days of piano-tuning as the only work option for the blind;

---

7. See chart and quote from Isabella Stone, page 131.

8. John Hills CBE, Professor of Social History at London School of Economics. Equality Report, 2009.

9. *Towards a Caring Economy,* October 2020.

skilled apprenticeships for the boys; nursing or hairdressing for the girls could be over, but there is still a long way to go. For example, the need for more house building to relieve homelessness is a stated objective of all political parties. The question of how to train more construction workers is raised but encouraging girls and women into construction work is seldom mentioned. Equally important is the need to encourage boys and men into caring professions like nursing, cleaning and teaching, but this also is seldom discussed.

Redefining the meaning of work takes us further down the road of economic modelling and helps identify how to encourage a care-based economy. Local action offers opportunities for fundamental change. I've described how the injection of limited capital and revenue investment enabled an excellent model of community based social care to be developed which brought together health and local authority services and sheltered housing. Constant monitoring by a relatively small body of staff measured the impact and brought new ideas into the project.

Successive governments have committed themselves to achieving the best system of social care, without following it up with action. During the pandemic central government failed to integrate environmental and public health staff, charities and local business. Lives were lost as central government tried to direct logistics from the centre, building temporary hospitals, and outsourcing mass testing at great expense to taxpayers without the investment in community based, primary and family care. It was a recipe for chaos, as was regularly pointed out at the time. Analysing the impact of the crisis upon the number of people in poverty, linked to gender, race, and disability, will help address some of these mistakes, as will the pressing need to pull together the full range of health and welfare institutions into a reforming model for Social Care.

More research using local, nationwide and Europe-wide examples will help. Other reports have shown that the political task is to pay far more attention to the socio-economic value of all forms of work.[10] In particular the work of caring, in any setting, demands proper recognition, pay, and training. Presenting successful local initiatives for wider consideration forms the basic story of this book, because reform devised at local rather than national level can be assessed and implemented with greater speed. The time is right, following the Covid-19 pandemic, to use initiatives at local level but include the NHS, local authorities and other relevant charities to resolve the crisis in social care. Positive results would be popular. Urgency is required if the old and frail and their loved ones are to avoid their latter years being dogged by constant worry.

These are big issues of global significance for the future. An urgency, driven by climate change, has also been highlighted by the coronavirus pandemic, not an obvious local government issue, but one which has been shown to deliver good and possibly better results when managed at a more regional than central government level. This reflects the message delivered constantly throughout this book that what was achieved in the radical days of the 80s was significant because it worked. Significant change requires a recognition that our position in the world is one of global interdependence, effectively lowering the role of national borders. My book has especially focussed on women because, quite simply, they make up 50% of the world population. They are more likely to believe that using diplomacy rather than violent confrontation and co-operation rather than competition, achieve better results in terms of well-being, care, love and social cohesion. So they are worth listening to. This will always require **patience**, **determination and courage**.

10. Grandparenting in Europe, 2013.

In 1866 Millicent Fawcett, aged only 19 helped to organise the collection of 1499 signatures in less than a month – without social media – to be delivered to Parliament by John Stuart Mill. Although this petition was unsuccessful, the Fawcett Society marks the moment as its foundation. They could not have anticipated that it would take 62 years and around 1600 more petitions before women would achieve voting parity in this country through the Equal Franchise Act of 1928. This was just a beginning.

Millicent Fawcett speaking in Hyde Park, 1913, whose statue now joins the men in Parliament Square[11] *and displays the words from a speech she gave in 1920.*

11. The statue by Gillian Wearing, unveiled in 2018, was comissioned by the Fawcett Society under the leadership of Sam Smethers with the support of London Mayor Sadiq Khan.

APPENDIX 1: **SHEFFIELD CITY CENTRE**

(Colours indicate period of construction or redevelopment)

Pre-study

1. Sheffield Cathedral
2. St. Marie's Roman Catholic Cathedral
3. Upper Chapel
4. City Hall
5. Town Hall
6. Central Library
7. Sheffield General Post Office (now an art college)
8. Sheffield Midland Station
9. Cutlers' Hall
10. University of Sheffield
11. Sheffield Polytechnic (now Sheffield Hallam University)
12. Transport House (T&GWU)
13. Bill Owen's bookshop
14. Sheaf and Castle Markets (now demolished)
15. Sheffield Telegraph and Star offices (repurposed)

1970s

16. Pond Street bus station
17. SYPTA Office
18. Common Ground (Women's Print Co-operative)
19. Crucible Theatre
20. AEU Headquarters

1980s

21. MSC Offices
22. Leadmill night club
23. Red Tape Studios
24. Sheffield Independent Film
25. Site Gallery
26. Showroom Cinema and Workstation
27. Science Park, Cooper Bdg
28. SHU Owen Building
29. Hyde Park/Park Hill flats
30. DEED offices, Palatine Chambers
31. SADACCA
32. Aizlewood's Mill
33. Kelham Island Museum.
34. SCCAU (now demolished)
35. Fat Cat public house
36. Globe Works
37. Former NUM Offices
38. Canal Basin redevelopment
39. Steelworker mural
40. Snow's (MONS co-operative)
41. West Street Employment Office (as seen in *The Full Monty*)
42. Womens Technology Training Centre, Tri-tech
43. Midland Bank Head Office (now demolished)

1990s and later

44. Meadowhall Centre
45. Lyceum Theatre
46. Afro-Caribbean Enterprise
47. BBC Radio Sheffield
48. Ponds Forge International Sports Centre
49. Sheffield Arena
50. Don Valley Stadium (now demolished)
51. NCPM (now SHU Students' Union)
52. Women of Steel Statue
53. Winter Garden
54. Millennium Gallery

—O— Supertram

SHALESMOOR
BOWLING GREEN ST.
RUSSELL ST.
ALMA ST.
GIBRALTER STREET
FURNACE HILL
CORPORATION ST.
SPITALFIELDS
River Don
NURSERY STREET
STANLEY STREET
BRIDGE STREET
WICKER
SPITAL HILL
SAVILLE STREET
DEREK DOOLEY WAY
BLONK STREET
VICTORIA QUAYS
Sheffield & Tinsley
Canal Basin
WEST BAR
SCOTLAND STREET
QUEEN ST.
HOLLIS CROFT
TENTER STREET
PARADISE SQ.
BANK ST.
CASTLE ST
EXCHANGE ST
WAINGATE
ANGEL ST.
HARTSHEAD
CAMPO LN
GARDEN STREET
HAWLEY ST.
HIGH STREET
COMMERCIAL ST.
PARK
SQUARE
SHEFFIELD PARKWAY
CHURCH STREET
TRIPPET LANE
ROCKINGHAM STREET
BAILEY LANE
LEOPOLD STREET
FARGATE
FLAT STREET
HYDE
PARK
DUKE STREET
PARK
HILL
WEST STREET
CARVER LN
BALM GREEN
BARKER'S POOL
SURREY ST.
NORFOLK ST.
TUDOR
SQ.
POND STREET
CARVER STREET
ROCKINGHAM LANE
DIVISION ST.
BACK FIELDS
CAMBRIDGE ST.
PEACE
GARDENS
PINSTONE STREET
SOUTH STREET
WELLINGTON STREET
ARUNDEL GATE
HOWARD STREET
SHEAF STREET
SHEFFIELD
MIDLAND STATION
SHEAF
SQ.
TALBOT STREET
FURNIVAL GATE
UNION ST.
CHARLES ST.
PATERNOSTER ROW
NORFOLK ROAD
CHARTER ROW
THE MOOR
FURNIVAL ST.
BROWN ST.
SHREWSBURY ROAD
EYRE STREET
MATILDA STREET
LEADMILL ROAD
SUFFOLK ROAD
LEADMILL ST.
CUMBERLAND STREET
GRANVILLE ROAD
Porter Brook
SHEFFIELD COLLEGE
ST MARY'S ROAD
EDMUND ROAD
River Sheaf
QUEENS ROAD
FARM ROAD
ST. MARY'S
CHURCH

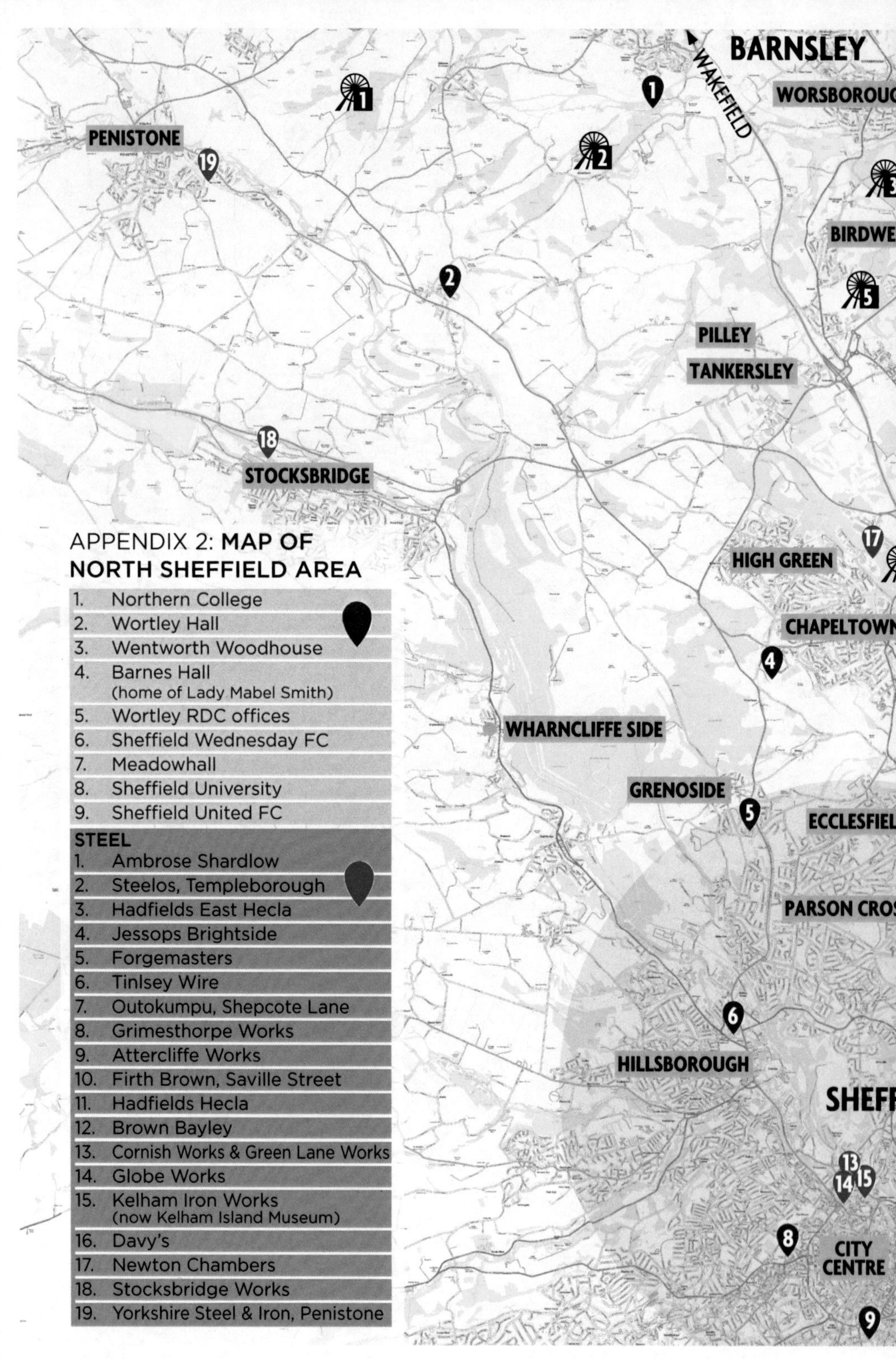
BARNSLEY
WAKEFIELD
WORSBOROUG
PENISTONE
BIRDWE
PILLEY
TANKERSLEY
STOCKSBRIDGE
HIGH GREEN
CHAPELTOWN
WHARNCLIFFE SIDE
GRENOSIDE
ECCLESFIEL
PARSON CROS
HILLSBOROUGH
SHEFF
CITY CENTRE
APPENDIX 2: MAP OF NORTH SHEFFIELD AREA
1. Northern College
2. Wortley Hall
3. Wentworth Woodhouse
4. Barnes Hall (home of Lady Mabel Smith)
5. Wortley RDC offices
6. Sheffield Wednesday FC
7. Meadowhall
8. Sheffield University
9. Sheffield United FC
STEEL
1. Ambrose Shardlow
2. Steelos, Templeborough
3. Hadfields East Hecla
4. Jessops Brightside
5. Forgemasters
6. Tinlsey Wire
7. Outokumpu, Shepcote Lane
8. Grimesthorpe Works
9. Attercliffe Works
10. Firth Brown, Saville Street
11. Hadfields Hecla
12. Brown Bayley
13. Cornish Works & Green Lane Works
14. Globe Works
15. Kelham Iron Works (now Kelham Island Museum)
16. Davy's
17. Newton Chambers
18. Stocksbridge Works
19. Yorkshire Steel & Iron, Penistone

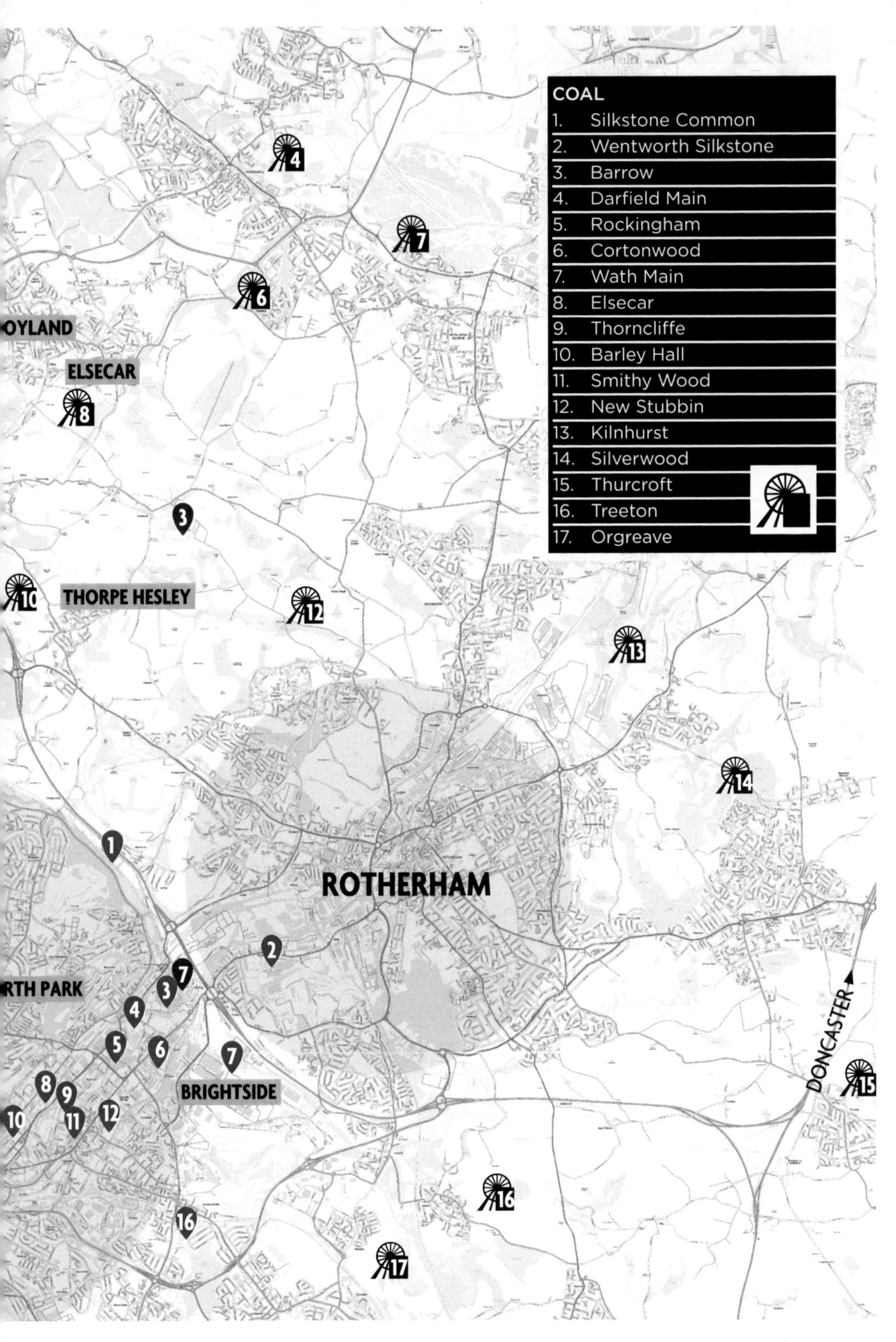
COAL
1. Silkstone Common
2. Wentworth Silkstone
3. Barrow
4. Darfield Main
5. Rockingham
6. Cortonwood
7. Wath Main
8. Elsecar
9. Thorncliffe
10. Barley Hall
11. Smithy Wood
12. New Stubbin
13. Kilnhurst
14. Silverwood
15. Thurcroft
16. Treeton
17. Orgreave
OYLAND
ELSECAR
THORPE HESLEY
ROTHERHAM
RTH PARK
BRIGHTSIDE
DONCASTER

Acronyms

ABI	Area Based Initiatives
ACAS	Advisory Conciliation and Arbitration Service
ACC	Association of County Councils
ACE	Afro-Caribbean Enterprise Centre
ADC	Association of District Councils
AEU	Amalgamated Engineering Union
AIMS	Association for the Improvement of Maternity Services
AMA	Association of Metropolitan Authorities
ANC	African National Congress
ASLEF	Associated Society of Locomotive Engineers and Firemen
ASRS	Amalgamated Society of Railway Servants
ASTMS	Association of Scientific, Technical and Managerial Staffs
BAFTA	British Academy of Film and Television Arts
BME	Black and Minority Ethnic
CBI	Confederation of British Industry
CCC	Coalfield Communities Campaign
CDG	Cooperative Development Group
CHP	Combined Heat and Power
CIIR	Catholic Institute for International Relations
CIQ	Cultural Industries Quarter

CLES	Centre for Local Economic Strategies
CND	Campaign for Nuclear Disarmament
CP	Communist Party
DEED	Department of Employment and Economic Development
DWP	Department of Work and Pensions
EC	European Community (from 1967)
EEC	European Economic Community
EOC	Equal Opportunities Commission
EPSU	Elderly Persons Support Unit
ERDF	European Regional Development Fund
ESF	European Social Fund
FE	Further Education
FSLN	Sandinista National Liberation Front
GLC	Greater London Council
GLEB	Greater London Enterprise Board
GMB	General Municipal and Boilermakers
HMRC	Her Majesty's Revenue and Customs
ISTC	Iron and Steel Trades Confederation
ITEC	Information Technology Training Centre
JNC	Joint Negotiation Committee
LGIU	Local Government Information Unit
MSC	Manpower Services Commission
NACODS	National Association of Colliery Overmen, Deputies and Shotfirers
NALGO	National Association of Local Government Officers
NCB	National Coal Board
NCPM	National Centre for Popular Music
NEC	National Executive Committee of the Labour Party
NF	National Front
NHS	National Health Service

NIWC	Northern Ireland Womens Coalition
NUM	National Union of Mineworkers
NUPE	National Union of Public Employees
NUR	National Union of Railwaymen
NUT	National Union of Teachers
ODA	Overseas Development Assistance
PPS	Parliamentary Private Secretary
PSE	Party of European Socialists
PTA	Passenger Transport Authority
RDC	Rural District Council
SADACCA	Sheffield and District Afro-Caribbean Community Association
SCAR	Sheffield Campaign Against Racism
SCCAU	Sheffield Coordinating Centre against Unemployment
SDP	Social Democratic Party
SERC	Sheffield Economic Regeneration Committee
SYCC	South Yorkshire County Council
SYPTA	South Yorkshire Passenger Transport Authority.
T&GWU	Transport and General Workers Union
TEC	Training and Enterprise Council
TOPS	Training Opportunities Schemes
TUC	Trades Union Congress
UCATT	Union of Construction, Allied Trades and Technicians
UDC	Urban District Council.
UDC	Urban Development Corporation
UNCDF	United Nations Capital Development Fund
UNIFEM	United Nations Women Committee
UN	United Nations
UP	Urban Programme

VAT	Value Added Tax
WAPC	Women Against Pit Closures
WEA	Workers' Educational Association
WEST	Women in Engineering Science and Technology
WINTT	Women in Non-Traditional Trades
WSG	World Student Games
WTTW	Women Technology Training Workshop

References

Adsetts, Sir Norman. 2017. *A Man of Sheffield – The Adsetts Story.*

Anderlini, Sanam Naraghi. 2000. *Women at the Peace Table.* UNIFEM.

Bailey, Catherine. 2008. *Black Diamonds. The Rise and Fall of an English Dynasty.* Penguin.

Ball, Malcolm and Hampton, William. 2004 (Edited). *The Northern College. Twenty-five years of Adult Learning.* NIACE (National Institute of Adult Continuing Education).

Barnsley Women – Women Against Pit Closures. 1985. Vol 2.

Blunkett, David. 1995 (Revised edition 2002). *On A Clear Day. An Autobiography.* Michael O'Mara Books Limited.

Blunkett, David and Jackson, Keith. 1987. *Democracy in Crisis. The Town Halls Respond.* Hogarth Press.

Branson. Noreen. 1979. *Poplarism 1919-1925. George Lansbury and the Councillors Revolt.* Lawrence and Wishart.

Coates, Ken and Barratt Brown, Michael. 1997. *Community under Attack. The Struggle for Survival in the Coalfield Communities of Britain.* Spokesman.

Cornwell, John. 2011. *Voices of Wortley Hall, the Story of Labour's Home 1951-2011.* Wortley Hall Ltd.

Darke, Jane. 1984. Making Space, Women in the Man Made Environment. In: *Matrix.* Taylor, Graham (ed.). Pluto Press.

Docherty, Charles. 1983. *Steel and Steelworkers – The Sons of Vulcan.* Heinemann Educational Books.

Gavin, Jean and Thoms, David. 1983. *Caring and Sharing, The Centenary History of the Co-op Womens Guild.* Co-operative Union,.

Grant, Jane W. 2016. *In the Steps of Exceptional Women, The Story of the Fawcett Society 1866-2017.* Francis Boutle.

Grayson, John. 1991. *Solid Labour. A Short History of the Yorkshire Regional Council of the Labour Party 1941-1991.* Yorkshire Regional Council of the Labour Party.

Greater London Council (Foreword by Michael Ward). 1985. *London Industrial Strategy.* Greater London Council.

Green, Geoff and Blunkett, David. 1987. Ends and Means. *New Soci*ety. Fabian Society.

Harvey, David. 1973. *Social Justice in the City.* Edward Arnold.

Hellewell, Scott D. 1996. *South Yorkshire's Transport 1974-1995.* Venture Publications.

Holderness, Margaret. 1983. *The Changing Role of Women in South Yorkshire 1960-1980.*

Hollis, Patricia. 1987. *Ladies Elect. Women in English Local Government 1865-1914.* Clarendon Press.

Holloway, Michael. 1993. *Portraits of a City Father – Appreciation of the Life of Bill Owen.* Sheffield Hallam University.

Mace, Jane and Yarnitt, Martin (Eds). 1987. *Time Off to Learn, Paid Educational Leave and Low Paid Workers.* Methuen and Co Ltd.

McGregor, Suzanne. 1988. *The Poll Tax and the Enterprise Culture.* CLES.

Melrose, Dianne. 1985. *Nicaragua. The Threat of a Good Example.* OXFAM.

Mendelson, J., Thorne, V., Pollard, S. and Owen, B. 1958. *Sheffield Trades and Labour Council, 1858 to 1958.*

Mowlam, Mo. 2002. *Momentum. The Struggle for Peace, Politics and the People.* Hodder and Stoughton.

Price, David. 2008. *Sheffield Troublemakers – Rebels and Radicals in Sheffield History.* Phillimore and Co Ltd.

Rowbotham, Sheila. 1973. *Womens Consciousness, Mans World.* Penguin.

Rowbotham, Sheila. 1999. *Threads Through Time.* Penguin.

Rowlinson, Alderman E.G. 1982. (Forward by Rt Hon Arthur Greenwood MP. Reprinted with Foreword by David Blunkett, 1982). *Six Years of Labour Rule in Sheffield 1926-1932.*

Seyd, Pat. 1987. *The Rise and Fall of the Labour Left.* Palgrave Macmillan.

Sheffield City Council. 1983. *The Rates Act; Rates, Services and Jobs.* Sheffield City Council.

Sheffield City Council. 1983. *Women in Sheffield.* Series from No 1: In Work out of Work. Sheffield City Council.

Sheffield City Council. 1984. *Sheffield's Health, Could We Care Less? People's Campaign for Health.* Sheffield City Council.

Sheffield City Council. 1986. *Health Care and Disease. A Profile of Sheffield Health Authority.* Sheffield City Council.

Sheffield City Council. 1986. *Putting You in the Picture.* Sheffield City Council.

Sheffield City Council. 1986. *Steel in Crisis.* Sheffield City Council.

Sheffield City Council. 1987. *Good Health for All.* Sheffield City Council.

Sheffield City Council. 1987. *Sheffield: Working it Out. An Outline Employment Plan.* Sheffield City Council.

Sheffield Women against Pit Closures. 1987. *We are Women. We are Strong.*

Sheffield Women against Pit Closures. 2018. *You Can't Kill the Spirit! Houghton Main Pit Camp, the Untold Story of the Women Who Set Up Camp to Stop Pit Closures.* Northern Print Solutions.

Stone, Isabella. 1*984. Positive Action Final Report.* Sheffield City Council.

Stone, Isabella. 1988. *Equal Opportunities in Local Authorities, Developing Effective Strategies for the Implementation of Policies for Women.* HMSO.

Taylor, Graham. 2017. *Ada Salter, Pioneer of Ethical Socialism.* Lawrence and Wishart.

Thane, Pat, 2018. *Divided Kingdom. A History of Britain, 1900 to the Present.* Cambridge University Press.

Todd, Selina. 2014. *The People. The Rise and Fall of the Working Class.* John Murray.

TUC. 1983. *Working Women. A TUC Discussion Book.* TUC.

Index

'A Birds Eye View of Porn' 151
Abortion Act 49
Adsetts, Sir Norman 262, 263
Advanced Metals and Manufacturing Centre 46
Advisory, Conciliation and Arbitration Service (ACAS) 97, 318
African National Congress (ANC) 225, 227, 308, 318
Afro-Caribbean Enterprise (ACE) 195, 314, 318
Agricultural Workers' Union 16
Ahern, Bertie 223
Ahtisaari, Martti 225
Aizlewood's Mill 259, 314
Albaya, Joe 49
Allende, Salvador 13, 85, 88
Alvarez, Bernabe 88
Alvarez, Ester 88, 89
Amalagamated Society of Railway Servants (ASRS) 144, 318
Amalgamated Engineering Union (AEU) 42, 46, 48, 50, 163, 165, 166, 314, 318
Anderlini, Sanam Naraghi 225
Annan Report 175
Anshan 46, 286, 287
Anti-ratecapping Campaign 236
Anti-slavery Society 40, 41
Archives Division 178
Ardron, Rose 68, 69, 151, 179
Area Based Initiatives 274, 318
Area Based Management 155
Arica 86, 89, 90
Arpillera 95
Asquith, Phil 193
Associated Society of Locomotive Engineers and Fireman (ASLEF) 97, 318
Association for the Improvement of Maternity Services (AIMS) 8, 318
Association of County Councils (ACC) 280, 318
Association of Direct Labour Organisations 146
Association of District Councils (ADC) 280, 318
Association of Metropolitan Authorities (AMA) 103, 280, 318
Association of Scientific, Technical and Managerial Staffs (ASTMS) 163, 318
Astor, Lady Nancy 32
A Tale of Two Cities: A Sheffield Project 51
Atkins, Mike 128
Atkins, Sue 64
Audit Commission 237, 247, 248
Autoways 173, 174, 176, 259

Bailey, Catherine 36
Bailey, Roy 120
Baird, Vera 298
Baldry, Tony 298
Ball, Malcolm 214, 215
Banham, Steve 248

Barker's Pool 49, 208
Barnsley 21, 22, 25, 31, 35, 52, 54, 62, 65, 71, 72, 101, 164, 203, 206, 209, 210, 215, 217, 322
Barnsley FE College 101
Barratt Brown, Michael 62, 63, 65
Barton, Joan 15, 17, 50, 104, 120
Barton, Roger 15, 17, 50, 91
Battersea Polytechnic 288
Bayley, Hugh 298
BBC Radio Sheffield 178, 314
Beauchief Abbey 145
Beckett, Margaret 16
Beijing Declaration and 'Platform for Action' 296, 298
Benington, John 126, 129, 159, 161, 167, 170, 196
Benn, Tony 80, 105
Bermondsey 187, 188
Bethlem, Juliana 69
Betts, Clive 16, 18, 23, 51, 101, 259, 267, 291
Bevan, Nye 12
Beveridge, Jeanette 56
Beveridge, William 56
Beyond the Fragments: Feminism and the Making of Socialism 113
Bickerstaffe, Rodney 307
Billings, Rev. Alan 111, 114, 120, 175, 242, 247, 251
Billy Elliott 205
Binfield, Clyde 40
Birkin, Graham 140, 141
Birmingham 39, 40, 146, 148, 260, 261, 284, 288, 290
Bishop Auckland 288
Black Country 39, 275
Black Diamonds 36, 203, 322
Black Lives Matter 294
Blair, Tony 81, 136, 223
Blunkett, David 4, 23, 84, 95, 99, 100, 102, 103, 104, 106, 110, 111, 115, 116, 118, 119, 121, 123, 124, 126, 140, 144, 146, 149, 219, 229, 232, 234, 235, 236, 241, 248, 267, 273, 280, 304, 324
Board of Guardians 204
Bochum 286
Bond, Steve 17, 140
Boston Women's Health Book Collective 68
Bower, Mike 196, 259, 265
Braddock, Jack and Bessie 10
Bradford 22
BRAKE 25
Brassed Off 205
Bretton Woods institutions 295
Brighton 234, 236, 253
Brightside constituency 14, 16, 28, 34, 85, 104, 154
Bristol 146
Brixton 108, 173
Bromley Judgement 30
Brooke, Anne 298
Brown, Colin 28
Bruegel, Irene 281
Brumwell, George 189, 284, 286
Brussels 19, 283
Burngreave 64, 69, 73, 94
Burns, Tom 43
Burrows, George 104, 149
Burslem 146, 247
Bustos Sierra, Felipe 88

Cabaret Voltaire 172
Caborn, George 42, 44, 50, 52, 76, 128, 129, 307
Caborn, Mary 8, 40, 41, 44, 45, 50, 52, 151, 225
Caborn, Richard 43, 44, 45, 46, 81, 157, 165, 166
Caja Laboral 302
Callaghan, James 13
Callow, Flis 211
Campaign for Nuclear Disarmament (CND) 285, 319

Canal Basin 260, 314
Capelin, Howard 107, 307
Capelin, Nicki 107
Caribbean 48, 76, 173, 195, 278, 308, 314, 318, 320
Carlyle, Robert 168
Carolus, Cheryl 226
Carpenter, Edward 41, 49, 307
Carpenter, M. 59
Carrs Lane Chapel 40
Carter, Bill 62
Cartwright, E.S. 57
Castle, Barbara 12, 69, 75, 80, 81
Catholic Institute for International Relations (CIIR) 90, 318
Cattaneo, Peter 168
Central constituency 165, 166
Centre for Local Economic Strategies (CLES) 280, 281, 282, 283, 285, 319
Chamber of Commerce 46, 167, 261, 262, 263, 267, 271, 286, 287
Channel 4 175, 177
Chapeltown 31, 34, 37, 101, 162, 204, 289, 317
Chartist movement 39, 40
Cheap fares 26, 27, 29, 96, 98, 99, 255
Cheetham, Graham 116
Childs, Anna 179, 180
Childs, David 163
Chile Human Rights Campaign 61
Chile Solidarity campaign 88
Chile Solidarity Committee 91
China 44, 45, 46, 286, 287, 296
Cities of Sanctuary 285
City Challenge 274
City Hall 44, 48, 74, 241, 243, 266, 303, 314
City Treasury 135, 137, 274
Civic gospel 40
Clarke, Sheena 68, 69, 70, 71, 130, 137, 156, 179
Clegg, Sir Alec 55
Clemmy, Mary 70
Clinton, Hillary 225
Coalfield Communities Campaign (CCC) 215, 318
Coates, Nigel 178
Cockburn, Cynthia 129
Coleg Harlech 128
Coleman, Pat 172, 178
Colenutt, Bob 282
Collets bookshop 197
Combined Heat and Power (CHP) 190, 191, 192, 283, 302, 318
Common Ground 68, 314
Common Market 23, 78, 79
Communist Party (CP) 45, 48, 49, 80, 210, 319
Community Charge 272
Community Development Project 59, 126
Community Work Apprenticeship 64
Comsat Angels 172
Concepcion 91
Confed 46, 163
Confederation of British Industry (CBI) 79, 271, 318
Connelly, James 49
Cook, Robin 81
Coombes, Keva 281
Cooper Brothers 8
Cooper Building 259
Cooperative Development Group (CDG) 196, 259, 318
Coopers and Lybrand 264, 271, 275
Cornwell, John 22, 23, 24, 50
Corporate Management Unit 110, 117, 123, 124, 125
Council for World Citizenship 262
Coventry Workshop 59, 112, 126, 274
Covid-19 pandemic 295, 296, 310, 312
Crick, Bernard 101
Cromar, Peter 170, 192, 196, 250
Crosland, Tony 55, 59, 60, 290
Crowther, Stan 23, 231
Croydon High School 288

Crucible Theatre 174, 266, 314
Cuban Revolution 85
Cultural Industries Quarter (CIQ) 176, 177, 178, 318
Cutlers Hall 213, 314

Daily Herald 100, 188
Dale, Reverend Robert 40
Darke, Jane 154, 187
Davey, Valerie 298
de Beauvoir, Simone 68
de Gaulle, Charles 78
Delors, Jacques 81
Democracy in Crisis: The Town Halls Respond 106, 246
Denmark 79
Department of Education and Science 100
Department of Employment and Economic Development (DEED) 156, 192, 195, 196, 197, 199, 201, 236, 259, 263, 267, 271, 274, 278, 319
Department of Work and Pensions (DWP) 309, 319
Desai, Jayaben 76
District Auditor 178, 201, 247
Divided Kingdom: A History of Britain, 1900 to the Present 75, 300
Dixon-Barrow, Dorothy 128
Docklands Development Corporation 275
Dodworth 31
Don Valley 15, 195, 264, 271, 275, 286, 314
Doncaster 20, 25, 52, 54, 217
Donetsk 286
Doughty, Sue 298
Douglas-Home, Alec 83
Dromey, Jack 284, 286
Drown, Julia 298
Dundee 291
Dunfermline West 292
Dyson Refractories 263

East coast ports 260
Ecclesfield Comprehensive School 22
Edge, Geoff 281
Educating Rita 59, 65
Education Department 62, 138
Elderly Persons Support Unit (EPSU) 102, 121, 265, 319
Elsecar 31
Employment Committee 123, 125, 159, 165, 167, 178, 198, 201, 231, 271
Employment Department 71, 123, 125, 129, 156, 158, 159, 161, 163, 166, 168, 171, 172, 179, 181, 186, 192, 193, 196, 197, 198, 241, 248, 250, 251, 276, 287
Enterprise Zones 274
Equal Opportunities Commission (EOP) 69, 70, 129, 130, 156, 161, 319
Equal Pay Act 69, 75
Escott, Karen 161, 171, 179
Essex Road Women's Centre 70
Esteli 219, 286
European 'Objective 2' 271
European Coal and Steel Community 78
European Community (EC) 78, 79, 81, 278, 319
European Economic Community (EEC) 16, 78, 79, 319
European Parliament 79, 81, 83, 215
European Regional Development Fund (ERDF) 295, 319
European Social Fund (ESF) 71, 81, 157, 186, 295, 319
European Union 82, 295

Faith in the City 111
Falklands 203, 246
Fat Cat 260, 314
Fawcett Society 298, 313, 323
Fawcett, Millicent 313
Field, Richard 263, 264
Firth Park 14, 15, 51, 100
Firth Park Labour Hall 14

Fitzwilliam, Earl 35
Flannery, Blanche 48, 74
Flannery, Kate 48
Flannery, Martin 48, 49, 289, 291
Flynn, Tosh 148
Foot, Michael 80, 105
Forging the Links 232, 234
Fox, Ernest 31, 33
Fox, Samuel 34
Fox's umbrellas 34
Freedom Charter 227, 308
Freeman, Arnold 44
Fuentes, Pedro 85-87, 91-92, 93
Furthering Socialism in a Cold Climate 3, 229, 251

Gale, Anita 298
Galvin, Angela 156
Gas Board 100
General Municipal and Boilermakers (GMB) 171, 319
George Street Congregational Chapel 40
Gill, Vi 48, 74, 153
Glasgow 15, 50, 88, 148, 282
Globe Works 261, 314
Good Friday Agreement 224
Granville, David 197
Grayson, John 214
Greater London 20, 30, 159, 198, 201, 281, 319, 323
Greater London Council (GLC) 30, 159, 198, 199, 230, 232, 234, 244, 245, 248, 261, 275, 279, 280, 281, 284, 319
Greater London Enterprice Board (GLEB) 159, 201, 319
Green Links to Europe 283
Green, Geoff 113, 117, 118, 121, 147, 175
Greenham Common Peace Camp 76
Greenwood, Gill 156, 179
Greenwood, Sylvia 48, 74
Grenfell Tower 301
Grenoside 31, 32, 33, 34, 36, 89, 204, 287
Grenoside Workhouse 204
Griffiths, Eddie 15, 18
Grosvenor Square 11
Grunwick 76, 77
Guardian 28, 111, 112, 120, 125, 141, 279
Gwenda's 72, 181, 182, 183, 184, 309, 310

Hadfields 105
Hague, Dave 166
Hampton, Bill 101, 215
Hannah, Simon 273
Hardie, Keir 43
Harding, Kath 197
Hardstaff, Veronica 293
Harpham, Harry 14
Hart, Judith 88
Hartshead 17
Harvey, Sylvia 176, 177
Hatton, Derek 10, 244
Hawker Hunter 14, 86
Hawkes, Gwenda 183
Hayman, Keith 196
Health and Safety Executive 190
Health Plan for Sheffield 121
Health Services Act 121
Health Visitor 288
Heath, Edward 13, 21, 54, 78, 79, 83, 84, 231
Heath, Pat 121
Heathfield, Peter 89, 91
Heaven 17 172
Hebblethwaite, B. 152
Hellewell, Scott D. 28, 256
Helvellyn 52, 53
Heseltine, Michael 29, 245, 246, 261
Higginbottom, Abiah 40
Hillcroft College 205
Hills, John 310
Hillsborough Co-operative Fellowship 44
Holderness, Margaret 205, 209
Hollis, Patricia 279

Holloway, Michael 42
Holmes, David 229, 242
Holtby, Winifred 21
Holyoake, G.J. 38
Home-Help service 102
Homes and Jobs 194, 283, 284, 286, 292
Homewood, Frances 114, 118, 129
Hood, Marianne 284
Hooley, Frank 165, 166
Hornsey Mere 50
Horton, Peter 62, 259, 266
Housden, Kate 66
Housing Department 138
Housing Improvement Areas 69
Howard, Nick 87
Howarth, Alan 298
Howson, George 48
Hoyland 31
Hughes, Beverley 298
Humber Estuary 260
Huyton 10, 34, 79
Hyde Park 187, 188, 191, 192, 313, 314

Image Working Party 263, 264, 271
In and Against the State 129
In Place of Fear 12
In Place of Strife 12, 54
Independent Labour Party 43, 188
Information Technology Training Centre (ITEC) 183, 319
Integrated Development Area 278
Iraq 81, 248
Iron and Steel Trades Confederation (ISTC) 163, 319
Ironmonger, Sir Ron 23, 24
Izal factory 34

Jackson, Keith 8, 10, 51, 56, 58, 59, 60, 61, 63, 64, 96, 106, 110, 129, 139, 143, 190, 196, 221, 241, 288, 291, 322
Jackson, Margaret 16
Jackson, Peter 11
Jara, Joan 94
Jara, Victor 13, 53, 90
Jenkin, Patrick 232, 246
Jenkins, Roy 25, 175
Joint Negotiation Committee (JNC) 149, 319
Joint Works Group 153, 155, 187, 188, 190, 193, 283
Jones, Jack 97
Joseph Rowntree Foundation 65

Kalisch, Angela 179
Keebler, Sally 298
Keele University 58
Kelham Island 259, 260, 314
Kennings 173, 176, 178, 259
Kettle, Liz 181
Khan, Sadiq 313
King Edward's School 8
King, Martin Luther 75
Kinnock, Glenys 298
Kinnock, Neil 174, 175, 234
Kirklees 170, 196, 251
Knight, Angela 185
Knight, Howard 247
Knowsley 10

Labour Representation Committee 39
Ladies Elect – Women in Local Government, 1865-1914 279
Lady's Bridge 260
Lancashire 9, 10, 27, 63, 173, 214, 261, 283
Lang, Isilda 93
Leadmill 176, 314
Leeds College of Art 289
Lennon, John 305
Leyland Bus Production Company 27
Lincoln 16
Liverpool 3, 7, 9, 10, 13, 14, 17, 19, 34, 59, 61, 64, 67, 73, 89, 108, 109, 114, 139, 244, 261, 282, 283
Liverpool University Institute for Extra-mural Studies 59

Livingstone, Ken 30, 199, 280
Llewellyn-Davies, Margaret 57
Lloyd, Tony 298
Loach, Ken 309
Local Government Act of 1982 248
Local Government Chronicle 101
Local Government Information Unit (LGIU) 248, 280, 319
London Docklands 261
London School of Economics 161, 310
Longton 56, 57, 58
Low Pay Campaign 156, 158
Lucas Aerospace 161, 193
Lyceum Theatre 266, 314

Macdonald, Ramsay 32
Mace, J. 140
Macmillan, Harold 78, 83
Making Space. Women in the Man Made Environment 154
Mallaber, Judy 248
Malmö 192, 302
Manchester 9, 39, 218, 260, 261, 280, 281, 283, 285
Manchester Ship Canal 9
Mann, Tom 43
Manpower Services Commission (MSC) 70, 71, 84, 107, 122, 162, 181, 314, 319
Mansbridge, Albert 56
Mansion House, London 271
Mao Tse-Tung 45
Marx, Karl 61
Mathews, Debbie 211
Mathews, George 104, 170
Maynard, Joan 16, 18, 19, 37, 50, 267
Mayo, Marjorie 281
McAvan, Linda 215, 298
McCormack, Inez 225
McCrindle, Jean 214
McDonald, Charlie 291
McGregor, Ian 202
McKay, Allen 95
McKechin, Anne 298
McWilliams, Monica 225
Me Too 294
Meade, Alf 114, 190, 191, 192, 283
Meadowhall 169, 269, 314, 317
Melrose, D. 220
Mendelson, John 34, 38, 95, 96
Metropolitan Counties 28
Meza, Juan 89, 90
Michie, Bill 23, 51, 71, 104, 111, 122, 123, 165, 166, 167, 172, 173
Militant 10, 109, 162, 166, 167, 172, 235, 244, 245, 305
Millennium Gallery 94, 314
Miners' Strike 3, 68, 92, 119, 201, 202, 210, 213, 214, 218, 308
Minimum Wage 158
Miskin, Jol 66, 162, 171, 172
Mitchell, Ruth 101
Momentum: The Struggle for Peace, Politics and the People 223
Mondragon 302
Mons 122, 123, 166, 193, 314
Morgan, Dave 173
Morgan, Julie 298
Morrison, Herbert 78
Mould, Nellie 57
Mowlam, Mo 222, 224
Mulhearn, Tony 244
Mulley, Fred 166
Municipal Socialism – Six Years of Labour Rule in Sheffield: 1926-1932 144
Murray, Robin 199, 280
Muscroft, Julie 250, 251
Myers, Winifred 57

Nae Pasaran 88
National Association of Colliery Overmen, Deputies and Shotfirers (NACODS) 95, 202, 319
National Association of Local Government Officers (NALGO) 163, 319

National Centre for Popular Music (NCPM) 177, 178, 314, 319
National Coal Board (NCB) 202, 203, 319
National Coal Mining Museum 206
National Executive Committee of the Labour Party (NEC) 16, 37, 234, 319
National Front (NF) 11, 80, 319
National Health Service (NHS) 73, 102, 121, 299, 304, 306, 312, 319
National Institute of Adult Continuing Education 322
National Pensioners' Convention 97
National Union of Mineworkers (NUM) 35, 52, 76, 78, 81, 89, 90, 95, 202, 203, 207, 208, 314, 320
National Union of Public Employees (NUPE) 163, 320
National Union of Railwaymen (NUR) 97, 320
National Union of Teachers (NUT) 48, 49, 163, 320
Neepsend 260, 261
Nelson, Ruth 179
New Statesman 160
Newcastle-under-Lyme 9
Newton Chambers 34, 162
Nicaragua 218, 219, 220, 222, 286, 287, 308, 323
Nissan 181, 183
Noches, Mario 89
Northern College 59, 60, 61, 63, 65, 66, 67, 82, 84, 140, 143, 154, 162, 171, 193, 194, 198, 199, 203, 210, 214, 215, 217, 222, 241, 288, 308, 322
Northern Ireland Women's Coalition (NIWC) 223, 225, 320
Northover, Baroness Lindsay 298
Norwich City Council 279
Nuttall, Phil 274

O'Grady, Frances 212
O'Neill, Pat 190
Oakey, Phil 174
On a Clear Day 100
Open University 59, 65, 307
Orgreave 206, 216
Ortega, Daniel 218, 220
Osborne, Sandra 298
Our Bodies, Ourselves 68
Overseas Development Programme 310
Owen, Bill 17, 38, 42, 44, 62, 64, 65, 76, 114, 129, 258, 259, 307, 314, 323
Owen, David 25
Owen, Tom 87
Owlerton 104
Oxford Delegacy for Extramural Studies 56

Paid Educational Leave 139, 140, 156, 186, 323
Paid Educational Leave and Low Paid Workers 'Time Off to Learn' 140
Pakistan Muslim Centre 195
Palatine Chambers 258, 263, 314
Pankhurst, Sylvia 47
Paris 11, 78
Park Hill 187, 188, 191, 192, 314
Parliamentary Private Secretary (PPS) 222, 290, 320
Parry, Sylvia 289
Party of European Socialists (PSE) 82, 320
Passenger Transport Authority (PTA) 255, 320
Peace and Reconciliation grant programme 225
Peace Process 222, 223, 308
Penistone 31, 32, 33, 34, 38, 95, 96, 97, 98, 102
People's Campaign for Health 121, 122, 324
Personnel Department 129, 130, 133
Peru 89
Philosophy, Politics and Economics (PPE) 262
Pilley 31
Planning and Land Act 1980 146
Poland, Caroline 179, 211

Poll Tax 272
Pollard, Sidney 38
Pompidou, Georges 79
Ponds Forge 174, 192, 314
Pons, Colin 175, 176, 177
Popular Unity 85, 88
Portraits of a City Father 42
Positive Action Final Report 139
Positive Action Project 71, 139, 158, 186
Positive Action Steering Committee 130
Positive discrimination 111, 120
Potteries 3, 7, 8, 9, 18, 56, 57, 58, 64, 66, 214
Powell, Enoch 11, 75, 76
Prescott, John 283, 285
Price, Christopher 264, 290
Price, David 41
Price, Kitty 288, 289
Price, Peter 23, 27, 265, 266
Price, Stanley 288
Programme for Action 298
Public transport 27, 28, 301
Publicity Department 197
Pupil teacher ratio 239, 240

Quilapayun 13
Quilley, Alan and Janet 224

Race Equality Unit 71, 128, 156
Race Relations Act 276
Ramaphosa, Cyril 225
Ratcliffe, Eva 33
Rates Act 229, 230, 233, 235, 247, 249, 250, 272, 324
Rates Bill 230, 245
Rawson, Mary-Anne 40, 41
Red Ladder 67, 114
Red Pepper 113
Red Tape 174, 198, 314
Redcliffe-Maud Report 20, 21, 54
Redcliffe-Maud, Lord 20
Redgrave, Vanessa 11
Republic of Ireland 79
Richardson, Jo 285
Right to Buy 154
Rippon, Geoffrey 231
River Don 260
Rivers of Blood 11
Road Transport Federation 255
Roberts, Matt 40
Robeson, Paul 44, 52
Robinson, Mary 225
Rodgers, Bill 25, 98
Rodgers, Frank 204
Ross, Ernie 298
Ross, Willie 80
Rotherham 23, 25, 34, 52, 54, 164, 217, 231
Round Chapel, Bethnal Green 199
Rowbotham, Sheila 113
Rowley, Eve 57
Rowlinson, E.G. 144
Royal Army Education Corps 56
Ruddock, Joan 298
Ruskin of the North 59, 60, 62
Russell Commission 60
Russell, Lord 60
Russell, Willy 59

Sagar, Pearl 225
Salisbury, Brian 196
Salter, Ada 187, 188, 325
Sandinista National Liberation Front (FSNL) 220, 319
Santiago 86, 87, 88
Saunderson, Ian 255
Scargill, Arthur 202, 203, 207, 234
Scotland Road 10
Scottish Rolls Royce 88
Second Chance to Learn 59, 61, 139
Section 137 123, 124
Segal, Lynne 113
Senior, John 146, 148

Sephton, Peter 256
Sequerra, Dan 129, 196
Sex Discrimination Act 69, 71
Shardlow's 89, 170
Shaw, Paul and Wendy 35, 36, 55
Sheffield & District Trades and Labour Party 23
Sheffield and District Afro-Caribbean Community Association (SADACCA) 195, 314, 320
Sheffield Bookshop 38
Sheffield Campaign Against Racism (SCAR) 47, 76, 128, 162, 320
Sheffield Co-operative Women's Guild 44
Sheffield College 73, 179, 180, 181
Sheffield Coordinating Centre Against Unemployment (SCAU) 107, 122, 171, 212, 314, 320
Sheffield DocFest 177
Sheffield Economic Regeneration Committee (SERC) 264, 275, 320
Sheffield Federation of Trades Councils 42
Sheffield Homestart 94
Sheffield Independent Film 175, 176, 314
Sheffield Insulations Group 262
Sheffield Midland Station 173, 314
Sheffield Morning Telegraph 229
Sheffield Partnerships 271
Sheffield Polytechnic 43, 162, 198, 264, 288, 314
Sheffield Royal Infirmary 261
Sheffield Science Park 258
Sheffield Trades and Labour Council 37, 40, 81, 324
Sheffield Vision 271
Sheffield Women Against Pit Closures 210, 211
Sheffield Women in Manual Trades 67
Sheffield Women's Development Trust 73
Sheffield Women's Film Co-operative 176
Sheffield Women's Network 162
Sheffield Women's Printing Co-op 144
Sheffield Works Department 71, 148
Shepherd's Bush 87
Sherwyn, Glyn 196
Shirecliffe FE College 71, 179, 189
Shore, Peter 80
Shoreham Street 173, 174
Short, Renée 231
Showroom Cinema 168, 176, 177, 314
Shrewsbury 100
Shutt, John 282
Silkin, John 80
Silkstone 31
Silva, Luis 89
Sinclair Reception Centre 87
Skelton, Paul 112, 113, 117, 118, 124, 147, 161, 172, 173, 175, 176
Skinner, David (Frederickson) 124, 287
Smethers, Sam 313
Smilie, John 123, 166
Smith, Arthur 10
Smith, Joyce 36
Smith, Lady Mabel 32, 35, 36, 43, 55, 72
Smith, Rennie 32
Snape, William 168
Snows 122, 166, 193
Social Care 3, 83, 102, 311
Social Strategy Steering Committee 120, 121
Society of Industrial Tutors 64
Somoza, President 220
South Africa 12, 218, 225, 226, 227, 297, 308
South Yorkshire County Council (SYCC) 21, 21, 22, 23, 24, 30, 50, 52, 63, 78, 85, 96, 116, 124, 230, 320
South Yorkshire Passenger Transport Authority (SYPTA) 22, 314, 320
Soviet Union 24, 286
Spanish Civil War 49, 97
Spring Bank Camps 50, 80, 114, 166, 265
Star 19, 115, 116, 186, 241, 261, 314
Stewart, Ann 284
Stocksbridge 14, 31, 34, 105, 289

Stoddart, Jude 71, 129, 130, 156, 161
Stoke-on-Trent 8, 56, 146
Stone, Isabella 130, 156, 298, 310
Storey, Maureen 68
Stringer, Graham 280, 281
Sturrock, Betty 15, 153
Sturrock, Jock 15, 16, 17, 22, 23, 50, 153
Sunderland 181, 183
Swingler, Stephen 9

Take Ten 139, 142, 156, 158, 186
Tams, Eric 57
Tatlow Stancer 173, 259
Tatlow, Matt 68
Taverne, Dick 16
Tawney House 58
Tawney, R.H. 56, 57, 58, 60
Taylor, G. 154, 188
Taylor, Richard 61
Tenants Federation 147, 284
Thane, Pat 5, 75, 300, 325
Thatcher, Margaret 83, 84, 92, 105, 146, 207, 213, 229, 243, 246, 269, 271, 300
The Full Monty 168, 309, 314
The Human League 172, 174
The Politics Of Partnership 3, 257
The Queen's College, Oxford 262
Thornbridge Hall 106
Thornes, Vernon 38
Thornton, Baroness Glenys 298
Tigwell, Tony 232, 236, 245
Tongue, Jenny 298
Toxteth 10, 73, 108
Trades Union Congress (TUC) 219, 320, 325
Trafalgar Square 12, 48
Training and Enterprise Council (TEC) 263, 320
Training Opportunities Scheme (TOPS) 70, 181, 320
Transport Act 24, 30, 254, 256
Transport and General Workers' Union (T&GWU) 10, 76, 169, 193, 284, 292, 314
Treasury 16, 132, 133, 134, 135, 138, 192, 196, 250, 274
Treaty of Paris 78
Tyneside 232, 282, 283

Uddin, Baroness Pola 298
Ullswater 50, 106, 243
UNDP 310
UNIFEM 225, 320, 322
Union of Construction, Allied Trades and Technicians (UCATT) 169, 190, 193, 284, 286, 292, 320
United Nations (UN) 225, 262, 295, 296, 320
United Nations Capital Development Fund (UNCDF) 262, 295, 296, 320
University of Sheffield 38, 62, 101, 120, 121, 162, 198
Urban Development Corporation (UDC) 278, 286, 320
Urban Programme (UP) 84, 110, 126, 127, 271, 273, 274, 277, 278, 320
Urban Theolology Unit 94

Valparaíso 91
Varadkar, Senni 128
Varley, Eric 80
Vasquez, Roberto and Eysen 89
Vietnam 11
Virago 69, 285

Wainwright, Hilary 113
Wakefield 20, 21, 54, 283
Waldegrave, William 245
Walker, Alan 120, 121
Wall, Ros 72, 182
Ward, Michael 159, 199, 201, 280, 281, 323
Warwick University 126, 196
Water Works building 208

Waterloo Bridge 218
Waugh, Alex and Pat 51
Wedgwood Memorial College 56
Wentworth Castle 62, 63, 203
Wentworth Woodhouse 35, 203
Wentworth, Thomas, 1st Earl of Strafford 62
West Indian community 128
West Indies 9, 76
West Riding of Yorkshire 20
West, Norman 81, 215
Wharncliffe Side 14
Wharncliffe, Earls of 31, 46
Whitehorn, Katharine 7
Whitehouse, Mary 151
Whitfield, Dexter 161
Whittaker, Baroness Janet 298
Wigfield, Alan 120
Wild, Ian 176, 177
Wilkinson, Gertrude 40
Williams, Annette 72, 181
Williams, Shirley 25
Wilson, Harold 9, 10, 11, 12, 13, 16, 20, 21, 24, 54, 59, 60, 69, 70, 75, 78, 79, 80, 82, 83, 84, 85, 88, 104, 111, 175, 285, 307
Wincobank Chapel 41
Windrush 48
Winter Gardens, Blackpool 96
Wollen, Roz 68, 69, 70, 71, 72, 101, 181
Woman's Own 300
Women Against Pit Closures (WAPC) 208, 211, 219, 321
Women Against Pit Closures. Barnsley Women 209
Women in Engineering, Science and Technology (WEST) 73, 181, 321
Women in Non-traditional Trades (WINTT) 73, 321
Women's Budget Group 310
Women's Joinery Training Workshop 71
Women's Liberation 66, 67, 70
Women's Officer 48
Women's Technology Training Workshop (WTTW) 179, 185, 186, 244
Womens Aid 68
Wood, Peter 114
Woodhead Tunnel 283
Woodward, Kate 57
Workers' Educational Association (WEA) 8, 42, 56, 57, 58, 66, 171, 307, 321
Works Department 71, 138, 144, 148, 154, 155, 189, 192, 238, 241, 286
Workstation 176, 314
World Peace Congress 37
World Student Games (WSG) 264, 265, 266, 321
World War One 32, 40, 183, 288
World War Two 33, 49, 218
Worthington, Tony 298
Wortley Hall 31, 46, 47, 62, 316, 322
Wortley Rural District Council 30, 32, 36, 102, 145
Wortley Union 31
Wulf-Mathies, Monika 225
Wyatt, Derek 298

Yarnitt, Martin 139
Yemen 76
Yorkshire Art Space 176, 178
Yorkshire WI 288
You Can't Kill the Spirit 211, 325
Young Women's Plastering Project 179

About the Author

Helen was born in 1939. She is a lifelong campaigner. She joined the Labour Party in 1963 to campaign for better maternity services. She studied History at Oxford, and later trained to be a teacher. After several years in Local Government, described here, she was elected MP for Sheffield Hillsborough in 1992. An assiduous constituency MP, she also served on the Environment Select Committee and became the Parliamentary Private Secretary to three Secretaries of State for Northern Ireland, with a brief to liaise with women and community groups there to win support for the Good Friday Agreement and its implementation.

She led cross-party work in Parliament on Water, Steel, South Africa and on the gender input into the Commission for Africa. She was elected onto the executives of the Labour Party's Parliamentary and National Committees.

Since stepping down from Parliament in 2005 she worked with the Equal Opportunities Commission to form the Women and Pension network. She was appointed to the Women's National Commission in 2007, and made a CBE in 2009 for services to the community of South Yorkshire and Women and Pensions. She was a Fawcett Society trustee, chaired the charity Grandparents Plus, and tutored on numerous courses about Politics and Public Life with the WEA. She now chairs the 'Friends' group of her local village green.